Basic Perspective Drawing:
A Visual Approach
Third Edition

John Montague

John Wiley & Sons, Inc.

New York • Chichester • Weinheim • Brisbane • Singapore • Toronto

Figure B on page 173 and Figures 1, 2, 3 on page 184 are used with
permission of Softkey: Design Center 3-D.

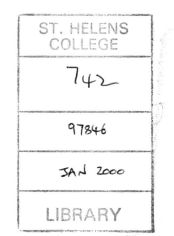
This publication is designed to provide accurate and authoritative informa-
tion in regard to the subject matter covered. It is sold with the understanding that the publisher is not engaged in rendering professional services. If
professional advice or other expert assistance is required, the services of a
competent professional person should be sought.

Library of Congress Cataloging-in-Publication Data

Montague, John, 1944–
    Basic perspective drawing : a visual approach / John Montague. —
3rd ed.
        p.   cm.
    Includes index.
    ISBN 0-471-29231-1
    1. Perspective.   2. Drawing—Technique.   I. Title.
NC750.M648   1998
742—dc21   97-44552

Printed in the United States of America.

10 9 8 7 6 5 4 3 2 1

Basic Perspective Drawing

For Julian and Alexandra

Contents

Preface

The goal of this book is to provide an accessible visual approach to perspective drawing. It is directed towards artists, illustrators, designers, and architects, who by natural inclination are visually oriented. Thus, unlike earlier texts on the subject, this book is designed wherever possible to "show" rather than to verbally describe.

In response to comments and suggestions from students and professionals who have used the book in its two earlier editions, this third edition has been further expanded and refined in keeping with its original intent. In this edition, four new chapters and an appendix have been added to supplement the original core chapters. The new chapters introduce sketching and rapid visualization techniques, the figure in perspective, shading and rendering techniques, and a very basic description of computer 3-D imaging. Finally, in the Appendix, some notes and suggestions have been added on teaching and studying perspective.

The book is organized to be studied sequentially and/or used as a convenient reference source. The first chapter provides a general orientation and overview, while subsequent chapters, including the four new ones, address more specific problems and techniques. In keeping with its original design, this new edition maintains the spare, linear style of illustration both for clarity and to invite direct participation. The book should be treated as a learning tool. It is meant to be drawn in.

Whether one works in conventional media or enters the fascinating world of 3-D animation and virtual reality, a firm grasp of perspective is a valuable orientation and foundation for understanding the optical world and how it works. Perspective drawing is a learnable skill but like other skills, to gain mastery and fluency, one needs to move deliberately, with practice and patience, from the known to the unknown, from the simple to the complex. This text is a guide for doing just that.

Basic Perspective Drawing

In normal experience, our eyes are constantly in motion, roving over and around objects and through ever-changing environments.

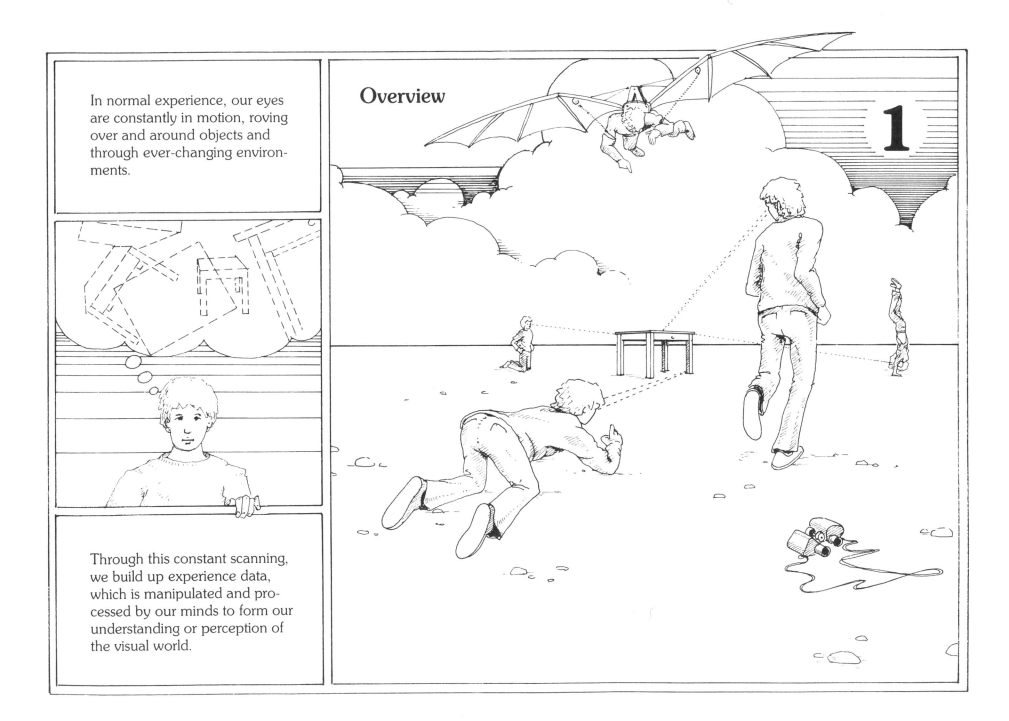

Overview

Through this constant scanning, we build up experience data, which is manipulated and processed by our minds to form our understanding or perception of the visual world.

These mental images of the visual world can never be in an exact one-to-one correspondence with what is experienced. Our perceptions are holistic; they are made up of all the information we possess about the phenomena, not just the visual appearance of a particular view.

As we gaze at the object or view, we sense this perceptual information all at once—colors, associations, symbolic values, essential forms, and an infinity of meanings.

Thus, our perception of even such a simple object as a table is impossible to express completely. Any expression of our experience must be limited and partial.

Our choice of what can or will be expressed is greatly affected by the various limits we self-impose or that are imposed upon us by our culture.

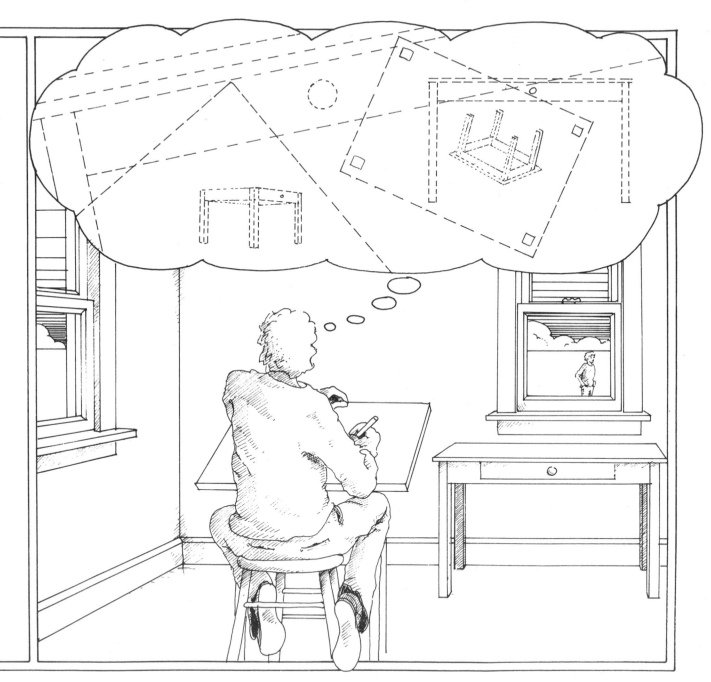

In expressing visual data, individuals and cultures as a whole make choices—some conscious, some unconscious—as to what aspects of their experience of a phenomenon can or should be expressed.

Consider the different images on the right.

Each of these drawings of a table is expressing different sets of information about the table— each is "correct."

A. Several views are presented simultaneously.

B. Parts are separated into measured plans and elevations.

C. Parts are arranged to express feeling, emotions, weight.

D. A single point of view is selected to produce an optical appearance.

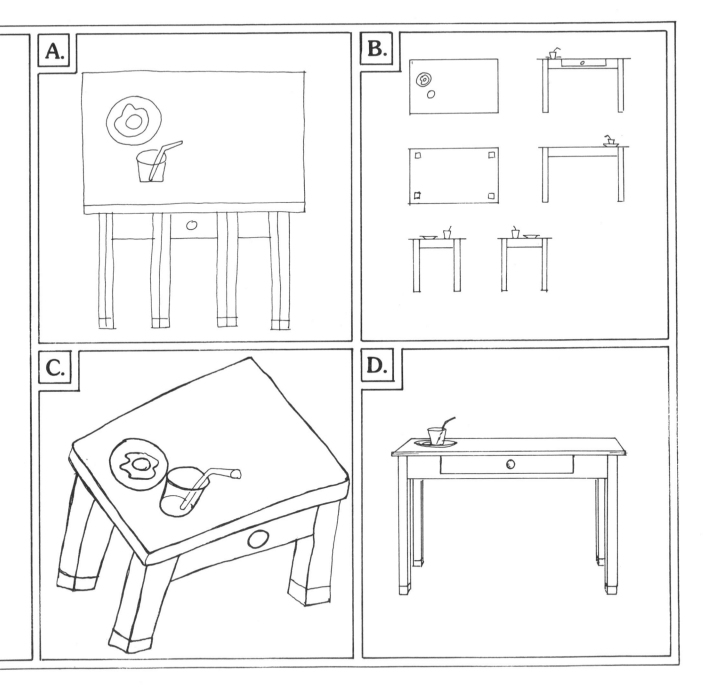

For every advantage gained from a particular system of representation, other possibilities are lost. Thus, linear perspective is only one of many representational systems and is certainly not always the most useful or appropriate technique.

Several Points of View

This system of representation has dominated art of the Middle Ages, nonwestern cultures, primitive art, the art of children, and much of the art of the twentieth century. This system represents what is important or what is known about the subject, not just the way the subject appears optically from a single point of view.

One Point of View

This system of representation was established at the time of the European Renaissance (c. 1450). It represents the appearance of reality; that is, appearance from a single point of view, as if traced on a window. Note that this "realistic" view prevents us from seeing the apples and the second cup.

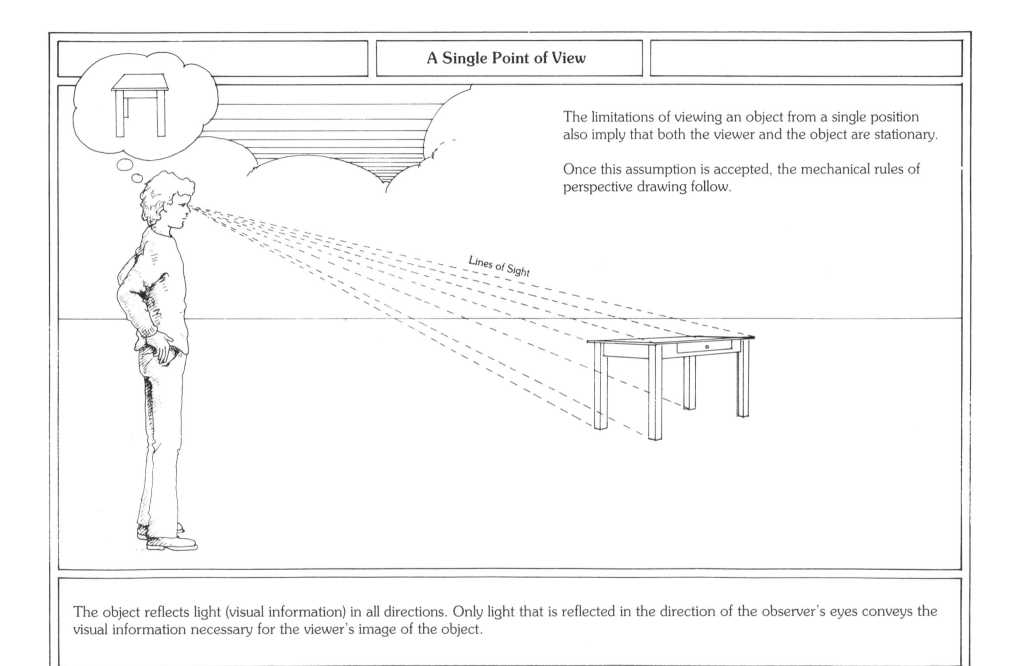

The limitations of viewing an object from a single position also imply that both the viewer and the object are stationary.

Once this assumption is accepted, the mechanical rules of perspective drawing follow.

Lines of Sight

The object reflects light (visual information) in all directions. Only light that is reflected in the direction of the observer's eyes conveys the visual information necessary for the viewer's image of the object.

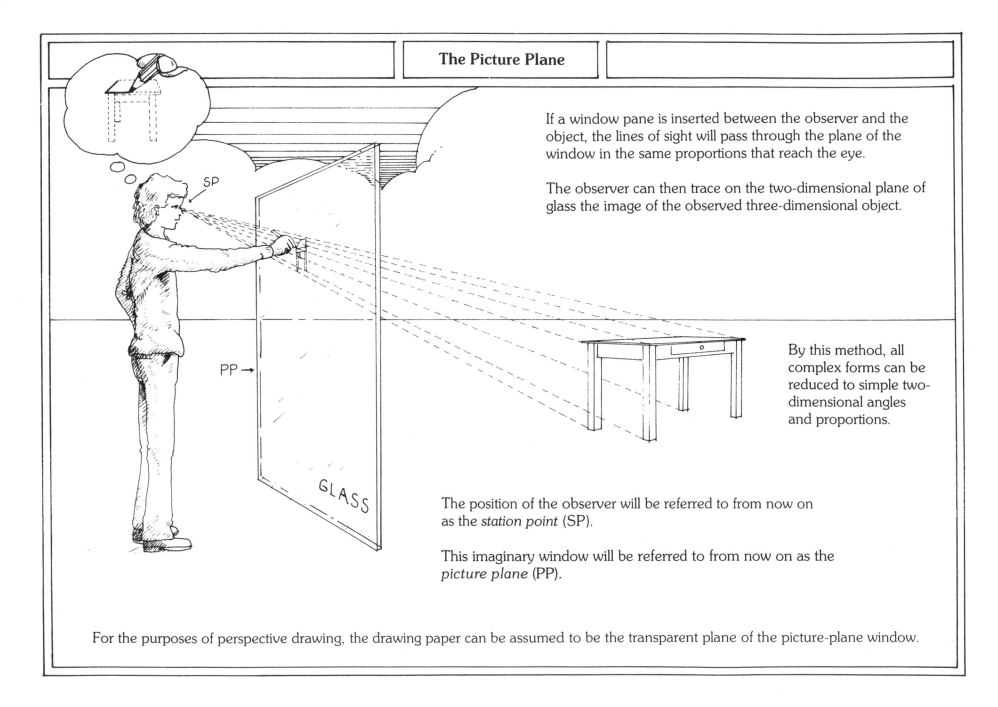

The Picture Plane

SP

PP →

GLASS

If a window pane is inserted between the observer and the object, the lines of sight will pass through the plane of the window in the same proportions that reach the eye.

The observer can then trace on the two-dimensional plane of glass the image of the observed three-dimensional object.

By this method, all complex forms can be reduced to simple two-dimensional angles and proportions.

The position of the observer will be referred to from now on as the *station point* (SP).

This imaginary window will be referred to from now on as the *picture plane* (PP).

For the purposes of perspective drawing, the drawing paper can be assumed to be the transparent plane of the picture-plane window.

The illusion of depth in linear perspective is suggested by the relative size, position, and shape of lines on the picture plane. The most obvious of these cues is size. The further away an object, the smaller it appears. This is demonstrated below.

Notice that the farther the object moves away from the observer, the narrower the lines of sight on the picture plane, and the closer those lines approach eye level.

If moved away far enough, the image will appear so small that it seems to disappear at eye level.

Eye Level

Lines of Sight

Ground Plane

SP

PP

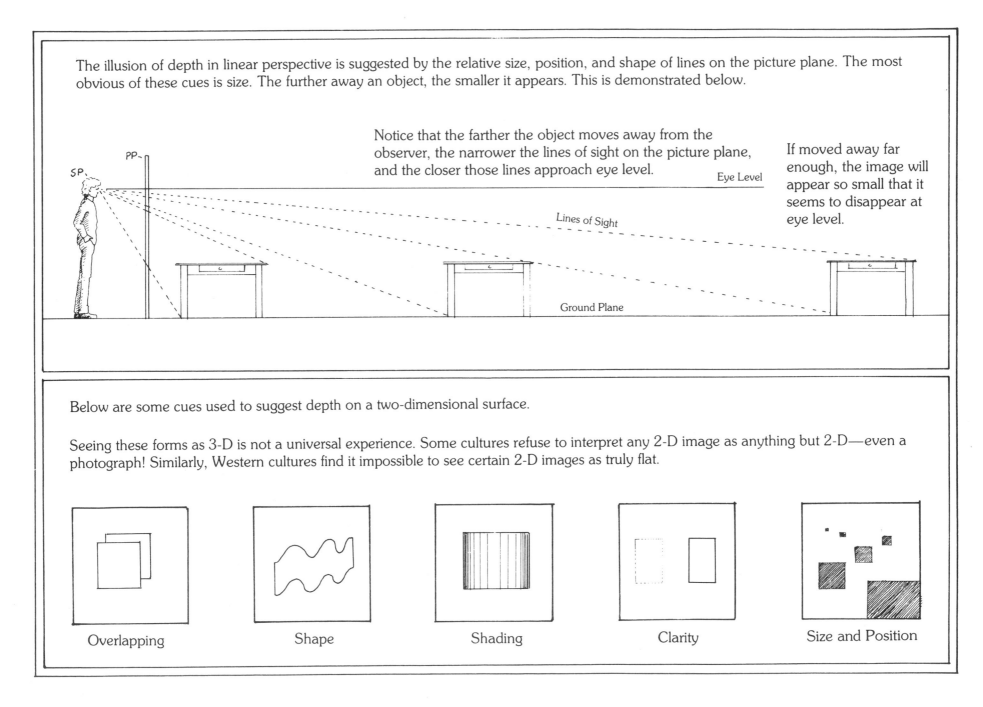

Below are some cues used to suggest depth on a two-dimensional surface.

Seeing these forms as 3-D is not a universal experience. Some cultures refuse to interpret any 2-D image as anything but 2-D—even a photograph! Similarly, Western cultures find it impossible to see certain 2-D images as truly flat.

Overlapping

Shape

Shading

Clarity

Size and Position

In relation to the picture plane, all objects moving away from the viewer gravitate toward the viewer's *eye level* while getting smaller at the same time.

Note that lines parallel to each other in the scene converge toward a common point at *eye level*, where the distance between them becomes so small, it seems to disappear.

The point at which lines converge is called the *vanishing point* (VP).

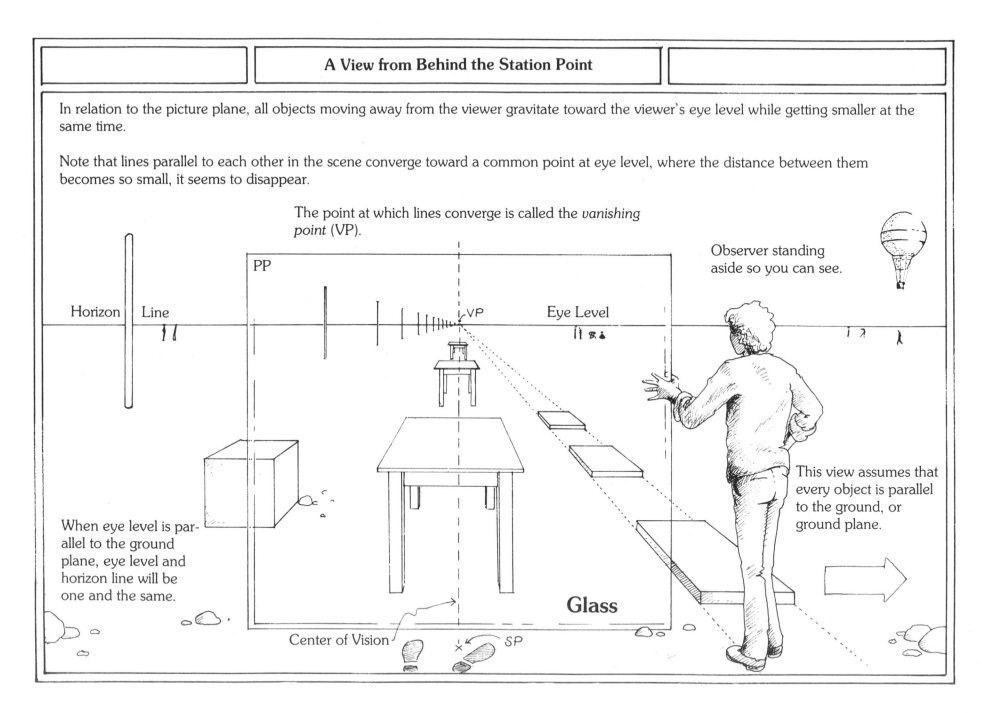

Horizon Line

PP

VP

Eye Level

Observer standing aside so you can see.

When eye level is parallel to the ground plane, eye level and horizon line will be one and the same.

This view assumes that every object is parallel to the ground, or ground plane.

Glass

Center of Vision

SP

From the observer's position in space, objects can recede in any direction, not just along lines parallel to the ground.

Therefore, for each observable object, there exists a *sphere of disappearance* encompassing the observer. An object receding in any direction from the observer's point of view (station point) will appear to decrease in size until it reaches the outer limits of its own sphere, vanishing completely.

The size and brightness of the object determine the magnitude of its sphere, if all other factors are equal.

There are as many concentric spheres of disappearance as there are objects observed.

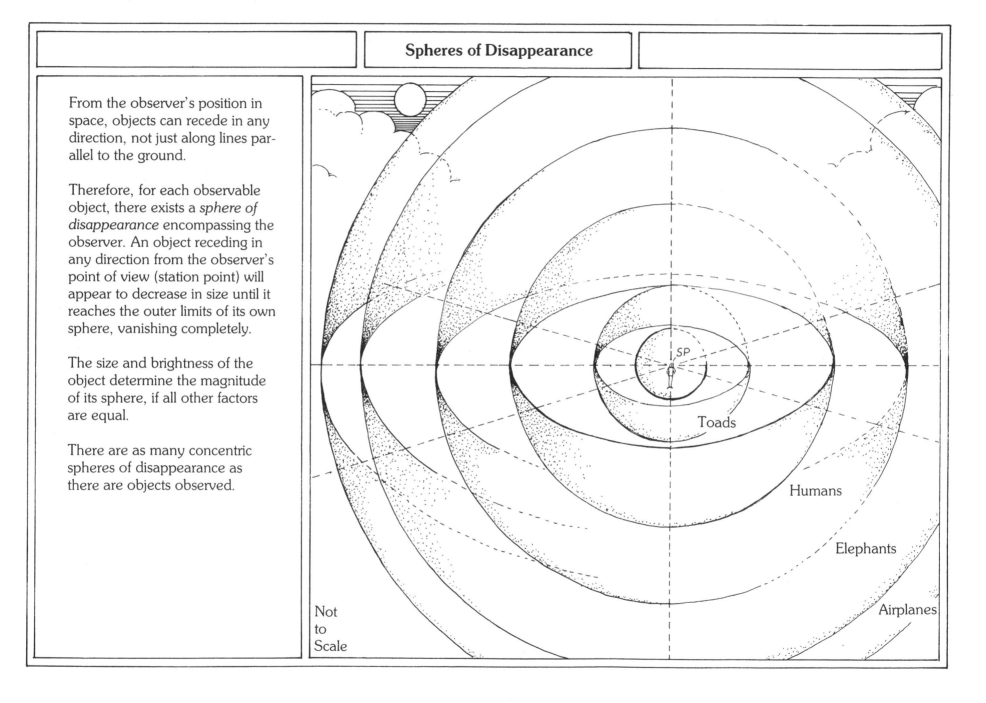

SP

Toads

Humans

Elephants

Airplanes

Not
to
Scale

9

Most of the time, people observe things while their feet are firmly planted on the ground. As a result, spheres of disappearance can be reduced, for practical purposes, to the following types:

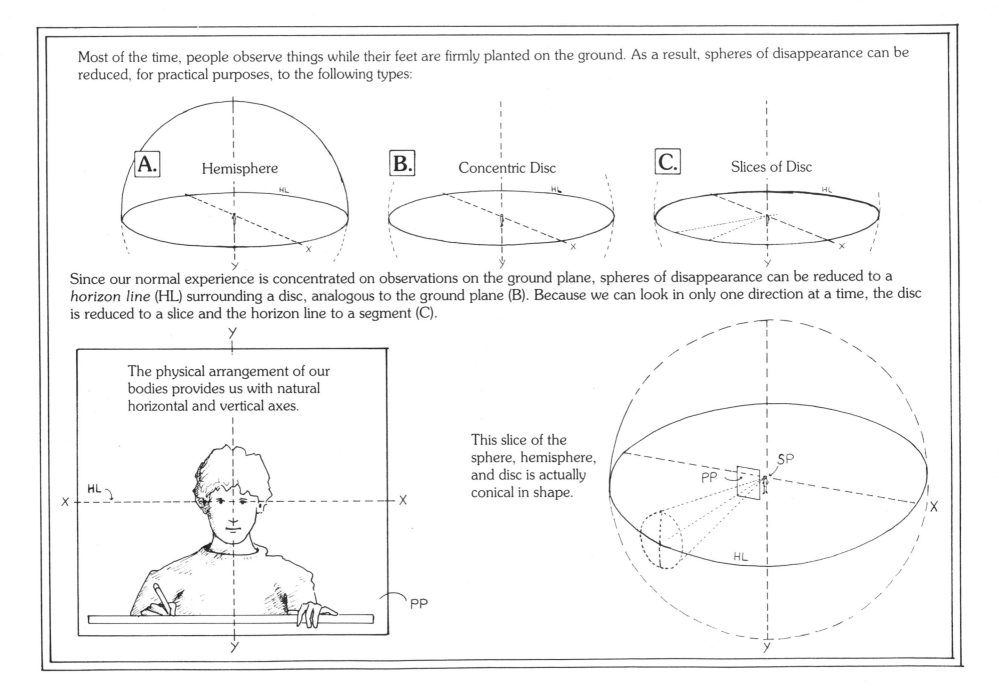

A. Hemisphere **B.** Concentric Disc **C.** Slices of Disc

Since our normal experience is concentrated on observations on the ground plane, spheres of disappearance can be reduced to a *horizon line* (HL) surrounding a disc, analogous to the ground plane (B). Because we can look in only one direction at a time, the disc is reduced to a slice and the horizon line to a segment (C).

The physical arrangement of our bodies provides us with natural horizontal and vertical axes.

This slice of the sphere, hemisphere, and disc is actually conical in shape.

Cone of Vision

The parts of our eyes that receive light are hemispherical, each gathering light from a cone of about 150 degrees. When these two cones overlap, we gather light from almost 180 degrees.

Only in the area where the fields from both eyes overlap does binocular vision occur.

Within this broad field of vision, we actually focus clearly through cones of about 30–60 degrees. When objects are outside of these standard cones of vision, we generally consider them to be distorted, as images appear through a wide-angle lens.

Vertically, our vision is limited to about 140 degrees, our sight being cut off by eyebrows, eyelids, and cheeks.

When we use both eyes, our cone of vision is a combination of two overlapping cones, one from each eye.

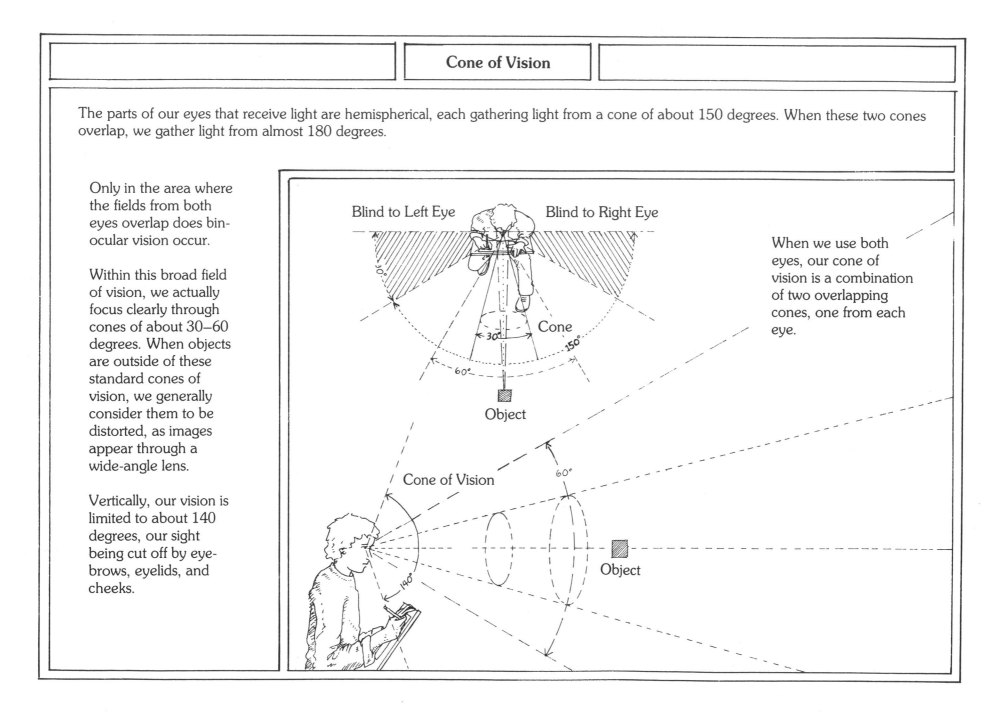

Optics of the Eye Relative to the Cone of Vision

Each eye perceives the object from a slightly different angle. This gives the brain a strong cue as to the depth of the object.

The brain harmonizes both two-dimensional views and creates a three-dimensional image.

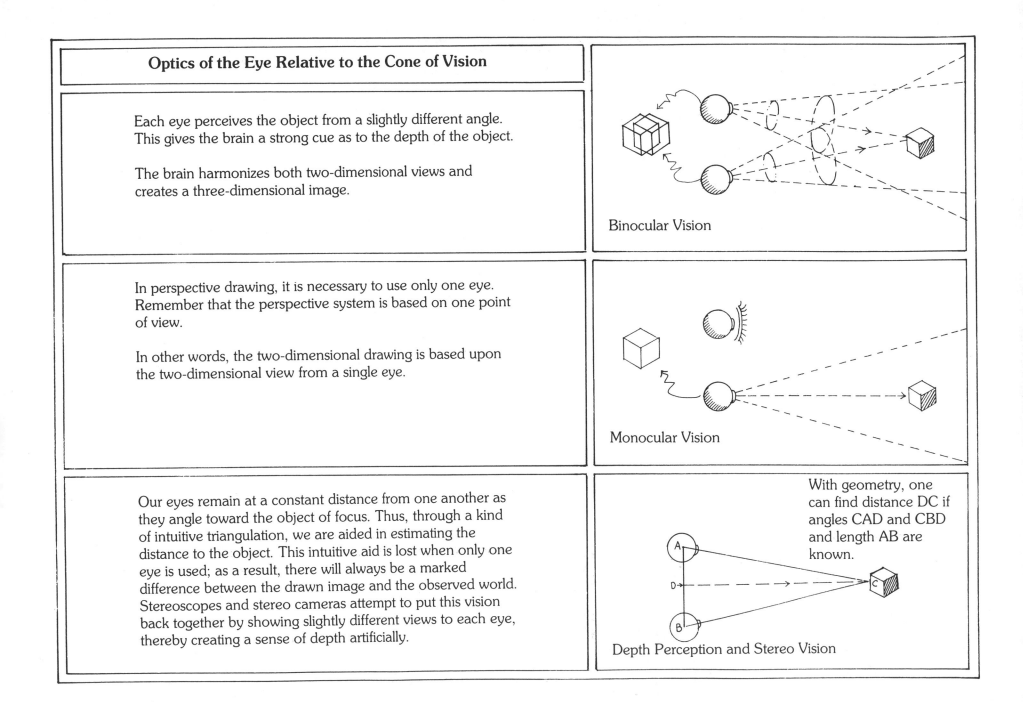

Binocular Vision

In perspective drawing, it is necessary to use only one eye. Remember that the perspective system is based on one point of view.

In other words, the two-dimensional drawing is based upon the two-dimensional view from a single eye.

Monocular Vision

Our eyes remain at a constant distance from one another as they angle toward the object of focus. Thus, through a kind of intuitive triangulation, we are aided in estimating the distance to the object. This intuitive aid is lost when only one eye is used; as a result, there will always be a marked difference between the drawn image and the observed world. Stereoscopes and stereo cameras attempt to put this vision back together by showing slightly different views to each eye, thereby creating a sense of depth artificially.

With geometry, one can find distance DC if angles CAD and CBD and length AB are known.

Depth Perception and Stereo Vision

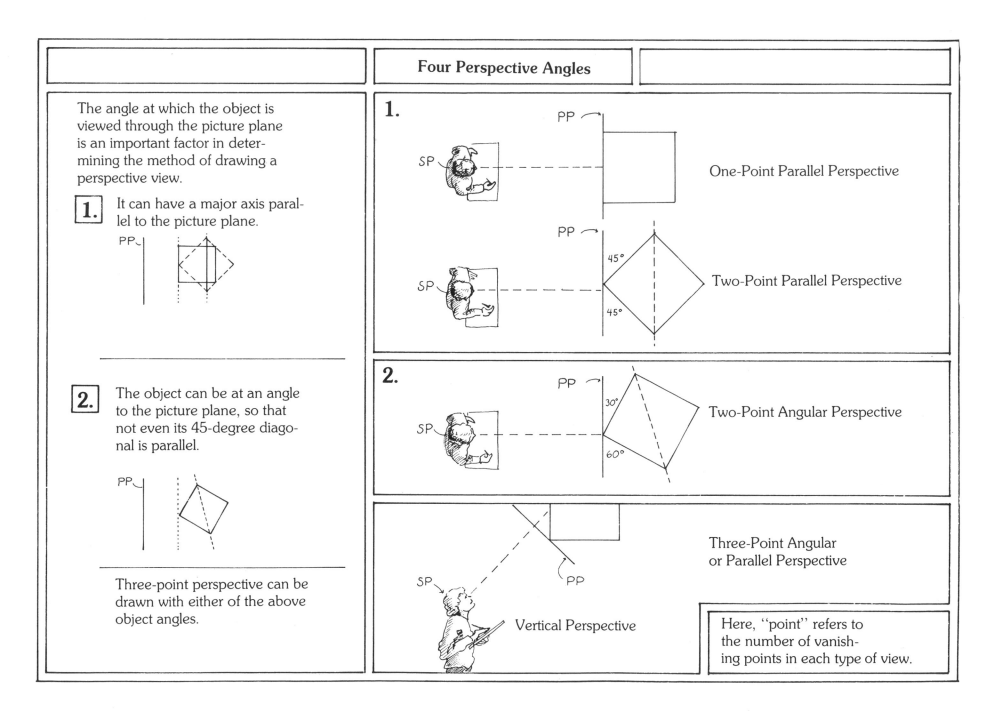

Four Perspective Angles

The angle at which the object is viewed through the picture plane is an important factor in determining the method of drawing a perspective view.

1. It can have a major axis parallel to the picture plane.

PP

2. The object can be at an angle to the picture plane, so that not even its 45-degree diagonal is parallel.

PP

Three-point perspective can be drawn with either of the above object angles.

1.

PP

SP

One-Point Parallel Perspective

PP

SP

45°

45°

Two-Point Parallel Perspective

2.

PP

SP

30°

60°

Two-Point Angular Perspective

PP

SP

Three-Point Angular or Parallel Perspective

Vertical Perspective

Here, "point" refers to the number of vanishing points in each type of view.

The rectilinear objects below have the following characteristics:

1. One set of planes parallel to the picture plane; and

2. One set of planes parallel to the ground and perpendicular to the picture plane.

As a consequence, the receding planes are also parallel to each other and converge on the same vanishing point.

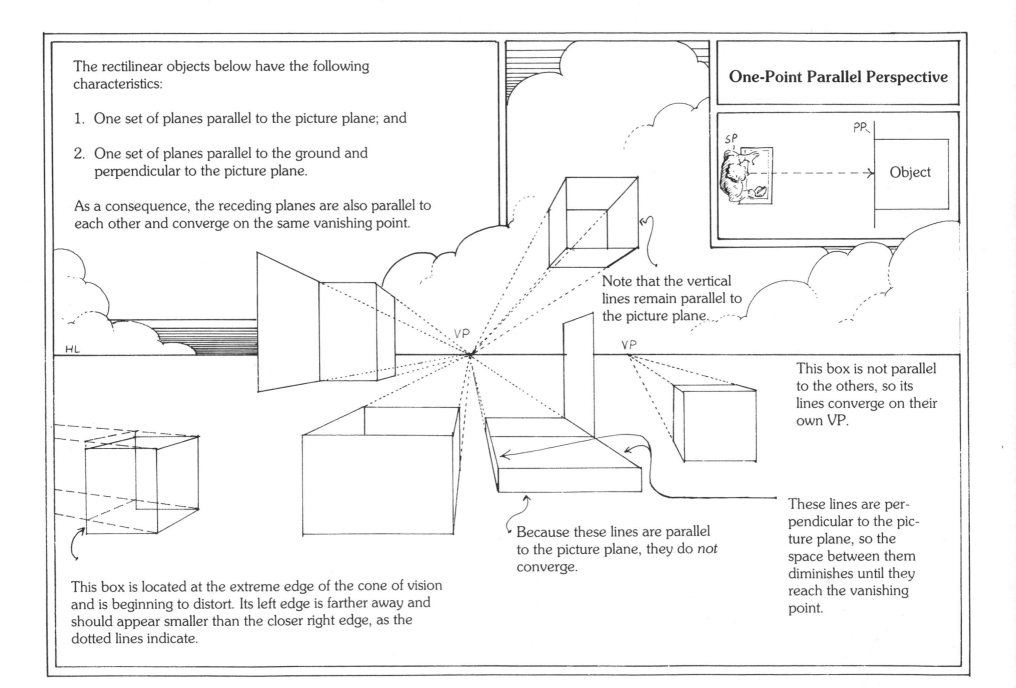

One-Point Parallel Perspective

Note that the vertical lines remain parallel to the picture plane.

This box is not parallel to the others, so its lines converge on their own VP.

Because these lines are parallel to the picture plane, they do *not* converge.

These lines are perpendicular to the picture plane, so the space between them diminishes until they reach the vanishing point.

This box is located at the extreme edge of the cone of vision and is beginning to distort. Its left edge is farther away and should appear smaller than the closer right edge, as the dotted lines indicate.

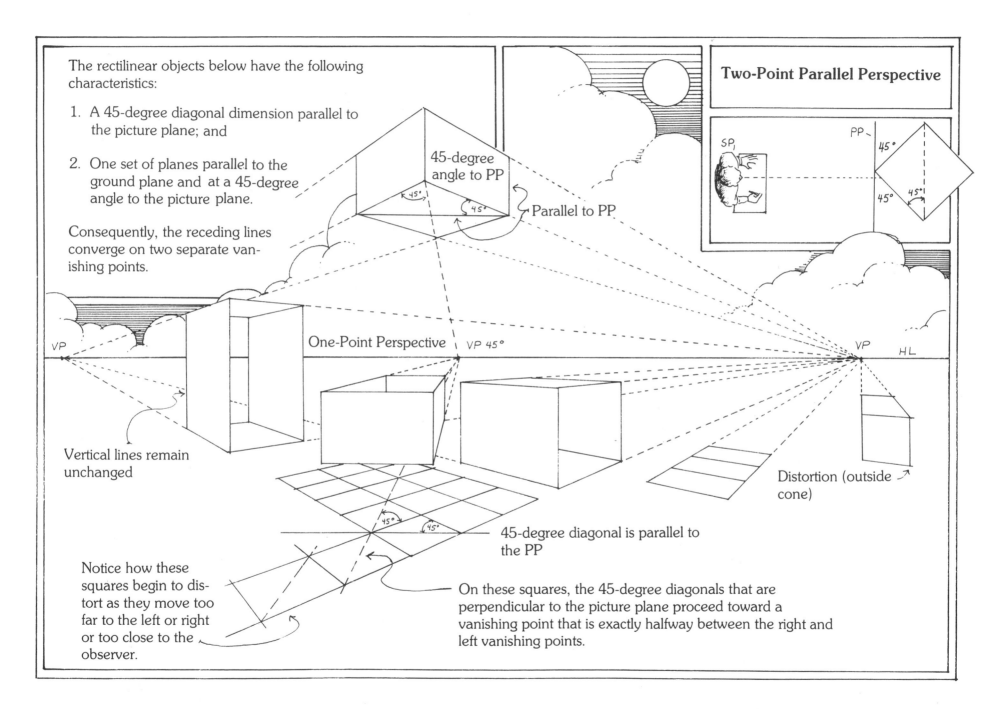

The rectilinear objects below have the following characteristics:

1. A 45-degree diagonal dimension parallel to the picture plane; and

2. One set of planes parallel to the ground plane and at a 45-degree angle to the picture plane.

Consequently, the receding lines converge on two separate vanishing points.

45-degree angle to PP

45°   45°

Parallel to PP

Two-Point Parallel Perspective

SP₁   PP
45°
45°   45°

Vertical lines remain unchanged

One-Point Perspective   VP 45°

VP

VP   HL

Distortion (outside cone)

45°   45°

45-degree diagonal is parallel to the PP

Notice how these squares begin to distort as they move too far to the left or right or too close to the observer.

On these squares, the 45-degree diagonals that are perpendicular to the picture plane proceed toward a vanishing point that is exactly halfway between the right and left vanishing points.

15

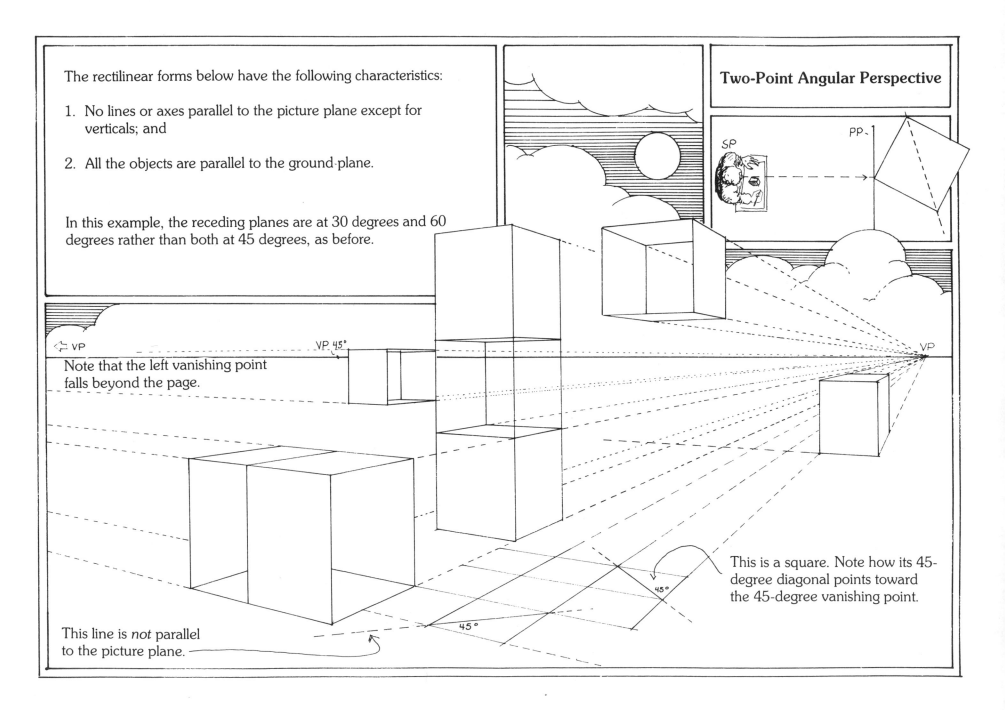

The rectilinear forms below have the following characteristics:

1. No lines or axes parallel to the picture plane except for verticals; and

2. All the objects are parallel to the ground-plane.

In this example, the receding planes are at 30 degrees and 60 degrees rather than both at 45 degrees, as before.

Two-Point Angular Perspective

SP

PP

Note that the left vanishing point falls beyond the page.

VP

VP 45°

VP

This is a square. Note how its 45-degree diagonal points toward the 45-degree vanishing point.

45°

45°

This line is *not* parallel to the picture plane.

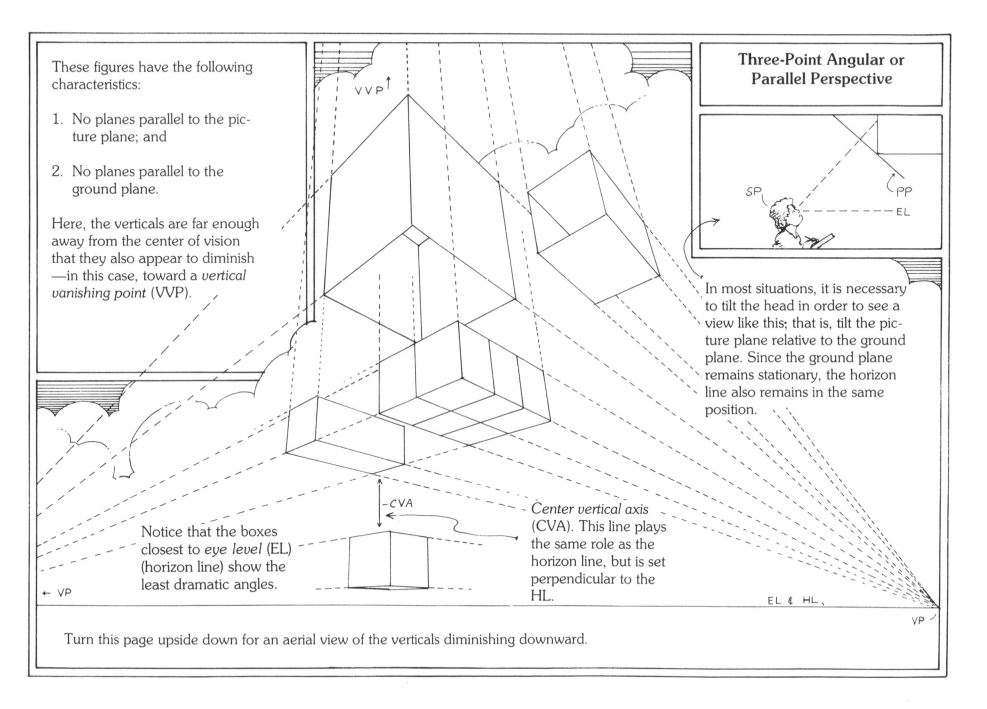

These figures have the following characteristics:

1. No planes parallel to the picture plane; and

2. No planes parallel to the ground plane.

Here, the verticals are far enough away from the center of vision that they also appear to diminish —in this case, toward a *vertical vanishing point* (VVP).

VVP↑

Three-Point Angular or Parallel Perspective

SP

PP

EL

In most situations, it is necessary to tilt the head in order to *see* a view like this; that is, tilt the picture plane relative to the ground plane. Since the ground plane remains stationary, the horizon line also remains in the same position.

CVA

Notice that the boxes closest to *eye level* (EL) (horizon line) show the least dramatic angles.

Center vertical axis (CVA). This line plays the same role as the horizon line, but is set perpendicular to the HL.

← VP

EL & HL

VP

Turn this page upside down for an aerial view of the verticals diminishing downward.

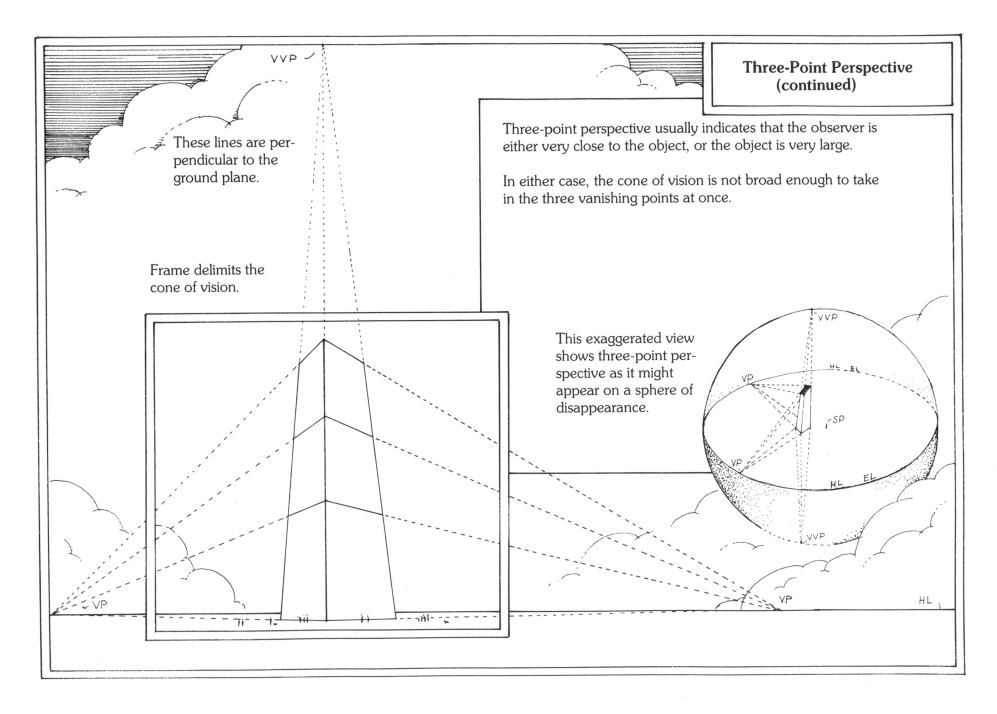

VVP

These lines are perpendicular to the ground plane.

Frame delimits the cone of vision.

Three-point perspective usually indicates that the observer is either very close to the object, or the object is very large.

In either case, the cone of vision is not broad enough to take in the three vanishing points at once.

This exaggerated view shows three-point perspective as it might appear on a sphere of disappearance.

VVP

HL EL

VP

SP

VP

HL EL

VVP

VP

HL

VP

HL

18

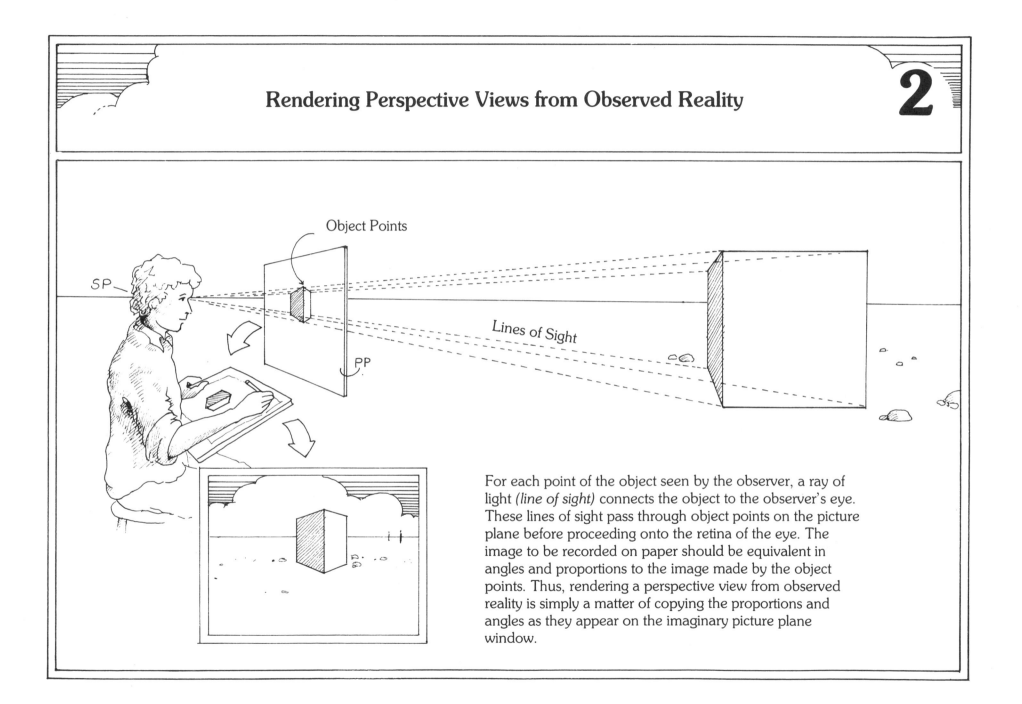

Rendering Perspective Views from Observed Reality

Object Points

SP

PP

Lines of Sight

For each point of the object seen by the observer, a ray of light *(line of sight)* connects the object to the observer's eye. These lines of sight pass through object points on the picture plane before proceeding onto the retina of the eye. The image to be recorded on paper should be equivalent in angles and proportions to the image made by the object points. Thus, rendering a perspective view from observed reality is simply a matter of copying the proportions and angles as they appear on the imaginary picture plane window.

Finding Proportions

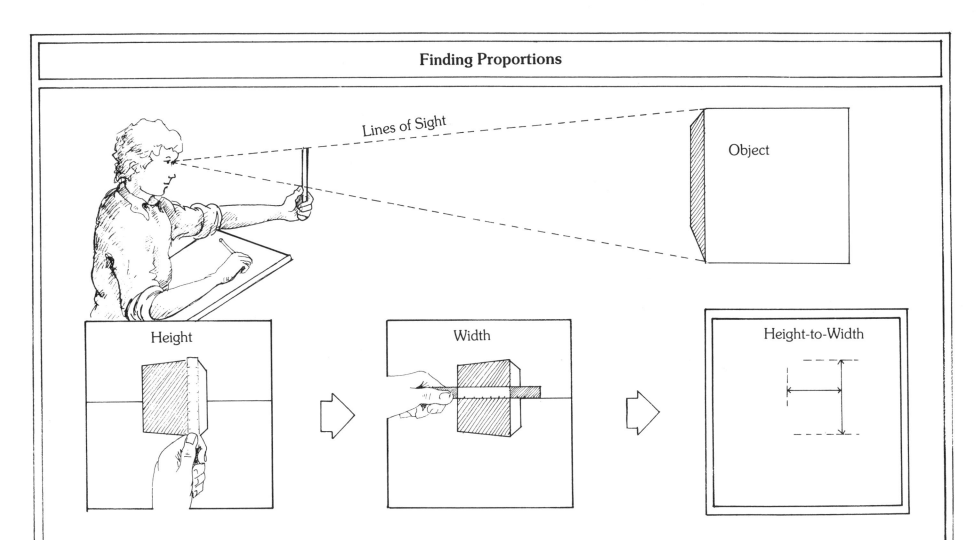

The proportions of an object can be taken from the picture plane window simply by viewing the object over a straightedge held at arm's length. By marking the lengths on the straightedge with the thumb, the height and width can be compared and transferred to the drawing at whatever scale is desired.

Hold the measuring arm straight so that it will always be the same distance from the eye. Remember that the straightedge represents the picture plane.

Finding Angles

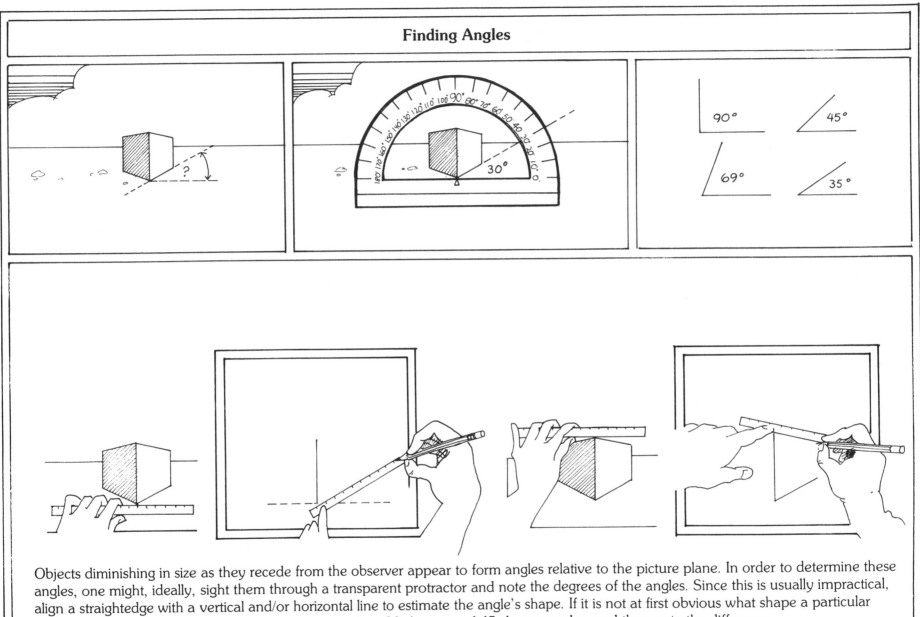

Objects diminishing in size as they recede from the observer appear to form angles relative to the picture plane. In order to determine these angles, one might, ideally, sight them through a transparent protractor and note the degrees of the angles. Since this is usually impractical, align a straightedge with a vertical and/or horizontal line to estimate the angle's shape. If it is not at first obvious what shape a particular angle takes, try comparing it to common angles, such as 90-degree and 45-degree angles, and then note the difference.

Finding the Angles of an Observed Object

If you can copy the angles and proportions of an object or scene, as discussed on the previous page, you can render a correct perspective of any object or space even without knowing the rules of linear perspective. Rendering the images from a view is really nothing more than making a one-to-one match of angles and proportions, as they appear on the imaginary picture plane.

A knowledge of perspective, however, has a twofold value:

1. It saves time, by minimizing the number of measures of proportions and angles that must be taken; and

2. The perspective system is self-correcting. Even if you misread one angle, the completed perspective will point out the error or, at worst, shift the viewpoint slightly.

The following three pages offer some simple steps for rendering perspective views from reality. Note that the basic procedure is to move from the simple to the complex—from essentials to incidentals.

It is critical in any view to establish the horizon line (viewer's eye level) first.

1. Find a vertical line on the object, preferably near you and your center of vision.

2. Find the angle of the receding plane off the vertical line. The farther above or below eye level, the better, since the angle will be more extreme and easier to estimate.

3. Find a second angle on the same side of the vertical line.

4. The point at which these two lines cross is the vanishing point.

5. Draw a line through this vanishing point parallel to the bottom of the paper (that is, parallel to the bottom of the picture plane). This is the horizon line (eye level).

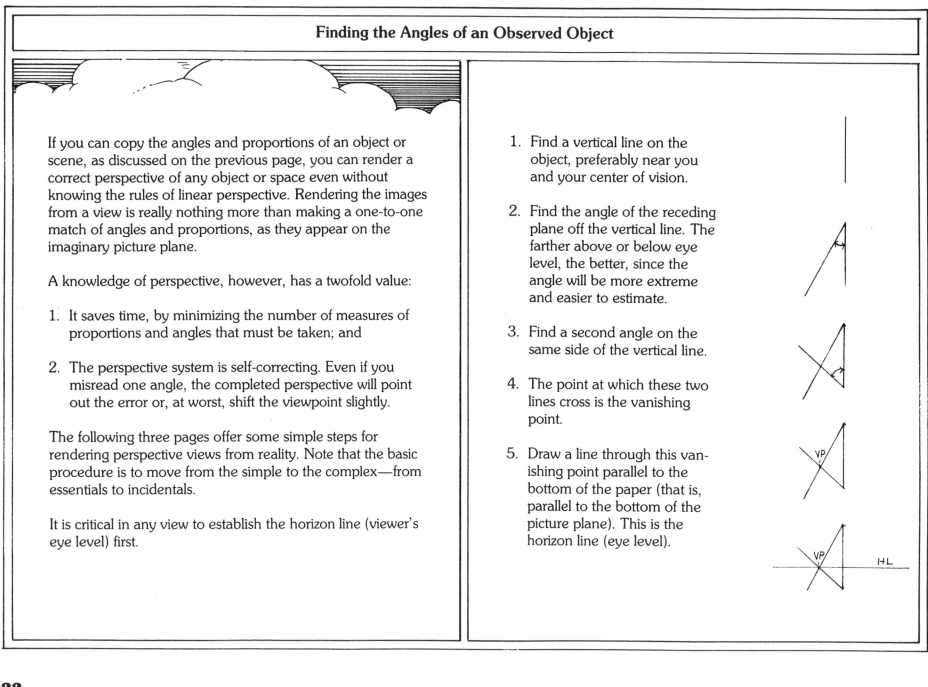

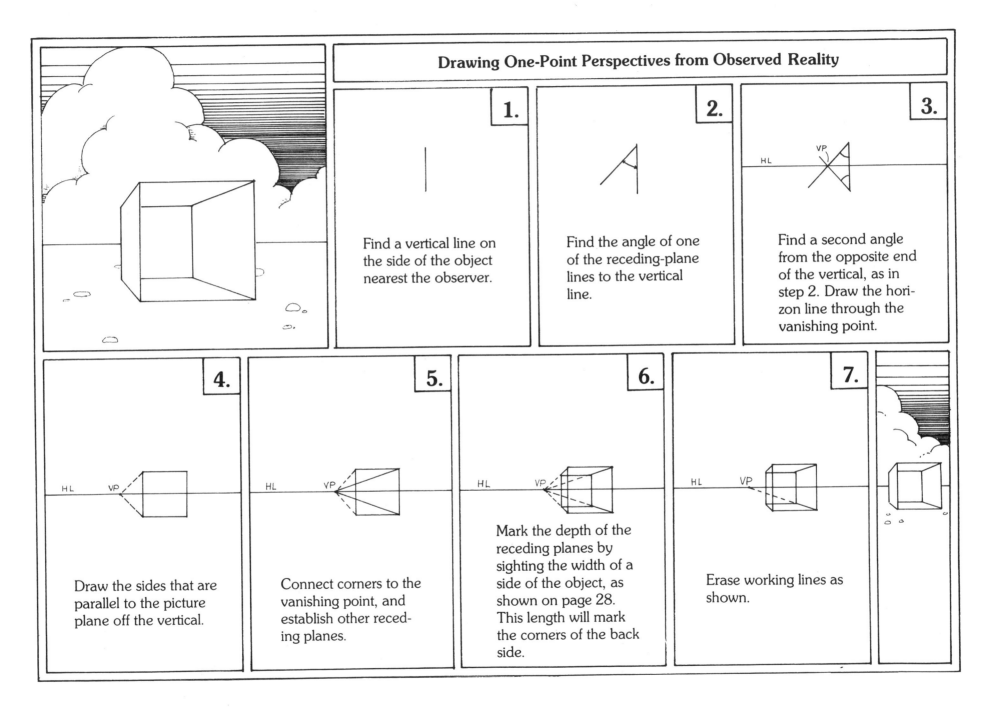

Drawing One-Point Perspectives from Observed Reality

1. Find a vertical line on the side of the object nearest the observer.

2. Find the angle of one of the receding-plane lines to the vertical line.

3. Find a second angle from the opposite end of the vertical, as in step 2. Draw the horizon line through the vanishing point.

4. Draw the sides that are parallel to the picture plane off the vertical.

5. Connect corners to the vanishing point, and establish other receding planes.

6. Mark the depth of the receding planes by sighting the width of a side of the object, as shown on page 28. This length will mark the corners of the back side.

7. Erase working lines as shown.

23

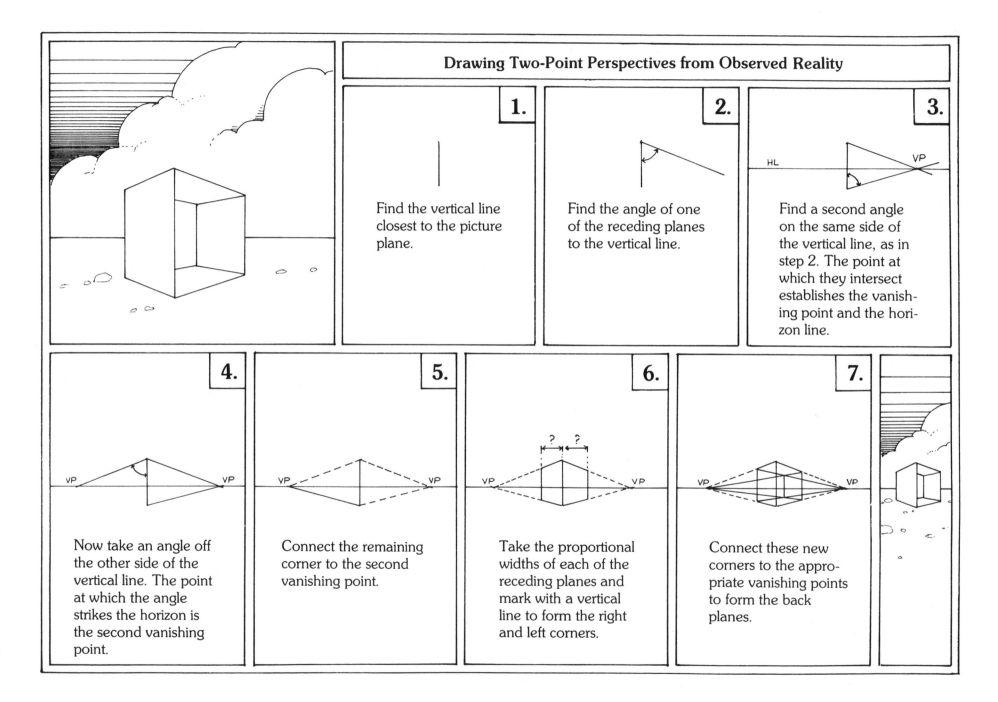

Drawing Two-Point Perspectives from Observed Reality

1. Find the vertical line closest to the picture plane.

2. Find the angle of one of the receding planes to the vertical line.

3. Find a second angle on the same side of the vertical line, as in step 2. The point at which they intersect establishes the vanishing point and the horizon line.

4. Now take an angle off the other side of the vertical line. The point at which the angle strikes the horizon is the second vanishing point.

5. Connect the remaining corner to the second vanishing point.

6. Take the proportional widths of each of the receding planes and mark with a vertical line to form the right and left corners.

7. Connect these new corners to the appropriate vanishing points to form the back planes.

24

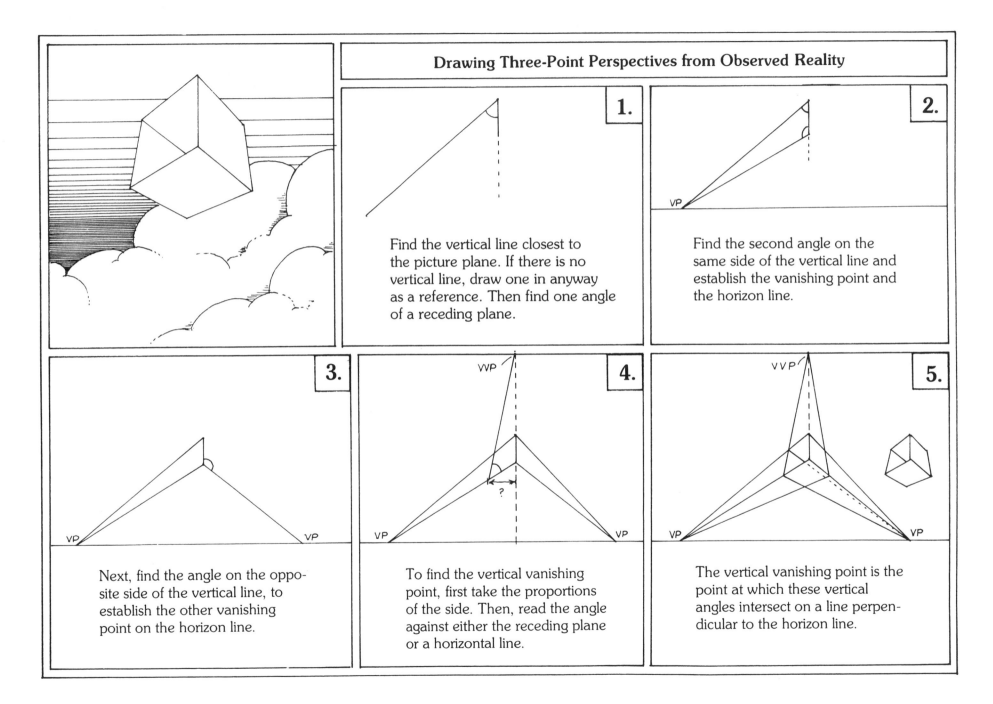

Drawing Three-Point Perspectives from Observed Reality

1. Find the vertical line closest to the picture plane. If there is no vertical line, draw one in anyway as a reference. Then find one angle of a receding plane.

2. Find the second angle on the same side of the vertical line and establish the vanishing point and the horizon line.

3. Next, find the angle on the opposite side of the vertical line, to establish the other vanishing point on the horizon line.

4. To find the vertical vanishing point, first take the proportions of the side. Then, read the angle against either the receding plane or a horizontal line.

5. The vertical vanishing point is the point at which these vertical angles intersect on a line perpendicular to the horizon line.

3

Plans, Elevations, and Paraline Projections

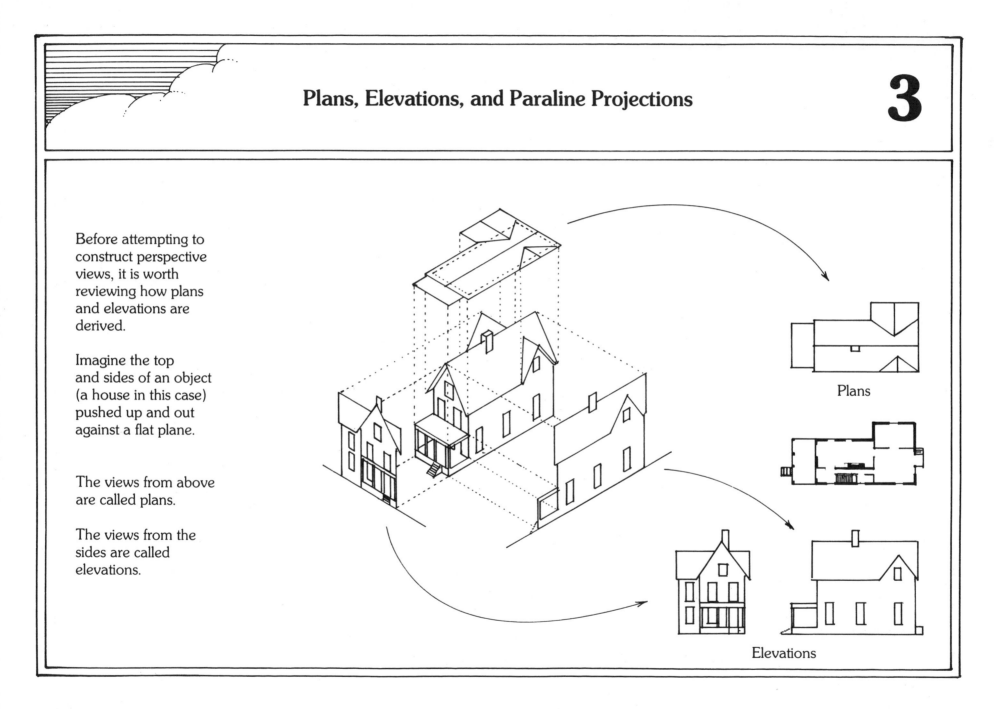

Before attempting to construct perspective views, it is worth reviewing how plans and elevations are derived.

Imagine the top and sides of an object (a house in this case) pushed up and out against a flat plane.

The views from above are called plans.

The views from the sides are called elevations.

Plans

Elevations

While the plan gives a view looking down on top of an object, it is often useful to slice a plane through the object to reveal important information.

In architectural drawings, for example, the plan is set up off the floor high enough to cut through and reveal windows and other important features.

Oblique of Floor Plan

Floor Plan

In the same way, elevations, or "sections," may be sliced vertically through the middle of objects in order to reveal interior arrangements.

Complex objects such as large buildings may require large numbers of such plans, elevations, and sections.

Elevation

Section Elevation

Complex curved objects,
such as boats and
airplanes, require
even more elaborate
methods of representation.

While the principles
remain the same, the
objects must be sliced
at numerous intervals
in order to mark off
reference points for
the curving lines.

Here, the simple plan
and elevations of
a canoe have been
subdivided into a
series of parallel
and intersecting planes.

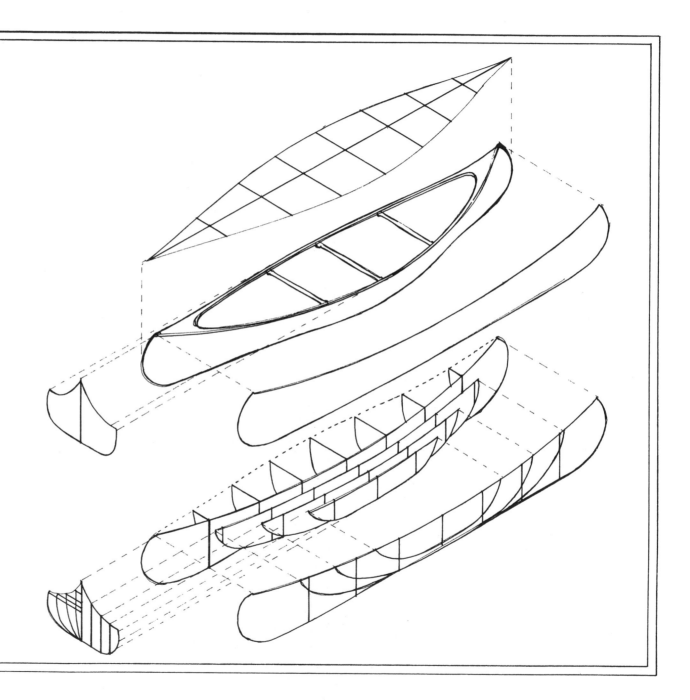

Paraline Drawing

Without resorting to the complexities of creating a fully "correct" optical perspective for an object, it is possible, and sometimes preferable, to employ paraline projection techniques. Paraline drawings are a kind of shorthand for creating a three-dimensional sense of an object and, as with all drawing techniques, they have their advantages and disadvantages.

One of the advantages of utilizing paraline drawings is that images can be drawn rapidly and to scale, using simple drafting tools (T square, triangles, and rule). Even in freehand, paraline drawings make it possible to conjure up credible three-dimensional images as part of the design process. More to our direct purpose of studying optical linear perspective, paraline drawings can be a tremendous aid in clarifying the basic lines, planes, and forms requisite for developing a full perspective or rendering.

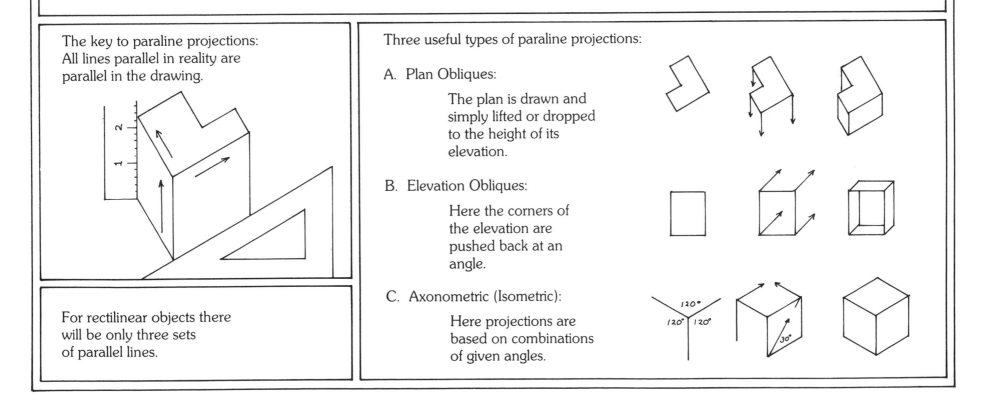

The key to paraline projections:
All lines parallel in reality are parallel in the drawing.

For rectilinear objects there will be only three sets of parallel lines.

Three useful types of paraline projections:

A. Plan Obliques:

The plan is drawn and simply lifted or dropped to the height of its elevation.

B. Elevation Obliques:

Here the corners of the elevation are pushed back at an angle.

C. Axonometric (Isometric):

Here projections are based on combinations of given angles.

To draw a plan oblique, first set up the plan so that it reveals the sides you are most interested in showing.

To facilitate the process it is practical to use a 45° or 60°/30° triangle.

Once the plan is down, drop or raise the vertical from the corners of the plan to the heights indicated by the elevation.

Depending on the project, sometimes it is easier to assume the plan is on top so that the elevation can be dropped to ground level. This saves having to draw in what will be hidden lines. On other occasions, it is better to raise the elevation off a plan laid on the ground, then erase the hidden lines.

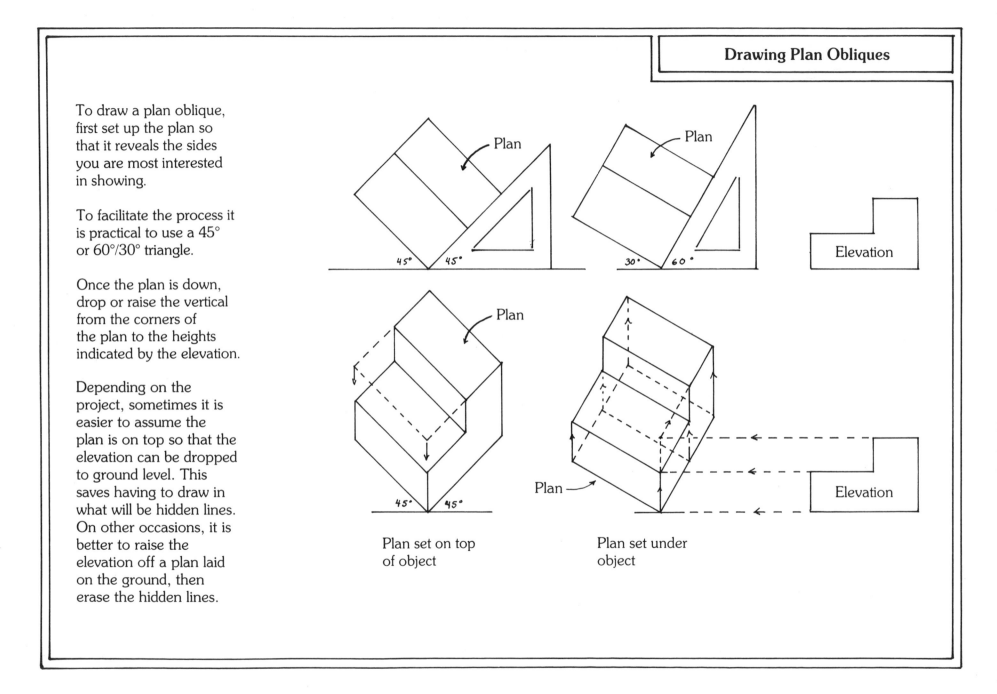

Plan set on top of object

Plan set under object

Like all other forms of paraline drawing, plan obliques have some important limitations when compared to fully developed optical perspectives.

All plan obliques limit the supposed angle of view to what would be about a 45° angle above or below the object.

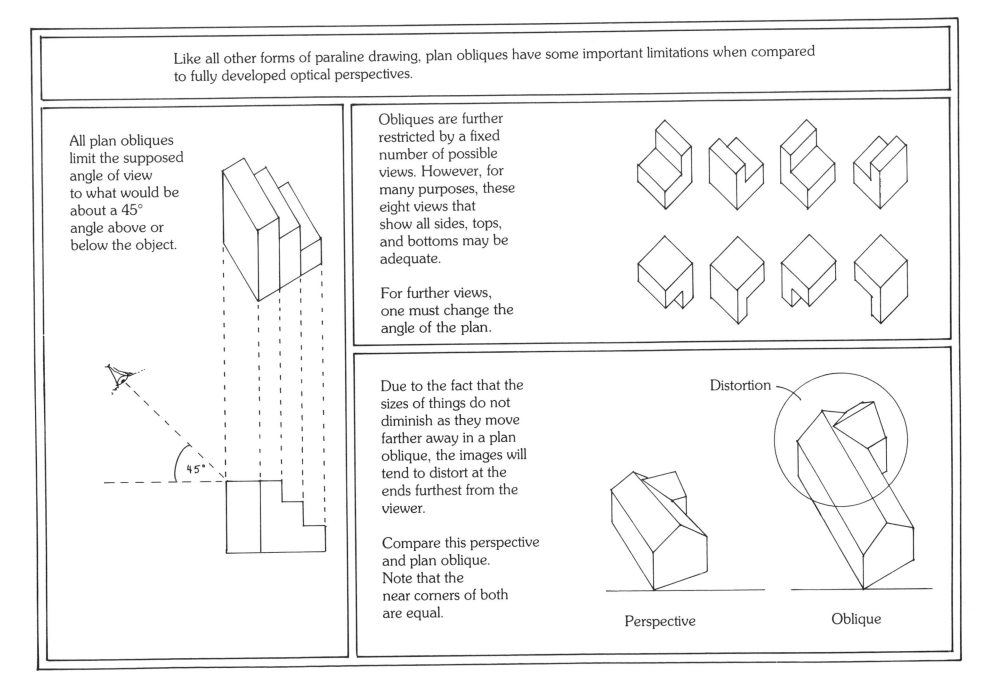

Obliques are further restricted by a fixed number of possible views. However, for many purposes, these eight views that show all sides, tops, and bottoms may be adequate.

For further views, one must change the angle of the plan.

Due to the fact that the sizes of things do not diminish as they move farther away in a plan oblique, the images will tend to distort at the ends furthest from the viewer.

Compare this perspective and plan oblique. Note that the near corners of both are equal.

Distortion

Perspective   Oblique

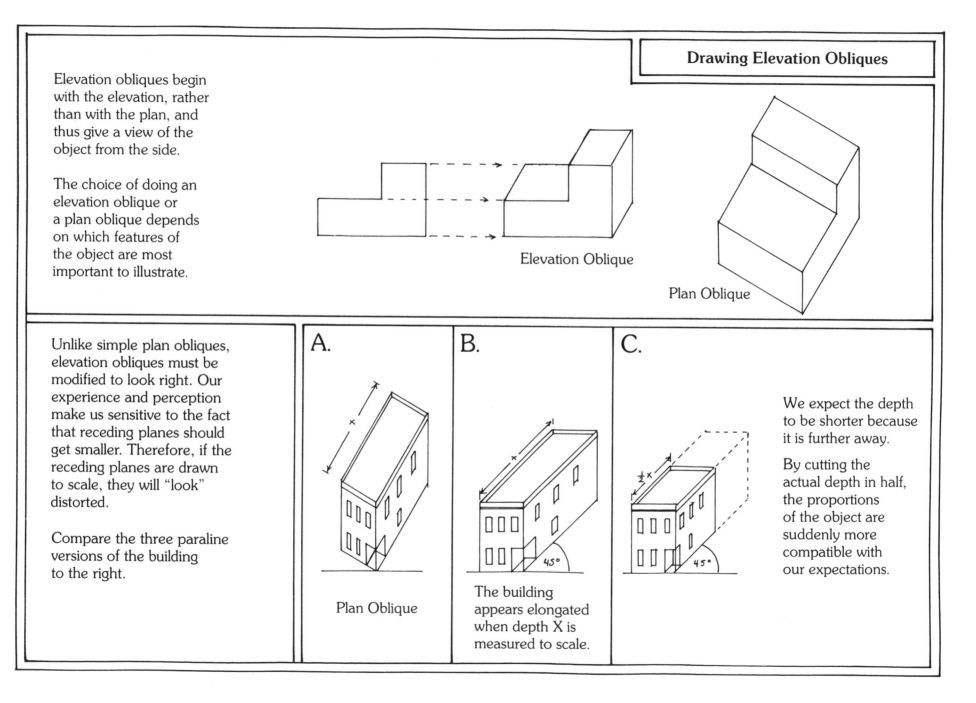

Elevation obliques begin with the elevation, rather than with the plan, and thus give a view of the object from the side.

The choice of doing an elevation oblique or a plan oblique depends on which features of the object are most important to illustrate.

Elevation Oblique

Plan Oblique

Unlike simple plan obliques, elevation obliques must be modified to look right. Our experience and perception make us sensitive to the fact that receding planes should get smaller. Therefore, if the receding planes are drawn to scale, they will "look" distorted.

Compare the three paraline versions of the building to the right.

A.

Plan Oblique

B.

The building appears elongated when depth X is measured to scale.

45°

C.

We expect the depth to be shorter because it is further away.

By cutting the actual depth in half, the proportions of the object are suddenly more compatible with our expectations.

45°

32

Fortunately, the lengths of the receding lines in an elevation oblique can easily be determined with the following formula:

The length of a receding line should be reduced by the percentage of a 90° angle that the receding angle represents.

For example: If the receding lines are at 45° (i.e., one-half of 90°), then each receding line should be cut to one-half of its correct measured length (see previous page).

Examples of corrections using standard 45° and 60°/30° triangles.

Note the distortion in these drawings of cubes, even though all sides are measured to equal lengths.

Here the cubes have been "corrected" by the formulaic reduction of the depth dimension.

As long as the reduction is applied, sides can still be scaled.

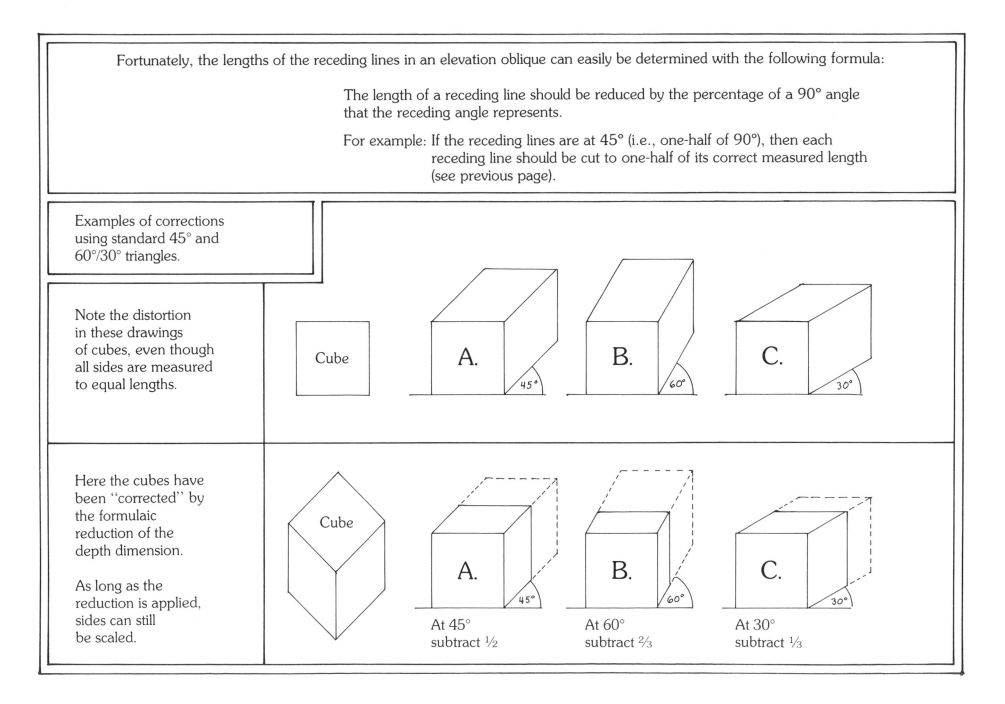

At 45° subtract ½

At 60° subtract ⅔

At 30° subtract ⅓

Isometric projections are a subcategory of axonometric techniques. Rather than starting with the plan or elevation, isometric drawings, like other axonometrics, are determined by the angles at which the three planes of a cube meet. The lengths of the three sets of parallel lines in an isometric can be measured to scale as in a plan oblique; however, right-angles are distorted to either 60° to 120°

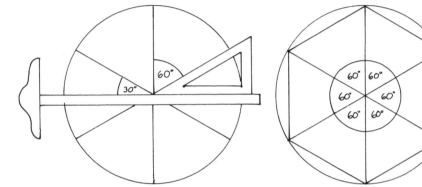
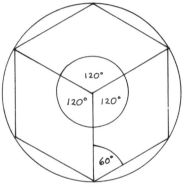
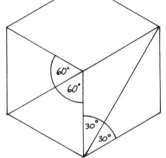

With the aid of a T square and a 60°/30° triangle, it is possible to construct forms to scale very rapidly with this method. Not only can planes be measured to scale, but squares and cubes can easily be found using 30° or 60° diagonals through the corners (i.e., 30° and 60° will be equal to 45° in plans or elevations).

As with the other paraline methods, isometric drawings will appear to distort on their far side, as the parallel receding lines violate the laws of diminishing size for receding objects.

Distortion

Isometrics and other axonometrics (dimetrics and trimetrics) are often used in engineering illustration. Numerous aids are available for precise axonometric drawings, such as special grids at given angles, and a variety of templates.

All attempts to create a three-dimensional illusion on a two-dimensional surface assume that the light reflected off the object passes through a picture plane where the object's image is recorded.

Paraline projections assume that those rays of light reflecting off the object remain parallel to one another.

Only in optical perspective is it assumed that the rays (lines of sight) converge at a finite point, i.e., the observer's eye (station point).

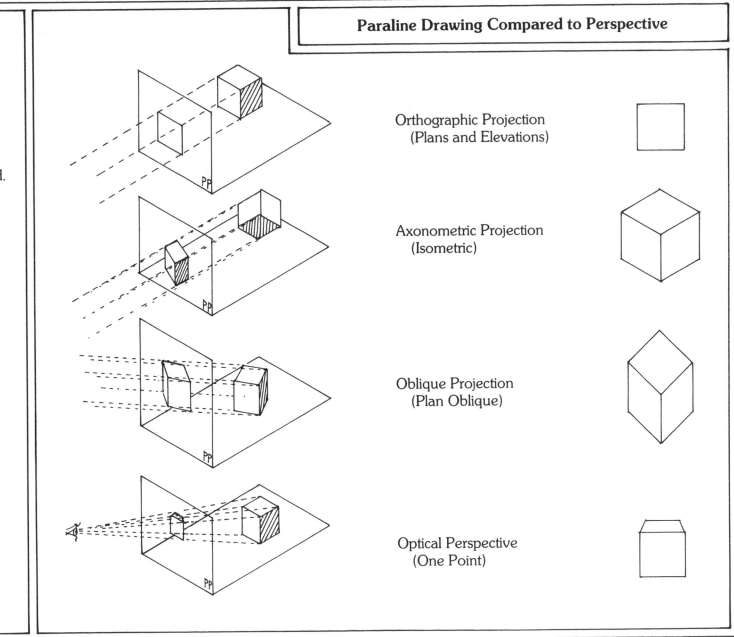

Orthographic Projection
(Plans and Elevations)

Axonometric Projection
(Isometric)

Oblique Projection
(Plan Oblique)

Optical Perspective
(One Point)

Constructing Perspective Views

When rendering perspective views from real objects or models, the view can be controlled only within certain limitations. The great advantage of constructing or making a perspective is that virtually any view can be represented, even if such a view would be impossible to see in a real situation.

In order to construct perspective views, it is necessary to take into consideration certain interconnected variables that will affect the final image.

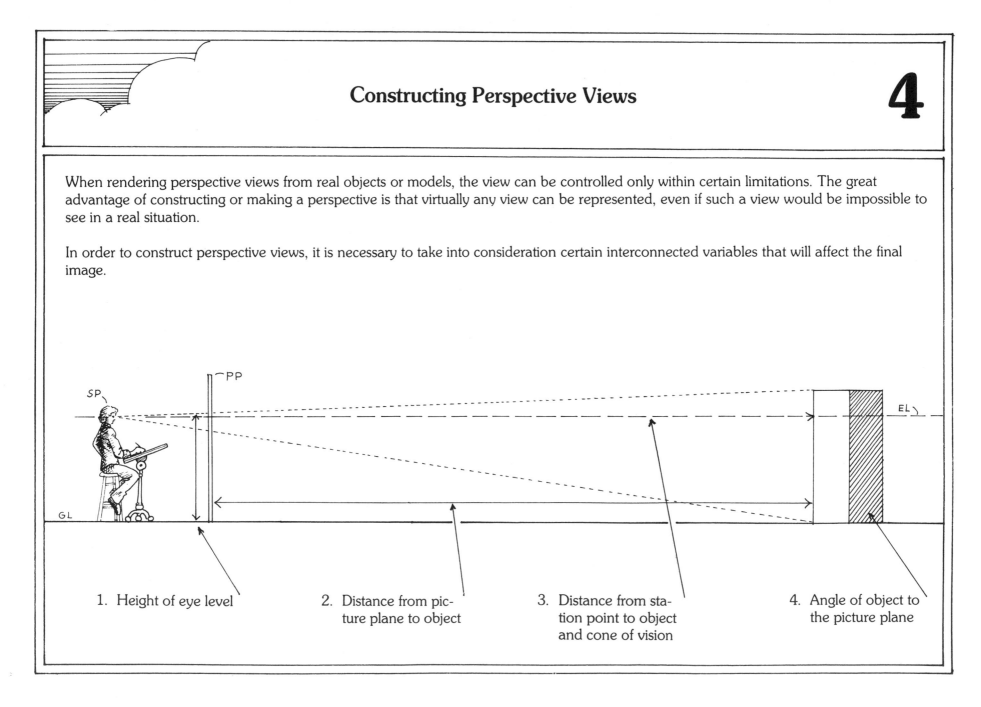

1. Height of eye level

2. Distance from picture plane to object

3. Distance from station point to object and cone of vision

4. Angle of object to the picture plane

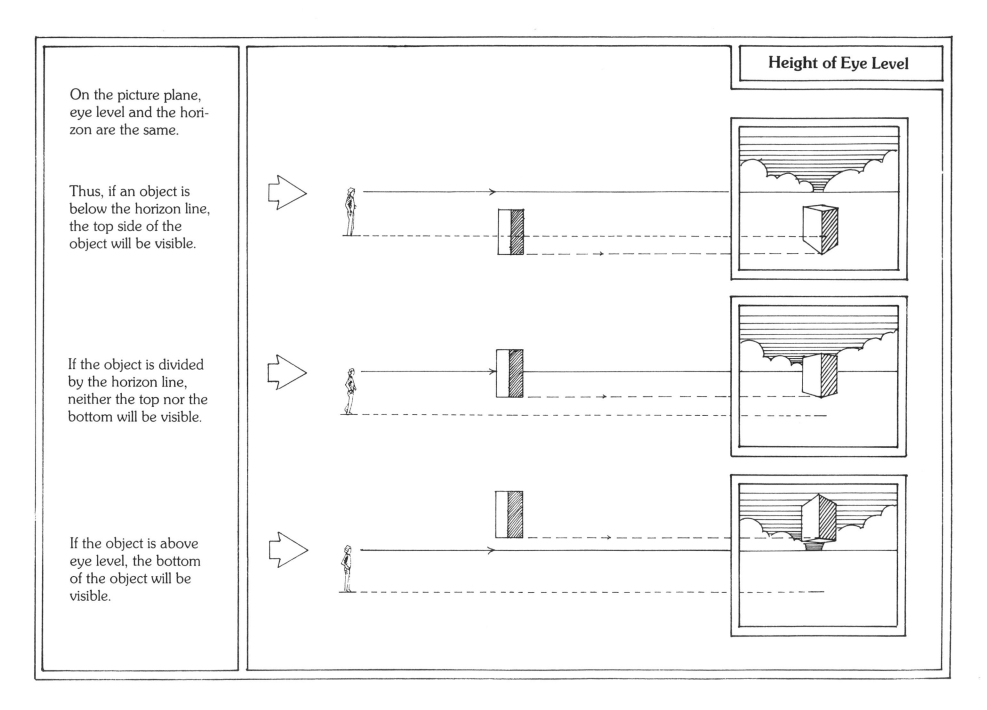

On the picture plane, eye level and the horizon are the same.

Thus, if an object is below the horizon line, the top side of the object will be visible.

If the object is divided by the horizon line, neither the top nor the bottom will be visible.

If the object is above eye level, the bottom of the object will be visible.

Height of Eye Level

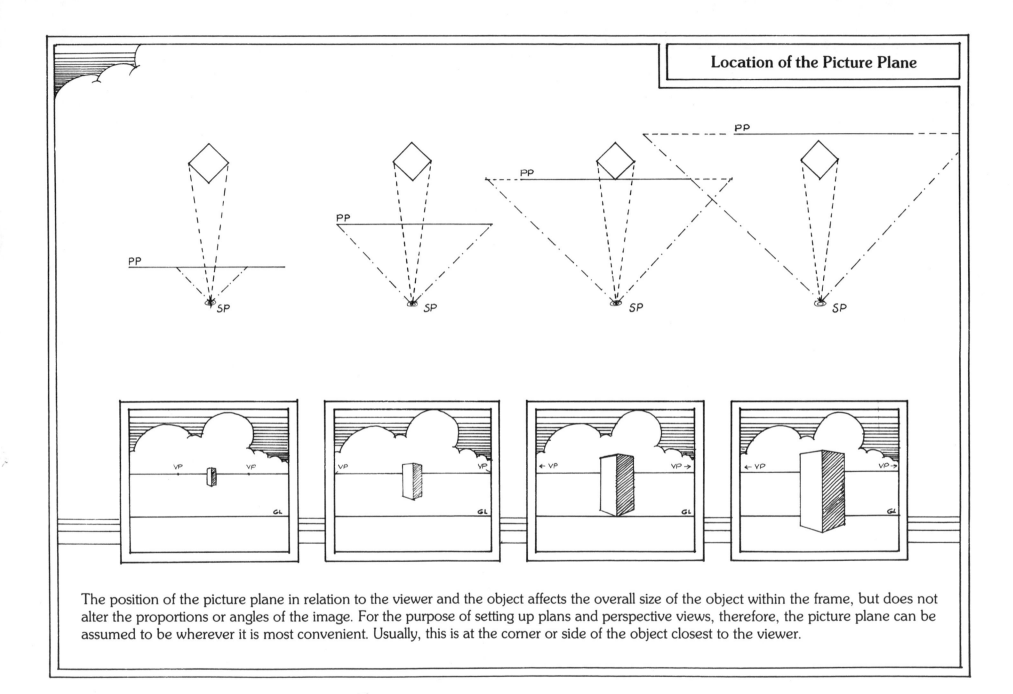

The position of the picture plane in relation to the viewer and the object affects the overall size of the object within the frame, but does not alter the proportions or angles of the image. For the purpose of setting up plans and perspective views, therefore, the picture plane can be assumed to be wherever it is most convenient. Usually, this is at the corner or side of the object closest to the viewer.

As our normal vision with one eye is limited to the spread of a 60° cone of vision, light received from outside that cone (i.e., peripheral vision) will appear distorted.

Thus, as we have seen, the circle at which the cone intersects the picture plane establishes the limits of the "normal" picture frame.

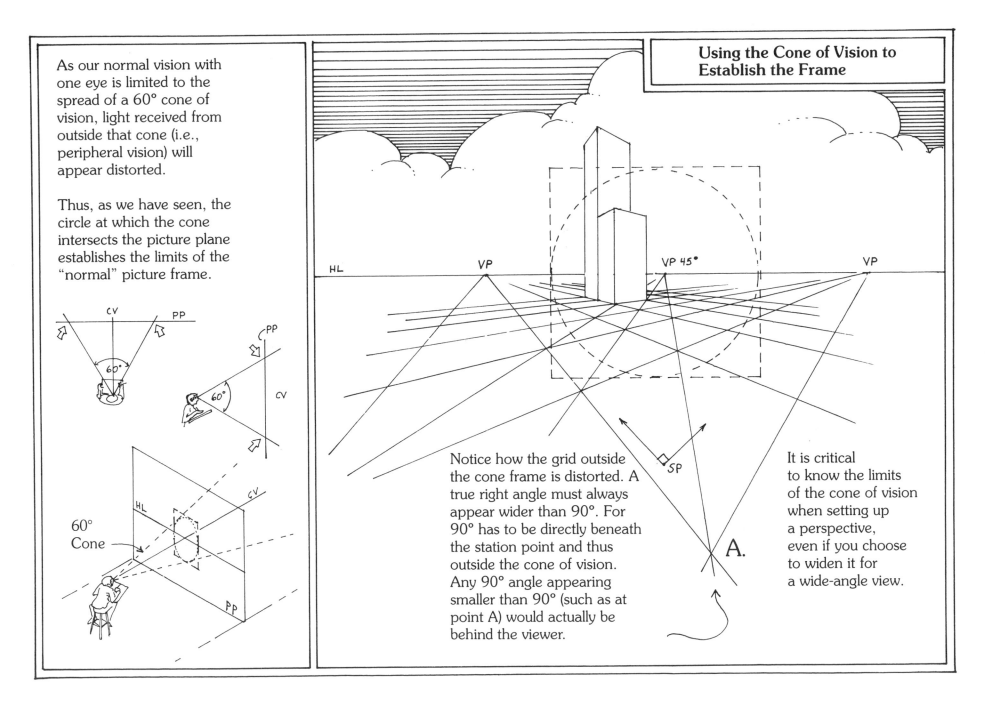

60° Cone

Notice how the grid outside the cone frame is distorted. A true right angle must always appear wider than 90°. For 90° has to be directly beneath the station point and thus outside the cone of vision. Any 90° angle appearing smaller than 90° (such as at point A) would actually be behind the viewer.

It is critical to know the limits of the cone of vision when setting up a perspective, even if you choose to widen it for a wide-angle view.

A.

The distance between the station point and the object determines:
1. The size of the drawn object.
2. The angle of the receding planes of the object.

Notice how the angles of the drawn object are more acute at 10 feet than at 40 feet: this explains why objects shot through a tele-photo lens appear flattened out.

Notice also that the cone of vision (60°) determines the frame of a normal view.

Thus, the "size" of the drawn view is relative to the frame (cone of vision) through which it is seen.

Once established, the frame can be cropped for composition.

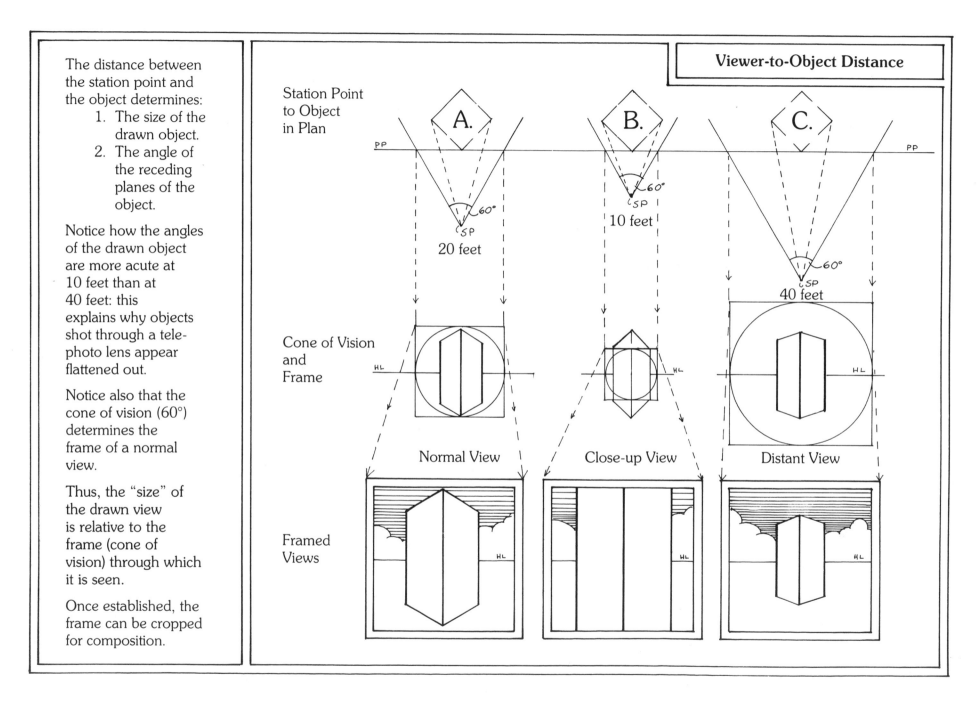

Viewer-to-Object Distance

Station Point to Object in Plan

PP

A.

B.

C.

60°
SP
20 feet

60°
SP
10 feet

60°
SP
40 feet

PP

Cone of Vision and Frame

HL

HL

HL

Normal View

Close-up View

Distant View

Framed Views

HL

HL

HL

The angle of the object to the picture plane determines which side or sides of the object will be visible. The angle of the object also determines the position of the vanishing points.

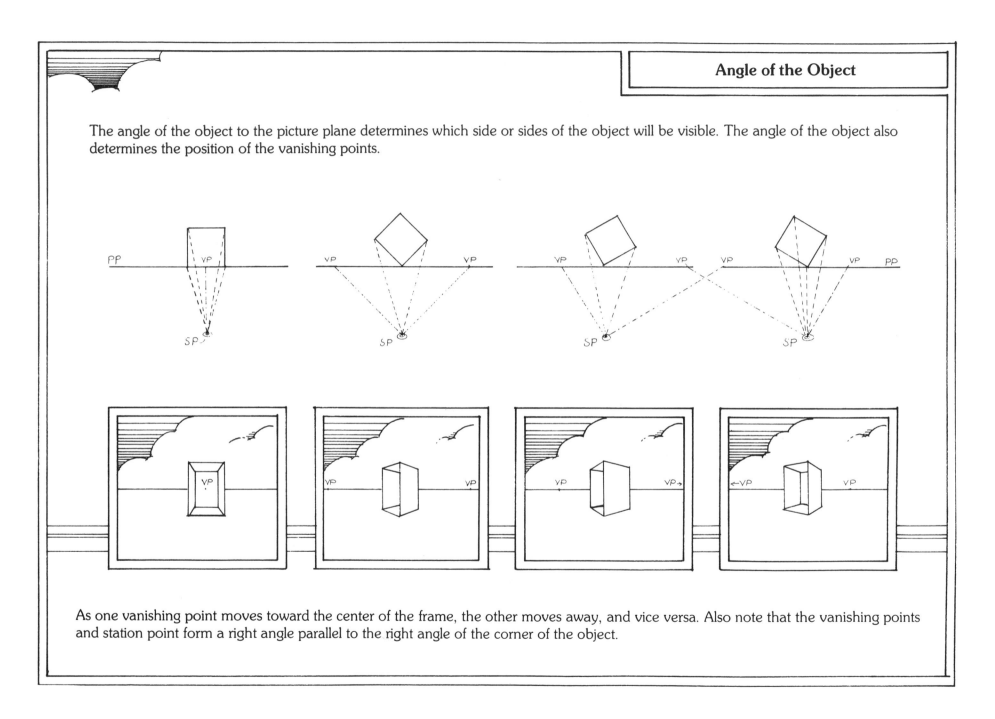

As one vanishing point moves toward the center of the frame, the other moves away, and vice versa. Also note that the vanishing points and station point form a right angle parallel to the right angle of the corner of the object.

41

Drawing a one-Point-Perspective View from a Plan

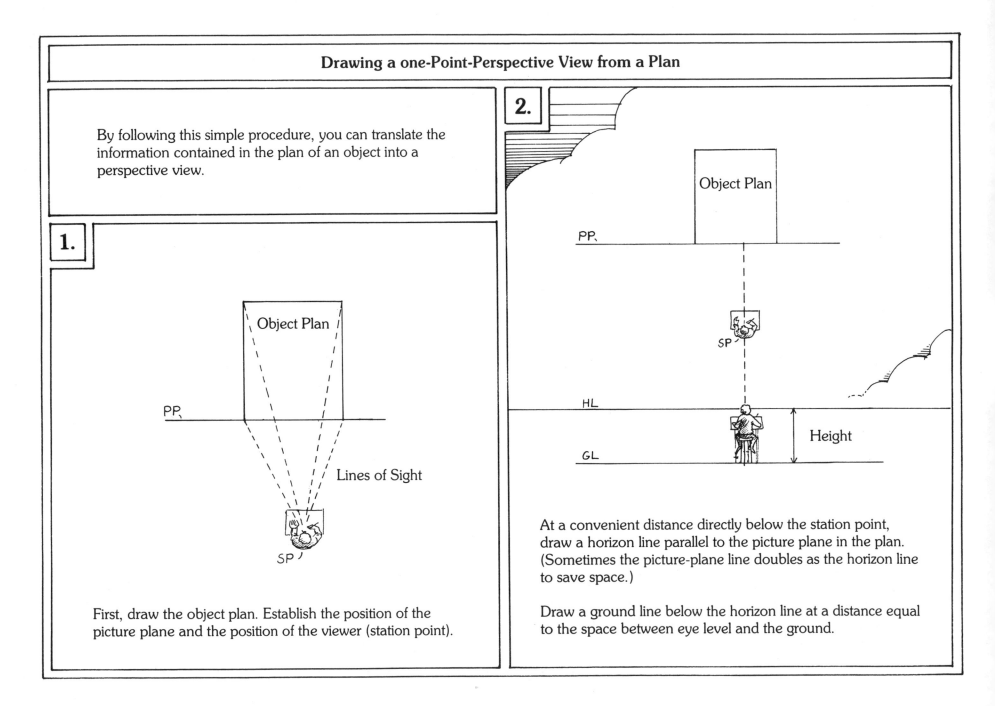

1.

By following this simple procedure, you can translate the information contained in the plan of an object into a perspective view.

Object Plan

PP.

Lines of Sight

SP

First, draw the object plan. Establish the position of the picture plane and the position of the viewer (station point).

2.

Object Plan

PP.

SP

HL

Height

GL

At a convenient distance directly below the station point, draw a horizon line parallel to the picture plane in the plan. (Sometimes the picture-plane line doubles as the horizon line to save space.)

Draw a ground line below the horizon line at a distance equal to the space between eye level and the ground.

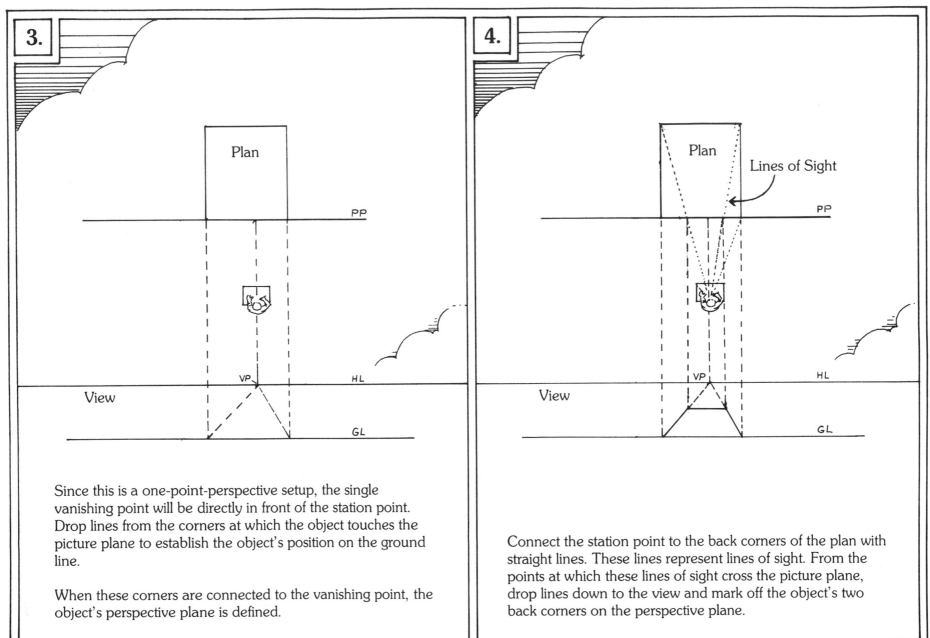

3.

Plan

PP

VP · · · · HL

View

GL

Since this is a one-point-perspective setup, the single vanishing point will be directly in front of the station point. Drop lines from the corners at which the object touches the picture plane to establish the object's position on the ground line.

When these corners are connected to the vanishing point, the object's perspective plane is defined.

4.

Plan

Lines of Sight

PP

VP · HL

View

GL

Connect the station point to the back corners of the plan with straight lines. These lines represent lines of sight. From the points at which these lines of sight cross the picture plane, drop lines down to the view and mark off the object's two back corners on the perspective plane.

In these more complex examples of one-point perspective, note how the lines of sight passing through the picture plane determine the corresponding position of the object in the view.

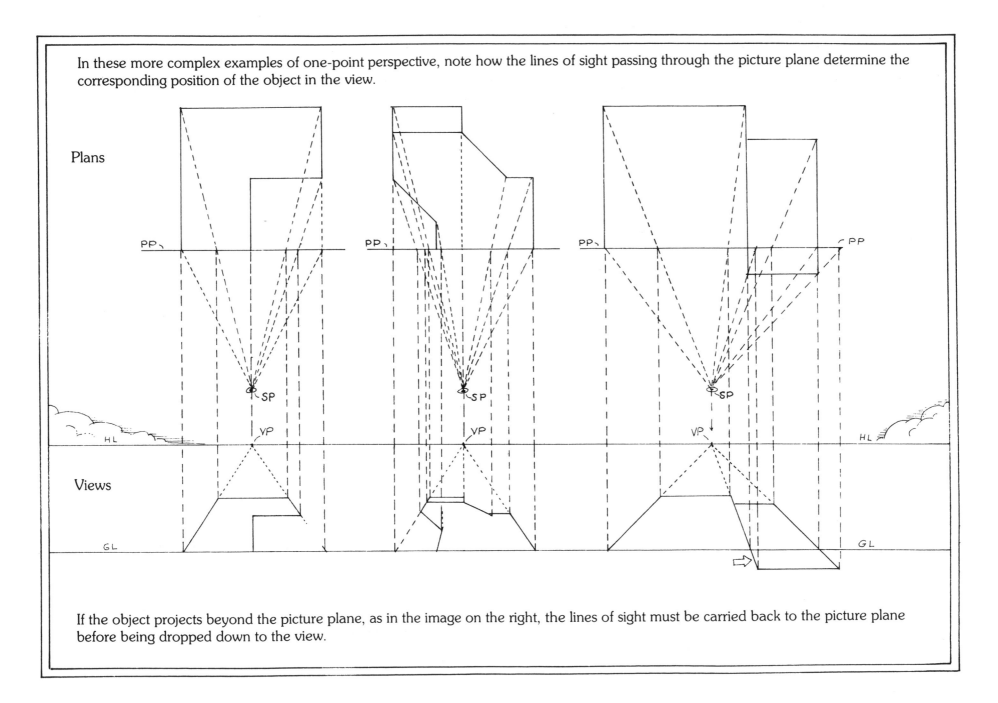

Plans

Views

If the object projects beyond the picture plane, as in the image on the right, the lines of sight must be carried back to the picture plane before being dropped down to the view.

Drawing a Two-Point-Perspective View from a Plan

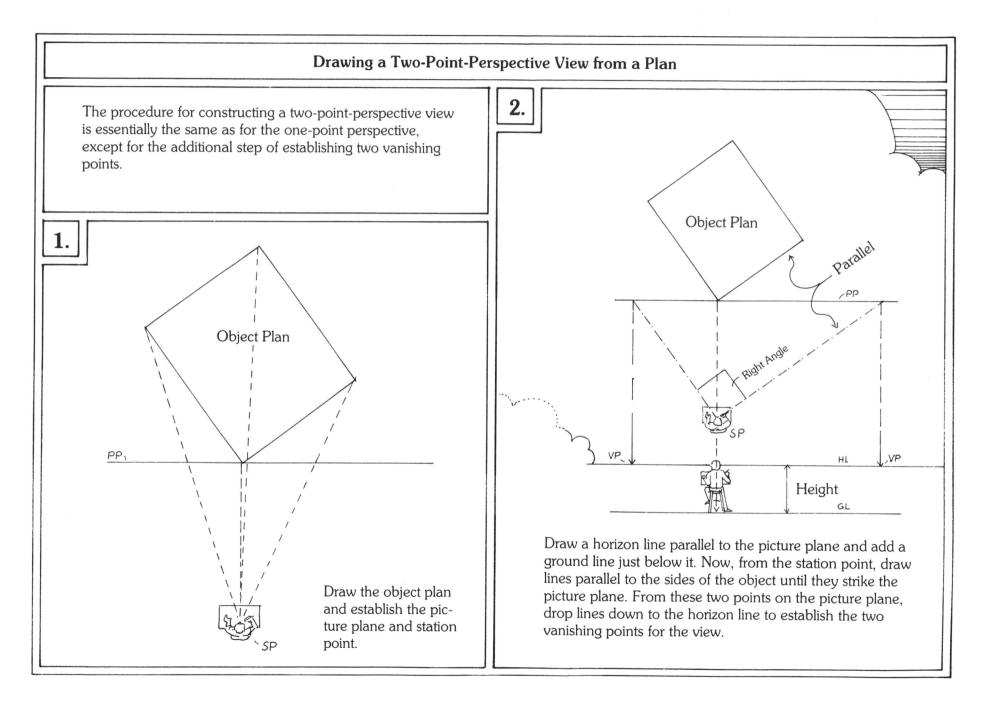

The procedure for constructing a two-point-perspective view is essentially the same as for the one-point perspective, except for the additional step of establishing two vanishing points.

1.

Object Plan

PP

SP

Draw the object plan and establish the picture plane and station point.

2.

Object Plan

Parallel

PP

Right Angle

SP

VP

HL

VP

Height

GL

Draw a horizon line parallel to the picture plane and add a ground line just below it. Now, from the station point, draw lines parallel to the sides of the object until they strike the picture plane. From these two points on the picture plane, drop lines down to the horizon line to establish the two vanishing points for the view.

45

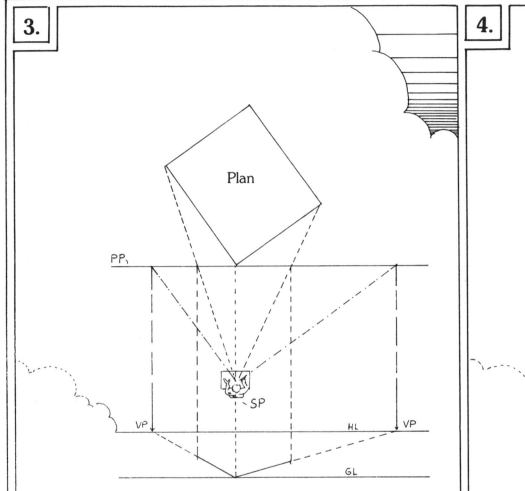

3.

Plan

PP,

VP · · · HL · · · VP

SP

GL

Drop a line from the corner of the object that touches the picture plane down to the ground line. Connect this point to the two vanishing points to establish the front receding planes of the object. The lines of sight from the right and left corners of the plan will mark points on the picture plane, which, in turn, will indicate the depth of the receding planes.

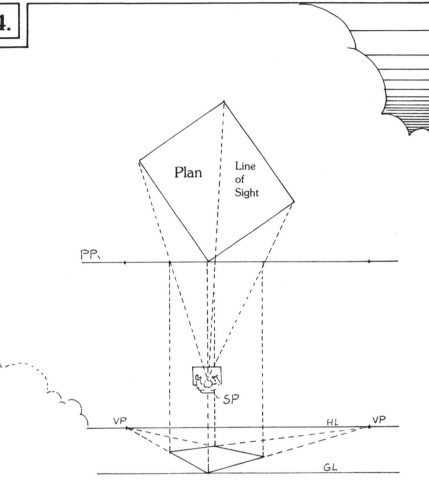

4.

Plan | Line of Sight

PP,

VP · · · HL · · · VP

SP

GL

The back planes of the object can now be found by connecting the left and right back corners of the front receding planes to their respective vanishing points. Note how these two lines intersect with the line of sight from the far corner of the object.

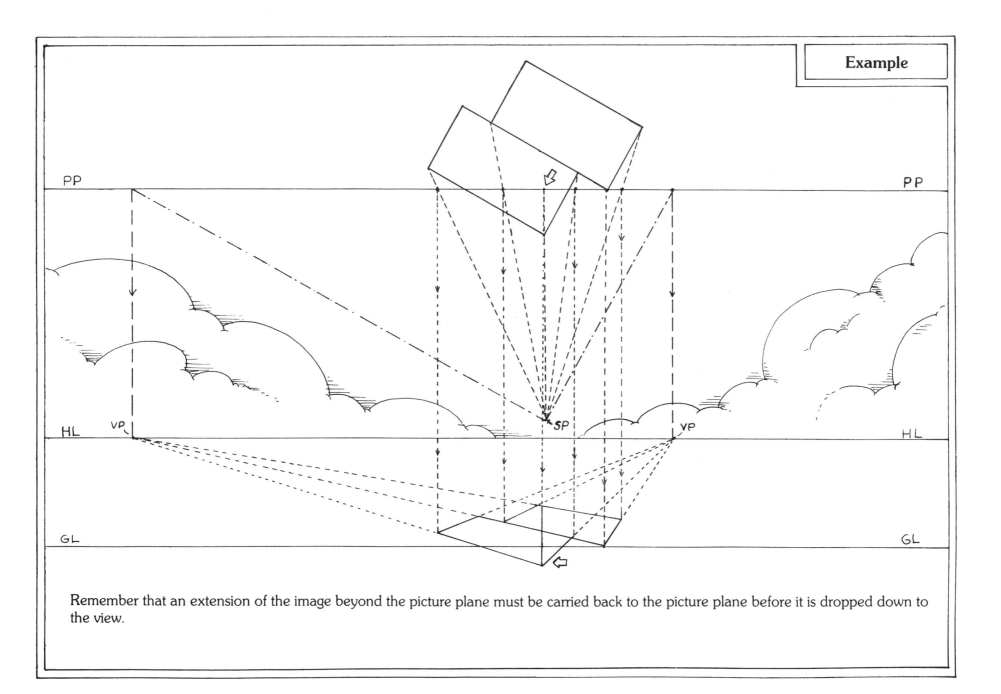

PP   PP

HL   VP   SP   VP   HL

GL   GL

Remember that an extension of the image beyond the picture plane must be carried back to the picture plane before it is dropped down to the view.

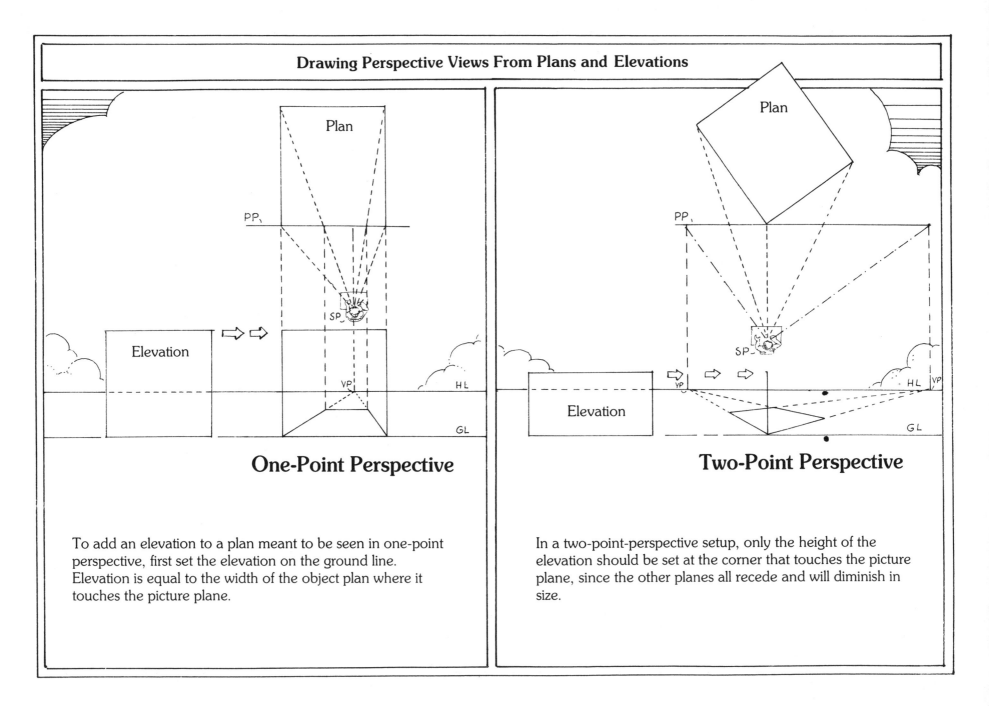

Drawing Perspective Views From Plans and Elevations

One-Point Perspective

To add an elevation to a plan meant to be seen in one-point perspective, first set the elevation on the ground line. Elevation is equal to the width of the object plan where it touches the picture plane.

Two-Point Perspective

In a two-point-perspective setup, only the height of the elevation should be set at the corner that touches the picture plane, since the other planes all recede and will diminish in size.

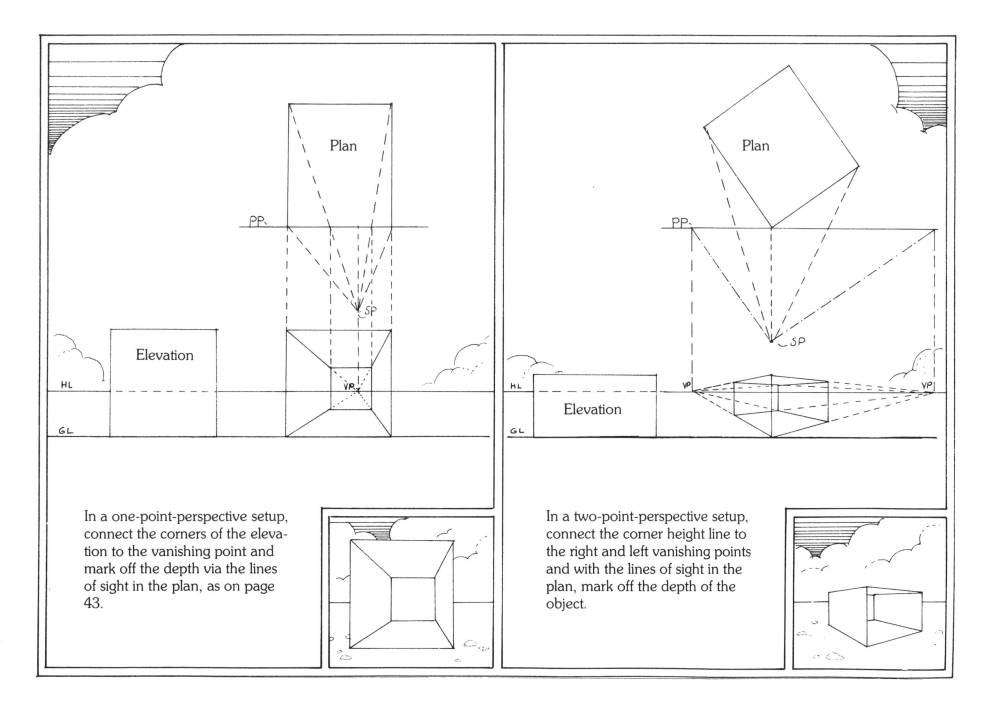

Plan

PP.

SP

Elevation

HL

VP

GL

In a one-point-perspective setup, connect the corners of the elevation to the vanishing point and mark off the depth via the lines of sight in the plan, as on page 43.

Plan

PP.

SP

HL

VP

Elevation

VP

GL

In a two-point-perspective setup, connect the corner height line to the right and left vanishing points and with the lines of sight in the plan, mark off the depth of the object.

In some situations, a single plan and elevation will be sufficient to reproduce a complete perspective of the object.

As the object becomes more and more complex, it becomes necessary to incorporate additional plans and elevations to convey the information.

By laying out plans and elevations separately, it is possible to position variations and details with great accuracy in the perspective view.

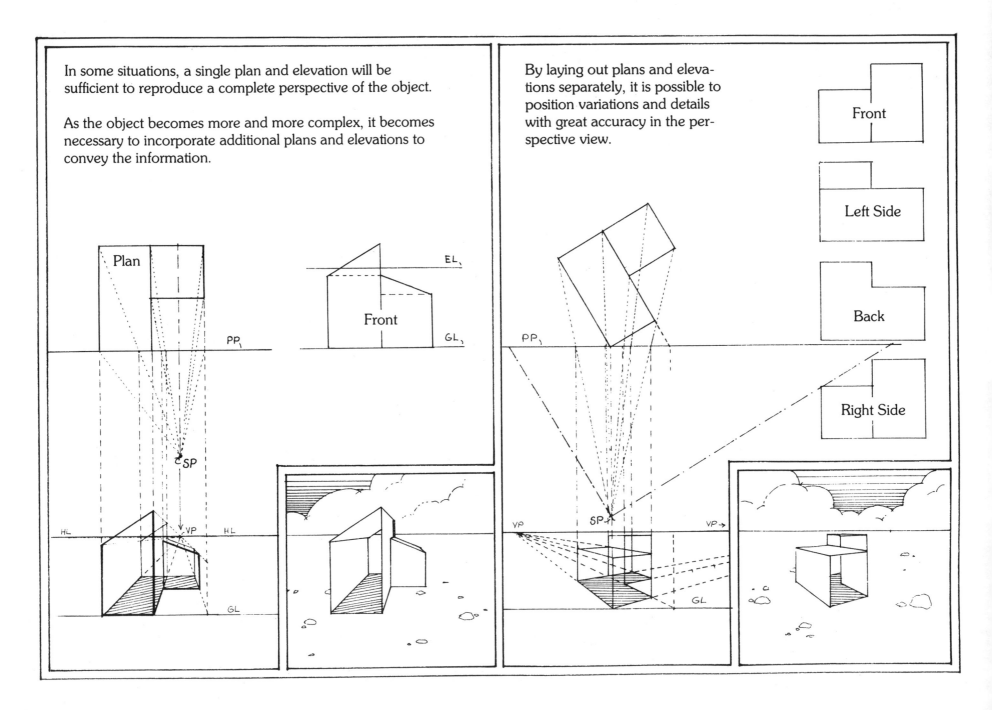

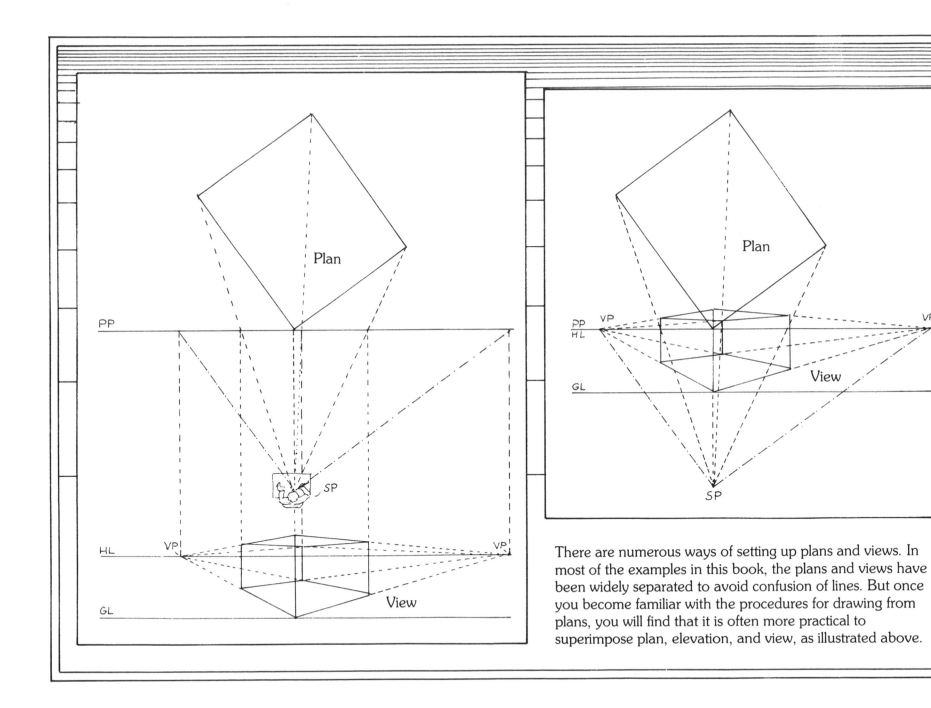

Plan

PP

SP

HL   VP   VP

GL   View

Plan

PP
HL   VP   VP

GL   View

SP

There are numerous ways of setting up plans and views. In most of the examples in this book, the plans and views have been widely separated to avoid confusion of lines. But once you become familiar with the procedures for drawing from plans, you will find that it is often more practical to superimpose plan, elevation, and view, as illustrated above.

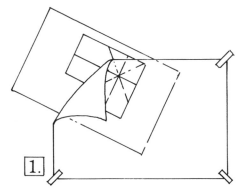

1. When taking plans into views it is usually most convenient to set the plan under a transparent drawing sheet, i.e., tracing paper or film.

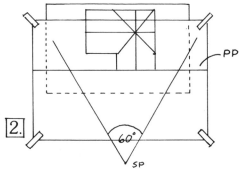

2. Draw in the picture plane (horizon line) where best for your composition. Set the station point so that the plan is inside the 60° cone of vision.

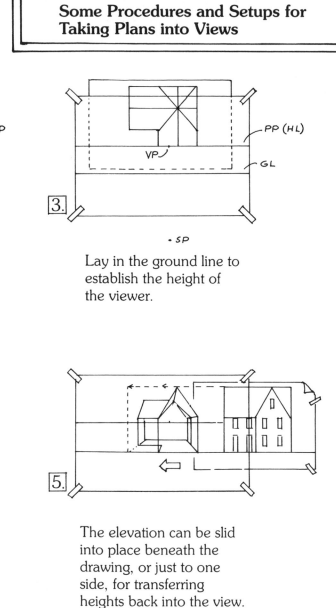

3. Lay in the ground line to establish the height of the viewer.

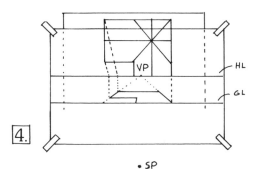

4. Drop the plan down into the view after setting up the vanishing point.

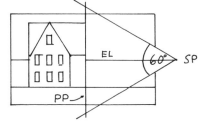

In the meantime, be sure to check the SP to PP distance against the elevation to make sure the elevation fits the cone as well.

5. The elevation can be slid into place beneath the drawing, or just to one side, for transferring heights back into the view.

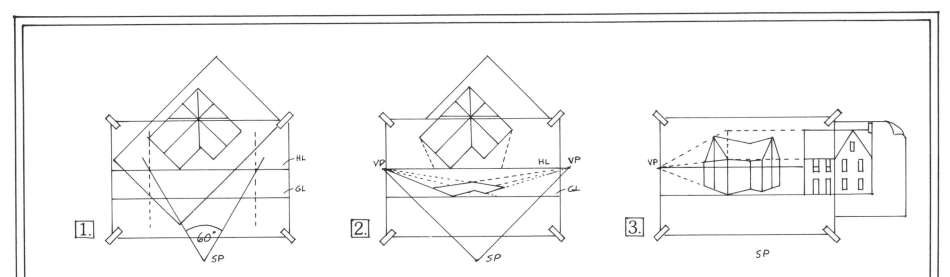

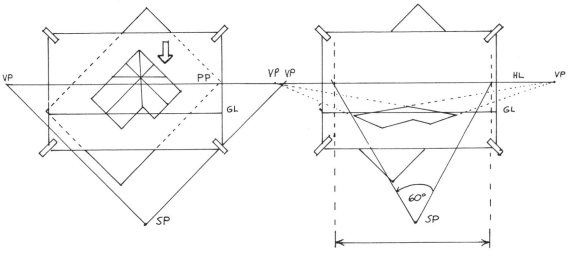

When setting up a two-point perspective, set the plan at the desired angle and proceed as just outlined for the one-point setup. Notice that here in the two-point perspective, the final image may appear considerably smaller than anticipated, relative to the size of the plans. This is due to the fact that all planes are receding behind the ground line (PP).

If you wish to enlarge the perspective image, simply move the plan forward of (downward from) the picture plane (compare to #1 above).

In order to keep the same point of view, be sure to move the station point back and keep it the same distance from the object.

Notice how the cone of vision (frame of view) is also correspondingly increased in size.

1. Before setting up an interior view it is a good idea to place the position of the viewer (station point) on the plan, and, using the 60° angle of the normal cone of vision, to check that the view will include the desired information.

2. If there are no objects or forms outside the normal 60° cone of vision that will call attention to the distortion, then the cone can be widened to include a broader view as might appear through a wide-angle lens.

3. Sometimes it is necessary to set the station point outside the interior space and to dissolve a wall for a clear view. This method is particularly useful with small spaces.

When setting up interior views, it is normally most practical to set the back wall or back corner of the plan against the picture plane. This allows the walls and space to proceed toward the viewer and into the viewer's peripheral vision.

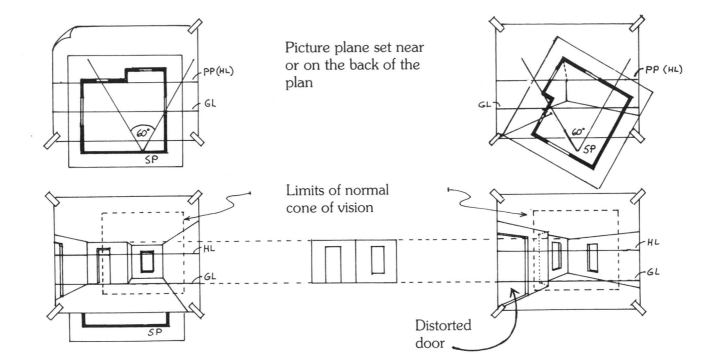

Picture plane set near or on the back of the plan

Limits of normal cone of vision

Distorted door

Here again, areas that extend beyond the cone of vision may be included if there are no objects of furniture to make the distortion obvious. Notice above how the door stretches to the left. Often, interior views are rendered in such a way that the walls are allowed to fade out—an effect similar to that experienced in our peripheral vision.

Constructing Perspective-Grid Systems

Perspective grids are extremely useful tools, particularly when objects and/or spaces to be drawn are complex. A grid is a series of lines perpendicular to one another that mark off units of uniform size, usually squares. When set in perspective, these units provide a ready reference for the size, angles, and proportions of objects within the same view. Using grid systems is a standard method in drawing objects to scale. In the following examples, techniques will be demonstrated for the construction of one-point and two-point grids.

Once a perspective grid is drawn, it can be enlarged, subdivided, and used again and again in other projects. In many cases, only a portion of a grid will be necessary to work out a particular detail or special problem; the whole system need not be drawn out every time. Grid systems in various scales and points of view are also commercially available.

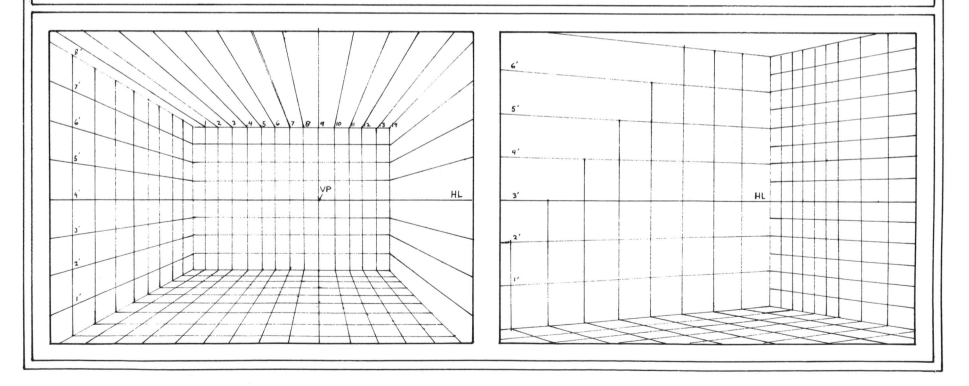

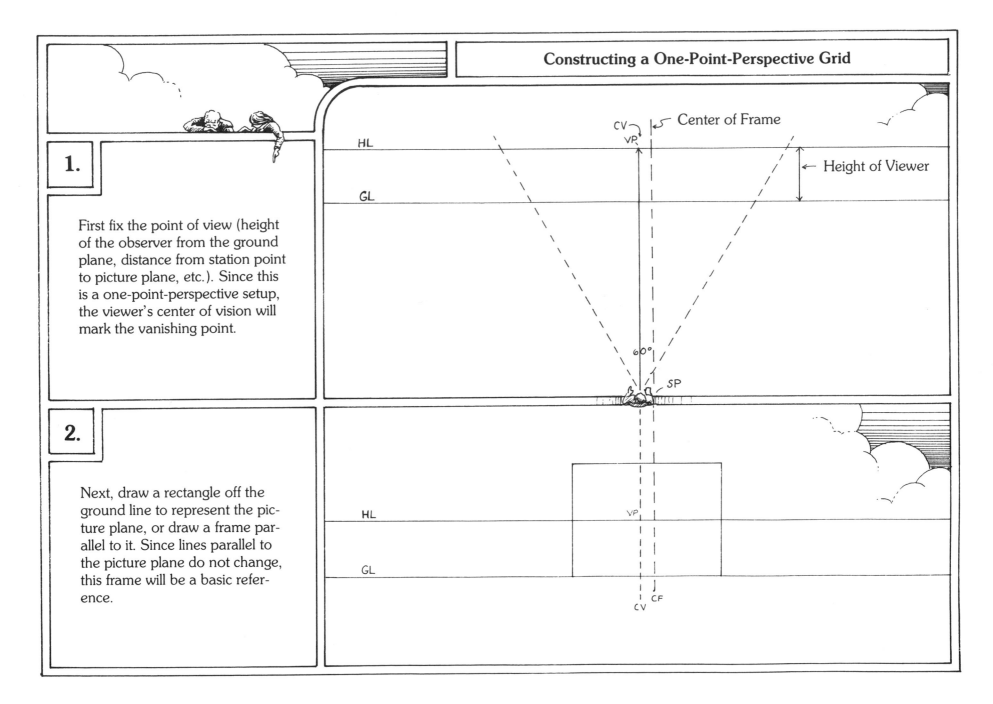

Constructing a One-Point-Perspective Grid

Center of Frame

CV

VP

HL

Height of Viewer

GL

1.

First fix the point of view (height of the observer from the ground plane, distance from station point to picture plane, etc.). Since this is a one-point-perspective setup, the viewer's center of vision will mark the vanishing point.

60°

SP

2.

Next, draw a rectangle off the ground line to represent the picture plane, or draw a frame parallel to it. Since lines parallel to the picture plane do not change, this frame will be a basic reference.

HL

VP

GL

CV

CF

57

3.

Mark the perimeter of the rectangle in equal units. Here the space will be 8 feet high and 12 feet wide. The observer is sitting slightly off to the left, with eye level at 4 feet off the ground.

4.

Draw lines through the equally spaced marks and connect them to the vanishing point. The space has now been divided into equal sized strips diminishing toward the vanishing point.

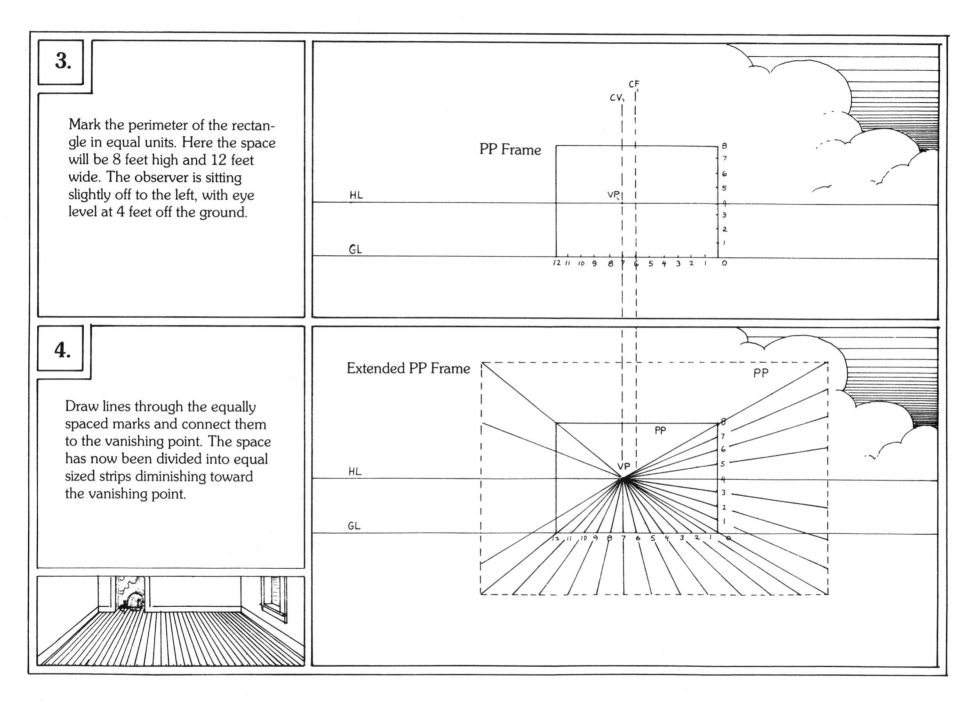

5.

In order to divide these parallel strips into square units, it is necessary to know the location of the 45-degree vanishing point. A line extended from this point across the receding lines at any given point will mark the positions for the lateral lines of the grid. Here, the 45-degree line was run through the corner of the frame.

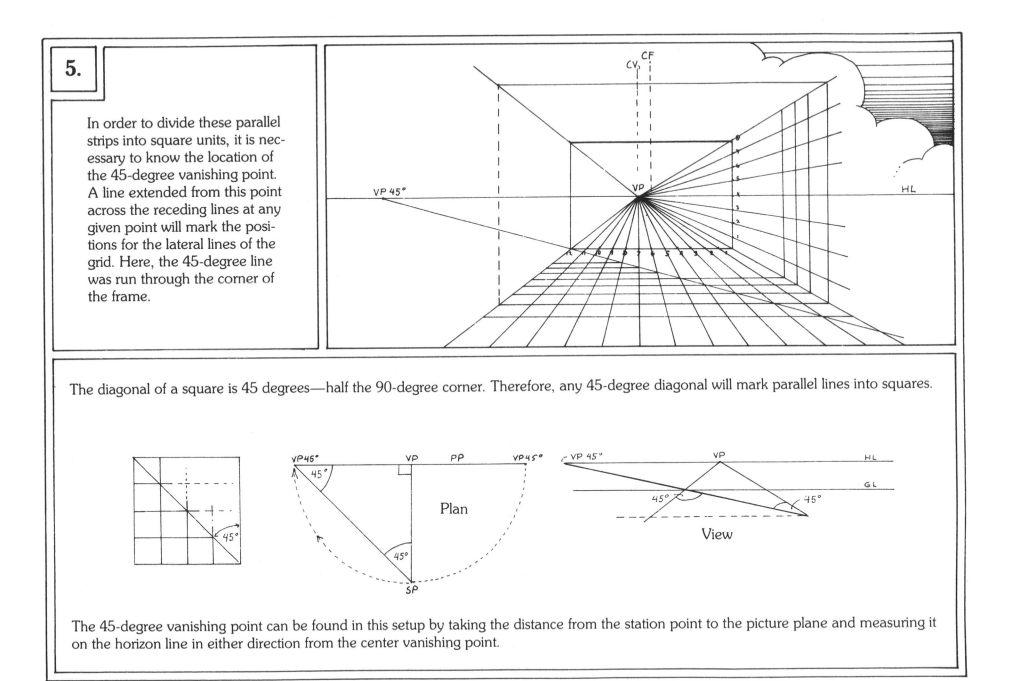

The diagonal of a square is 45 degrees—half the 90-degree corner. Therefore, any 45-degree diagonal will mark parallel lines into squares.

Plan

View

The 45-degree vanishing point can be found in this setup by taking the distance from the station point to the picture plane and measuring it on the horizon line in either direction from the center vanishing point.

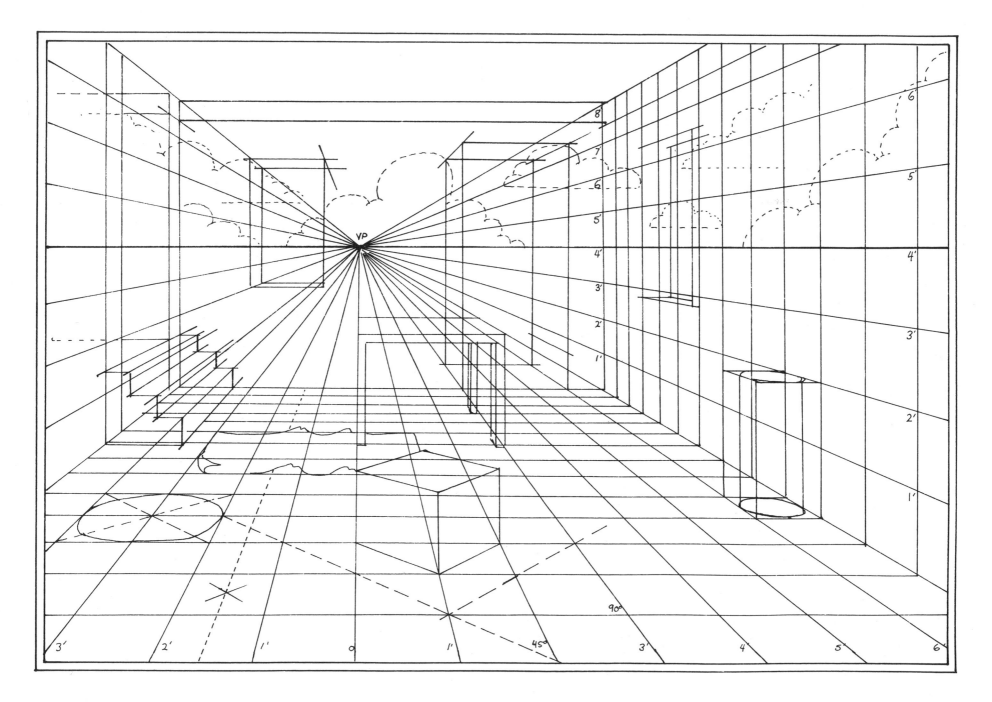

60

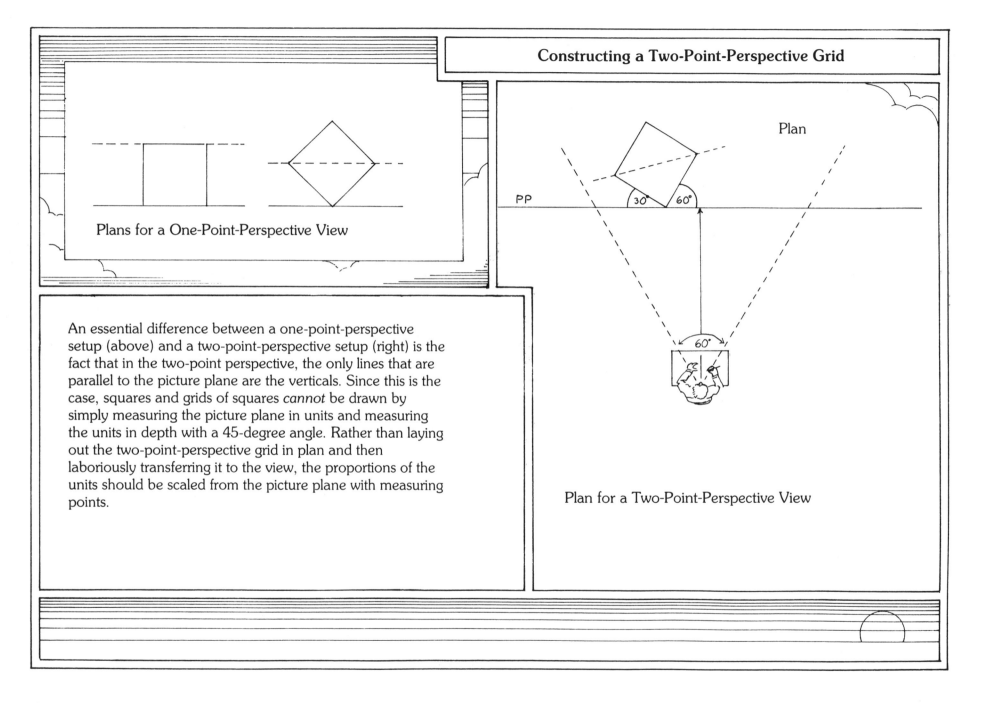

Plans for a One-Point-Perspective View

Plan

PP   30°   60°

60°

Plan for a Two-Point-Perspective View

An essential difference between a one-point-perspective setup (above) and a two-point-perspective setup (right) is the fact that in the two-point perspective, the only lines that are parallel to the picture plane are the verticals. Since this is the case, squares and grids of squares *cannot* be drawn by simply measuring the picture plane in units and measuring the units in depth with a 45-degree angle. Rather than laying out the two-point-perspective grid in plan and then laboriously transferring it to the view, the proportions of the units should be scaled from the picture plane with measuring points.

1.

Set up the point of view, as described earlier, and establish the vanishing points for the angle at which the grid is to be seen.

Note in this example that the viewer's center of vision is to the right of the point where the angle touches the picture plane.

2.

Measuring points must now be found for each vanishing point. To find a *measuring point* (MP), first measure the distance from the vanishing point to the station point with a compass. Next, measure and note this same distance from the vanishing point toward the other vanishing point on the picture plane. This noted length will be the measuring point for that vanishing point. In other words, the VP-SP line is equal to the VP-MP line. The left vanishing point's MP will be to the right of the center of vision, while the right VP's measuring point will be located at the left of the center of vision.

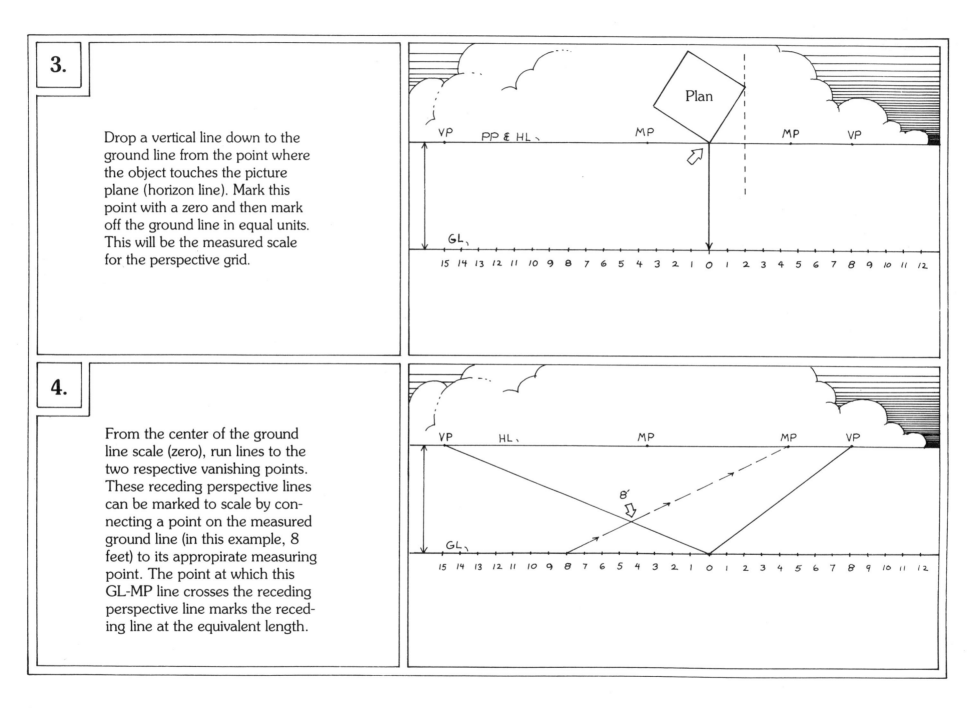

3.

Drop a vertical line down to the ground line from the point where the object touches the picture plane (horizon line). Mark this point with a zero and then mark off the ground line in equal units. This will be the measured scale for the perspective grid.

Plan

VP   PP & HL   MP   MP   VP

GL

15 14 13 12 11 10 9 8 7 6 5 4 3 2 1 0 1 2 3 4 5 6 7 8 9 10 11 12

4.

From the center of the ground line scale (zero), run lines to the two respective vanishing points. These receding perspective lines can be marked to scale by connecting a point on the measured ground line (in this example, 8 feet) to its appropriate measuring point. The point at which this GL-MP line crosses the receding perspective line marks the receding line at the equivalent length.

VP   HL   MP   MP   VP

8'

GL

15 14 13 12 11 10 9 8 7 6 5 4 3 2 1 0 1 2 3 4 5 6 7 8 9 10 11 12

5.

Using the procedure shown on the previous page, mark the other receding line at an equal length (8 feet). Connect these receding-line points to their respective vanishing points, to form a two-point-perspective square. In this example, the square is 8 feet by 8 feet.

Draw a diagonal of the square to establish a 45-degree vanishing point. Forty-five degree vanishing points can be helpful in both checking and expanding the grid system.

6.

Additional evenly spaced points can be marked off on the receding perspective lines (now the two front sides of a square). When these points are connected to their vanishing points, they form a scaled grid.

Here, the grid squares are 2 feet by 2 feet.

7.

The vertical dimensions of the two-point-perspective grid can be drawn with the aid of a *vertical measuring line* (VML). To make a vertical measuring line, simply set a vertical at the zero point on the scaled ground line and mark it to the same scale. The points of this vertical scale can be transferred to any point over the base grid by connecting a given point to its correct vanishing point. In this example, the 10-foot height has been carried 8 feet toward the left vanishing point.

8.

By transferring the points on the vertical measuring line to other verticals, vertical grids can be easily set up in coordination with the lines of the base grid. Note in this illustration how the 8 foot by 10 foot vertical grid plane is related to the base grid and the vertical measuring line.

The entire three-dimensional space can be gridded in two-point perspective by expanding this system.

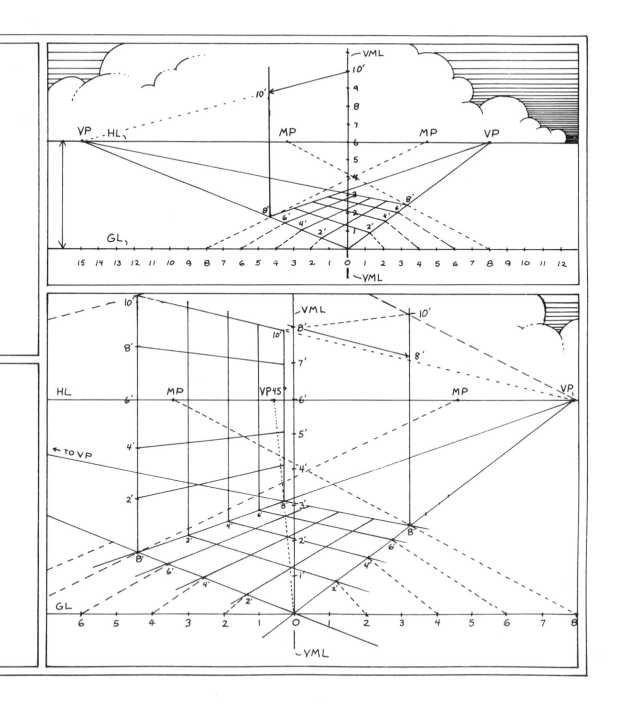

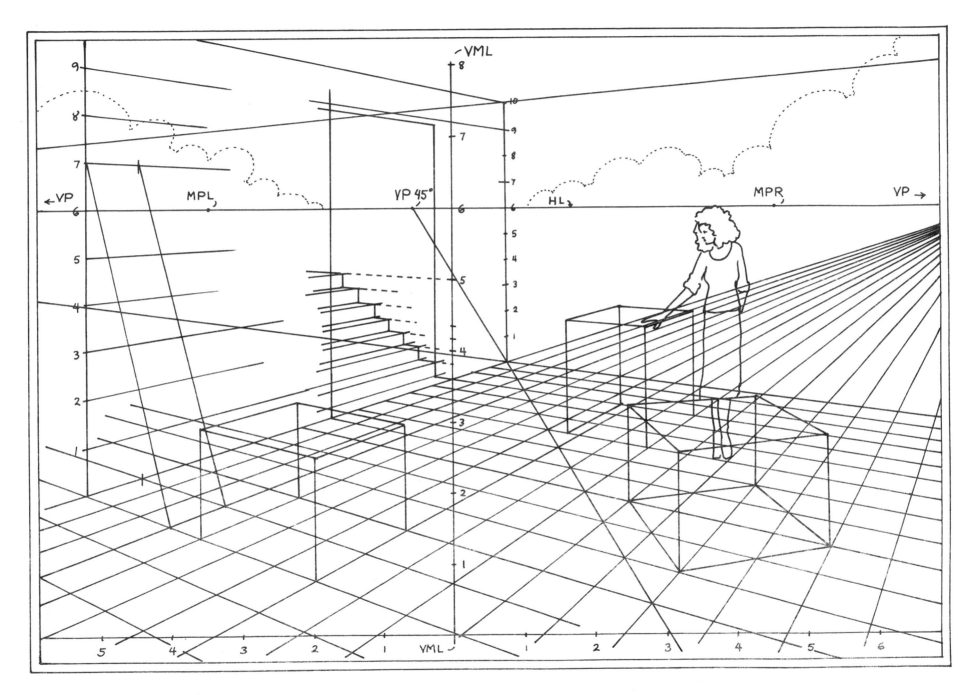

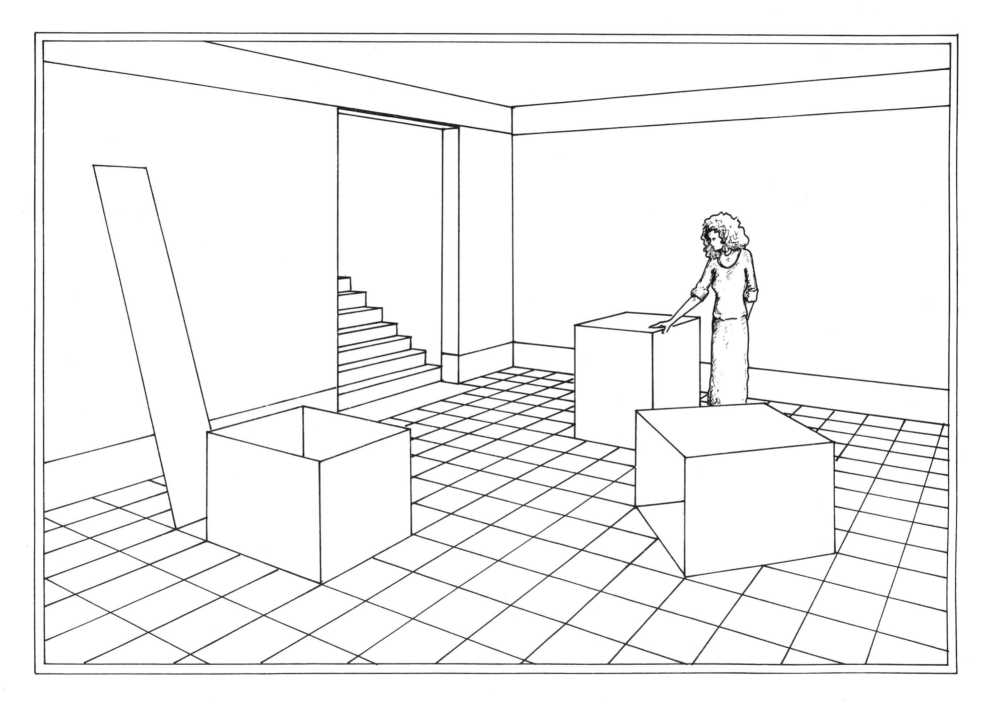

Geometric Tools: Diagonals, Squares, and Cubes

Diagonals

In addition to their use in constructing perspective grids, diagonals serve several useful functions in the drawing of perspective views.

One basic rule is that diagonals of any rectangle will cross at the center of that rectangle; this is also true of rectangles viewed in perspective.

Finding the center automatically means that rectangles can be subdivided and multiplied geometrically in the perspective system.

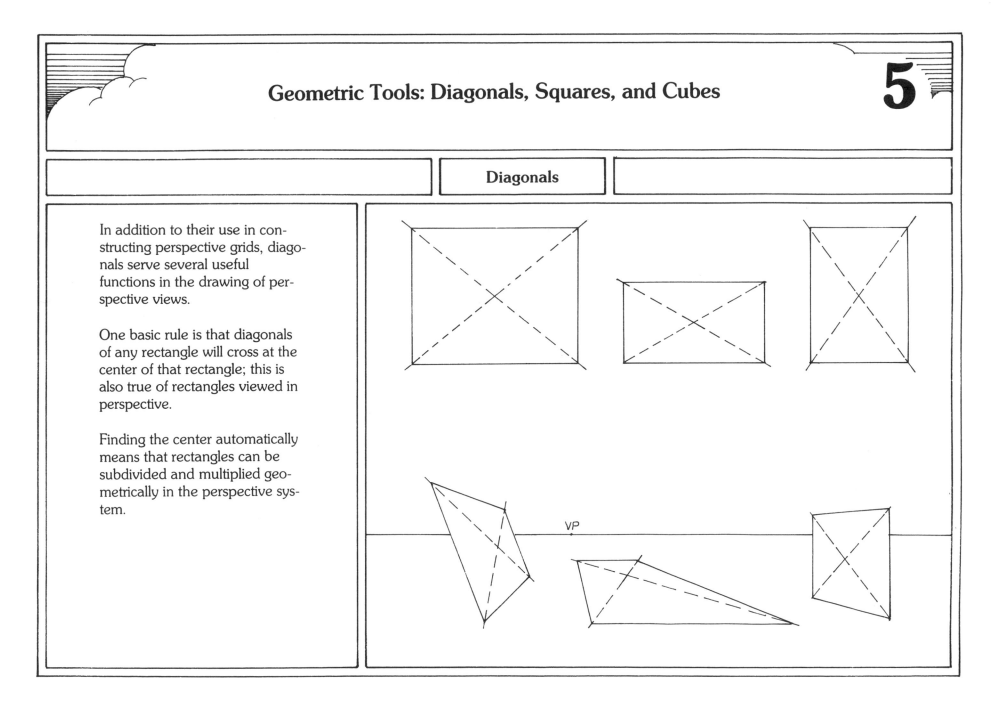

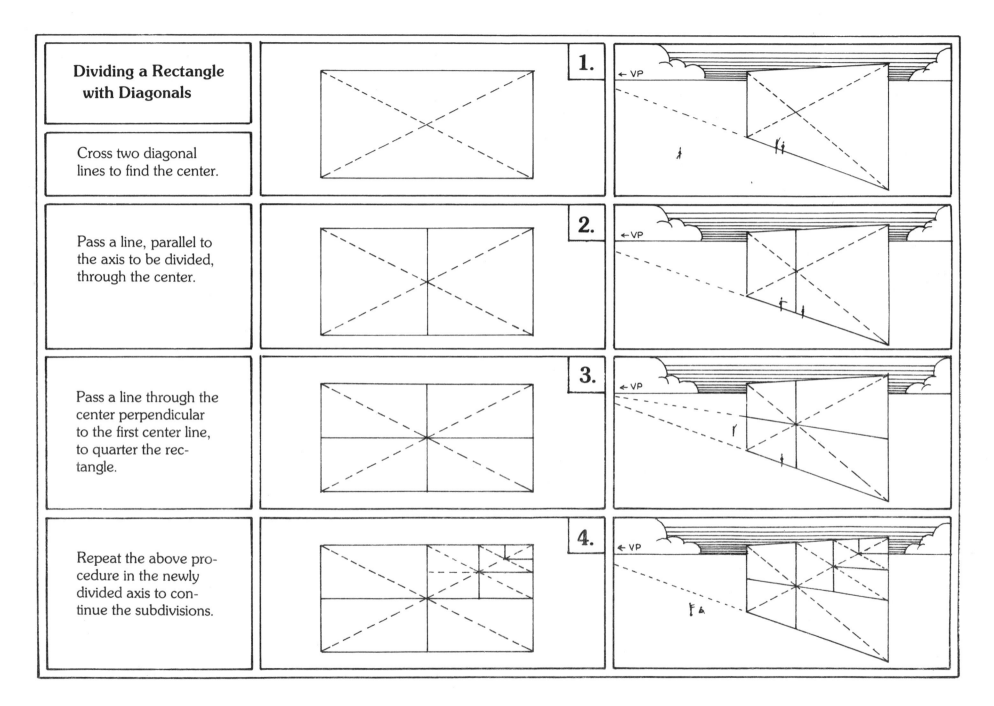

Dividing a Rectangle with Diagonals

Cross two diagonal lines to find the center.

1.

Pass a line, parallel to the axis to be divided, through the center.

2.

Pass a line through the center perpendicular to the first center line, to quarter the rectangle.

3.

Repeat the above procedure in the newly divided axis to continue the subdivisions.

4.

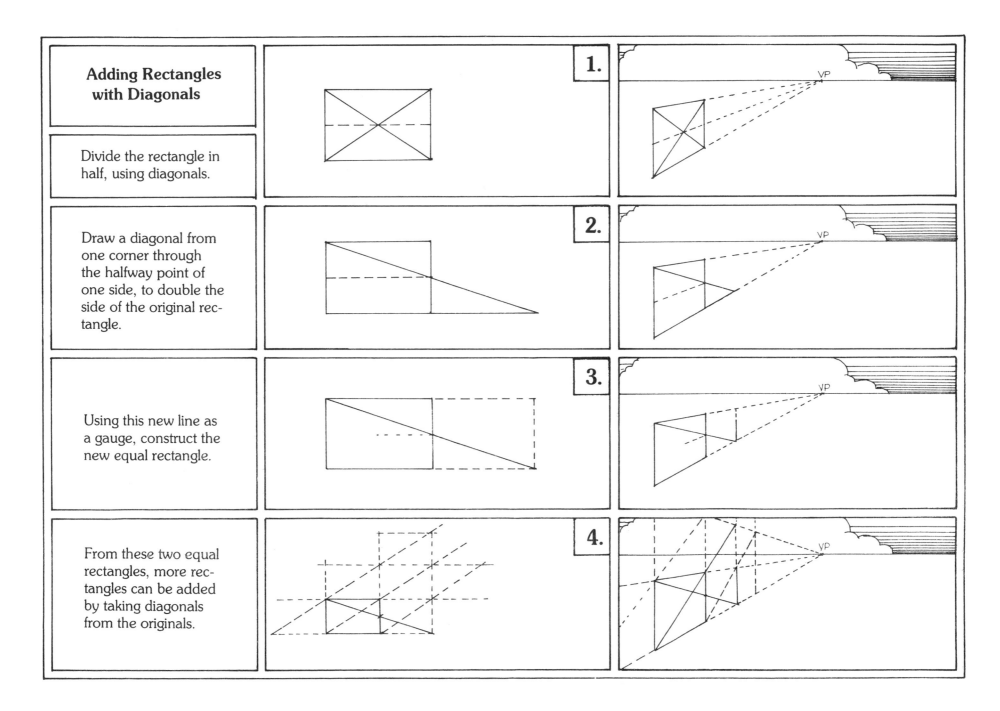

Adding Rectangles with Diagonals

1. Divide the rectangle in half, using diagonals.

2. Draw a diagonal from one corner through the halfway point of one side, to double the side of the original rectangle.

3. Using this new line as a gauge, construct the new equal rectangle.

4. From these two equal rectangles, more rectangles can be added by taking diagonals from the originals.

VP

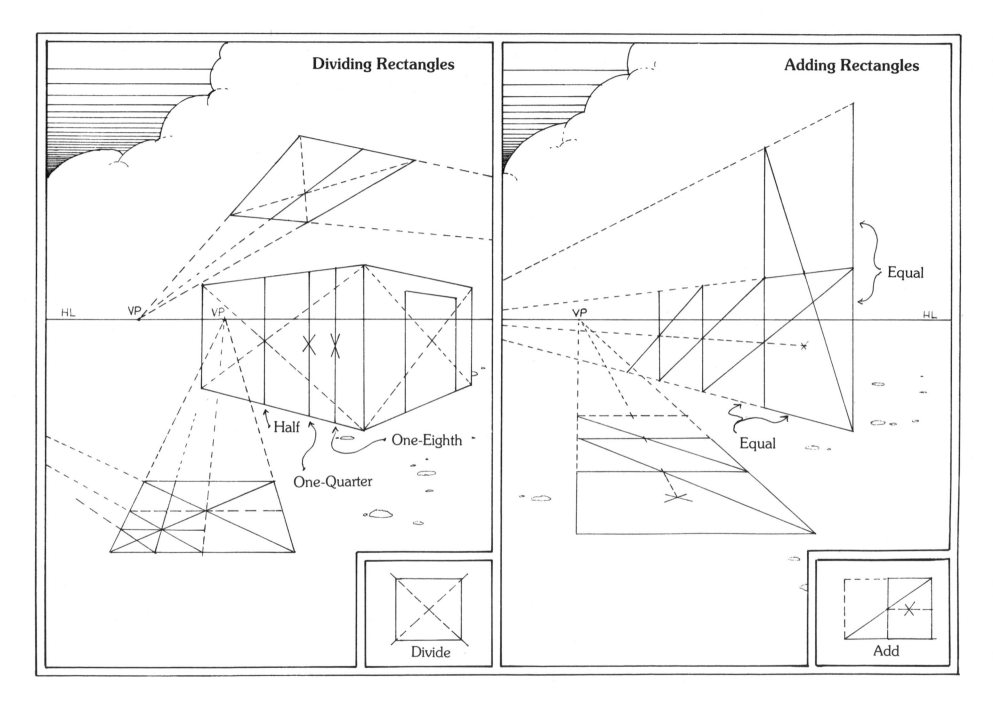

Dividing Rectangles

Adding Rectangles

HL

VP

VP

Half

One-Eighth

One-Quarter

Divide

Equal

HL

VP

Equal

Add

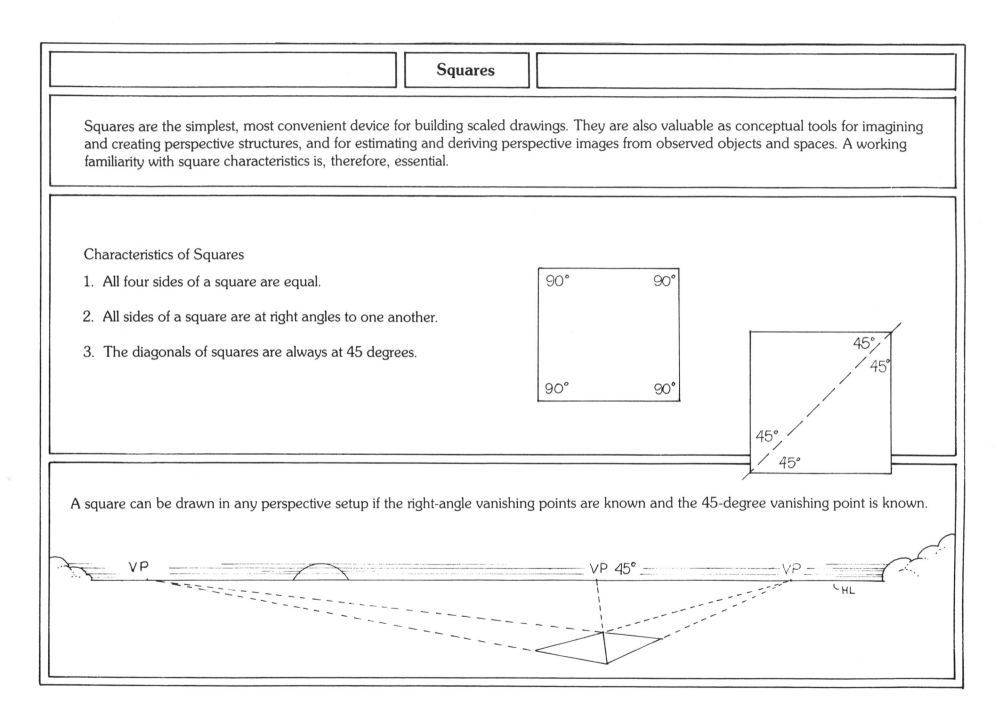

Squares

Squares are the simplest, most convenient device for building scaled drawings. They are also valuable as conceptual tools for imagining and creating perspective structures, and for estimating and deriving perspective images from observed objects and spaces. A working familiarity with square characteristics is, therefore, essential.

Characteristics of Squares

1. All four sides of a square are equal.

2. All sides of a square are at right angles to one another.

3. The diagonals of squares are always at 45 degrees.

90°   90°

90°   90°

45°
45°

45°
45°

A square can be drawn in any perspective setup if the right-angle vanishing points are known and the 45-degree vanishing point is known.

VP   VP   VP 45°   VP

HL

There are numerous ways in which to draw squares in perspective views. The following are some of the most basic and common.

A.

Draw the square or combination of squares in the plan and bring the dimensions down into the view. (See pages 39–43.)

B.

In a one-point-perspective setup, find the 45-degree vanishing point or estimate its position, and then mark off the receding plane at the point where the diagonal crosses.

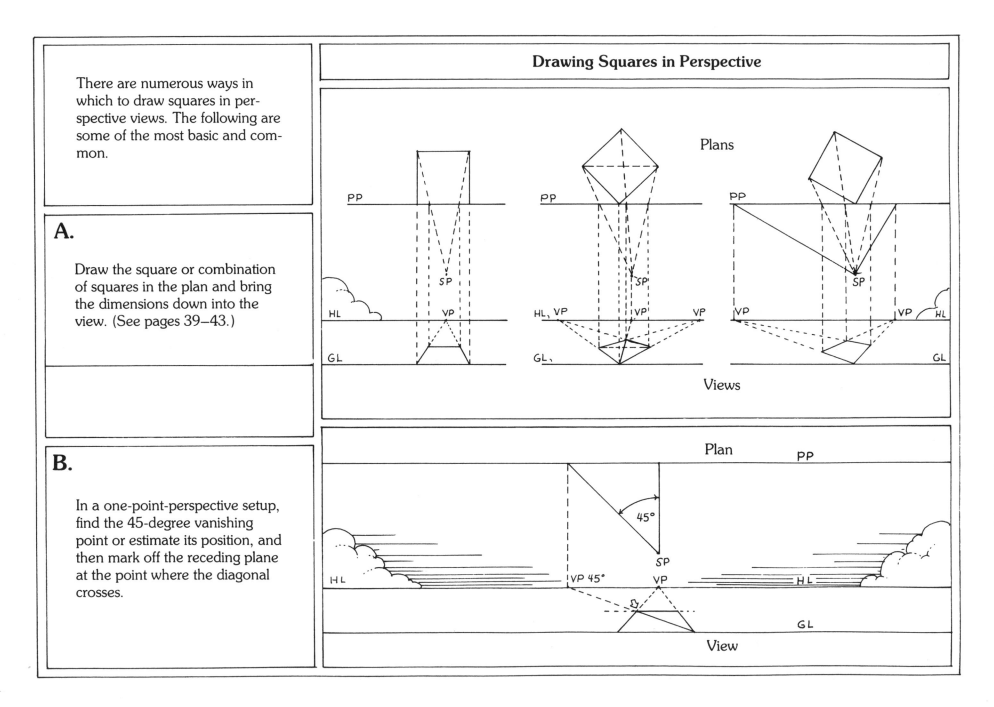

Drawing Squares in Perspective

Plans

Views

Plan

View

C.

For two-point-perspective setups, find the measuring points and connect them to equal lengths on the ground line (the bottom of a scaled picture plane).

D.

With practice and experience, you will develop a sensitivity to the shapes and proportions of drawn perspective squares, so that you can recognize or correct them.

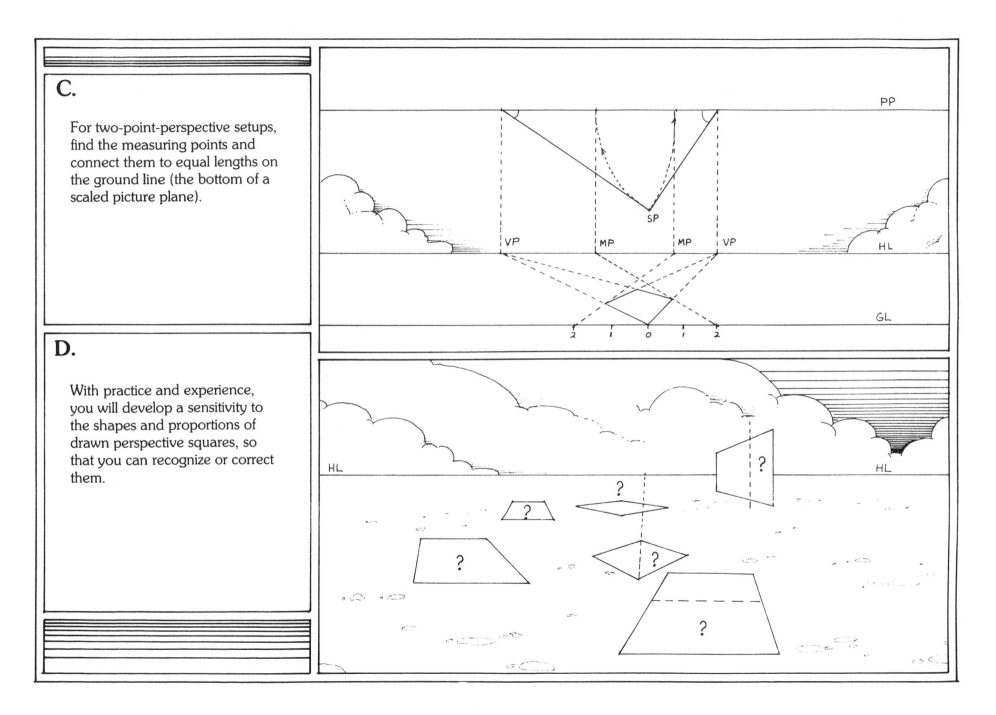

Cubes

Cubes are a combination of six squares. The methods of constructing them in perspective views, then, are essentially the same as the methods used for squares.

Characteristics of Cubes

1. All six sides of a cube are equal square planes.

2. All six side planes are joined at right angles.

3. The diagonals of the sides (squares) are always at 45 degrees.

As with squares, a cube can be drawn in any perspective setup if the right-angle vanishing points are known and the 45-degree vanishing point is known.

The basic methods for drawing cubes in perspective are virtually the same as those for squares, except for the addition of an elevation.

A.

Draw the cube in plan and elevation. After the plan has been brought down into the view as described earlier (see pages 39–44), set the whole elevation over the view to coincide with the ground plane (for a one-point perspective) or set the corner elevation at the corner of the view (for a two-point perspective).

B.

For a one-point-perspective setup, draw a base square, add the elevation, and complete the cube as illustrated.

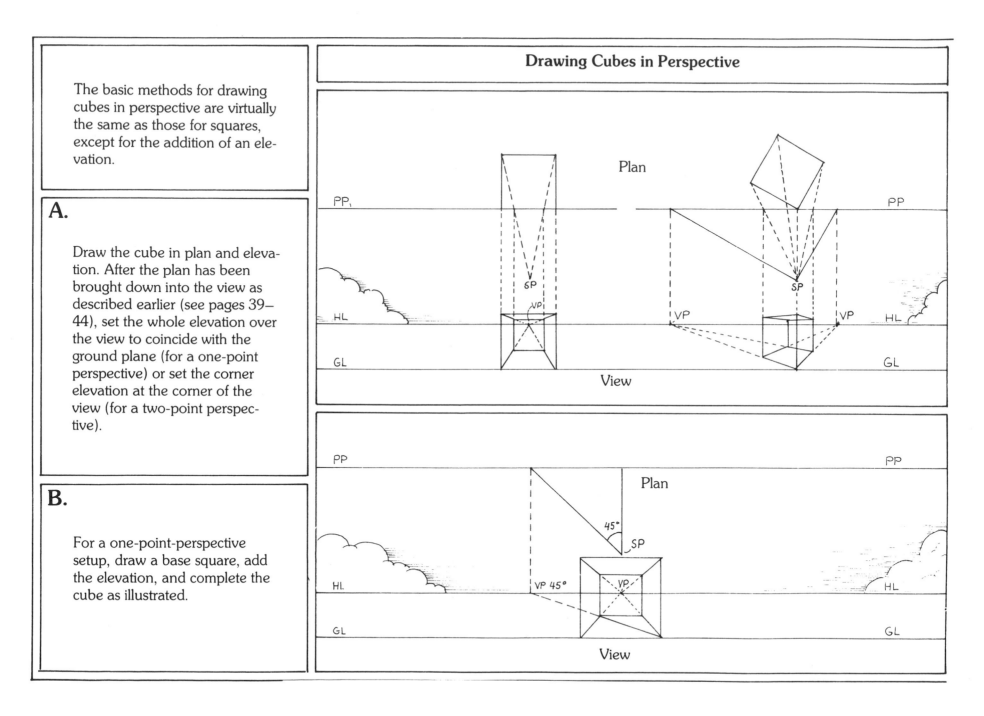

Drawing Cubes in Perspective

Plan

PP

SP

VP

HL

GL

View

PP

SP

VP

VP

HL

GL

View

PP

PP

Plan

45°

SP

HL

VP 45°

VP

HL

GL

GL

View

C.

To establish the base square for a two-point-perspective cube, find the measuring points and connect them to the scaled ground line. Where a corner of the cube touches the ground line, draw a vertical measuring line and mark it off at the height of the elevation.

D.

As with squares, try to develop the ability to recognize and estimate the proportions and angles of perspective cubes. Try adding and subtracting from various planes until the shape seems correct.

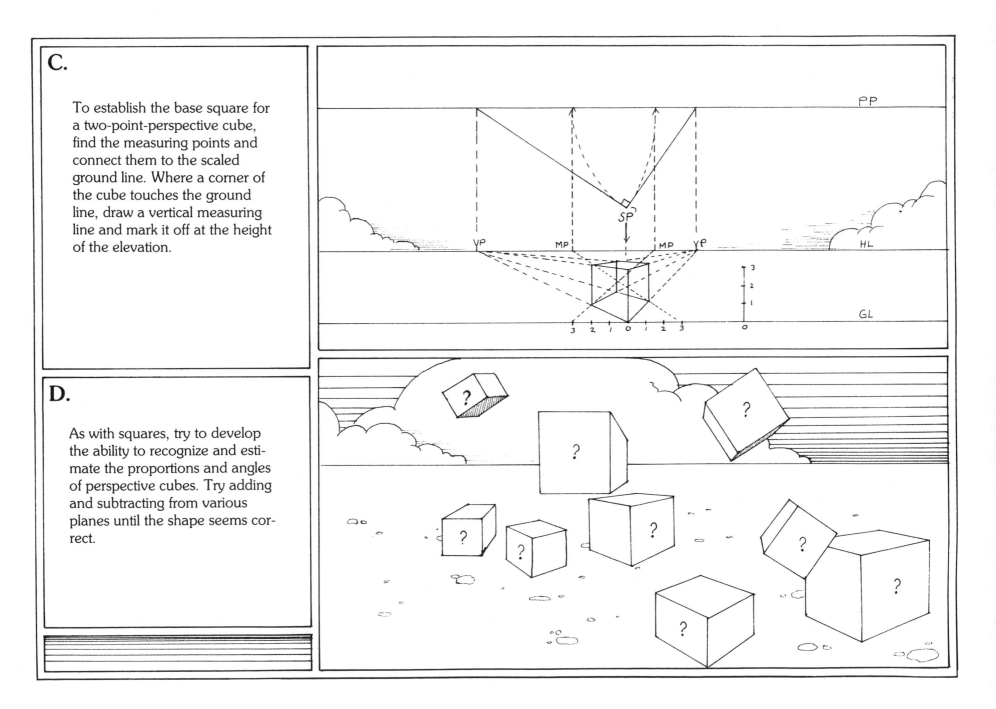

E.

In three-point perspective, none of the planes of the cube are parallel to the picture plane. Therefore, even the elevation of the cube will diminish toward a vanishing point.

Since the viewer is in the center of the view, all the vanishing points will be an equal distance apart, forming an equilateral triangle connecting three horizons. The three 45-degree vanishing points will also be equidistant and in the centers of their respective horizons.

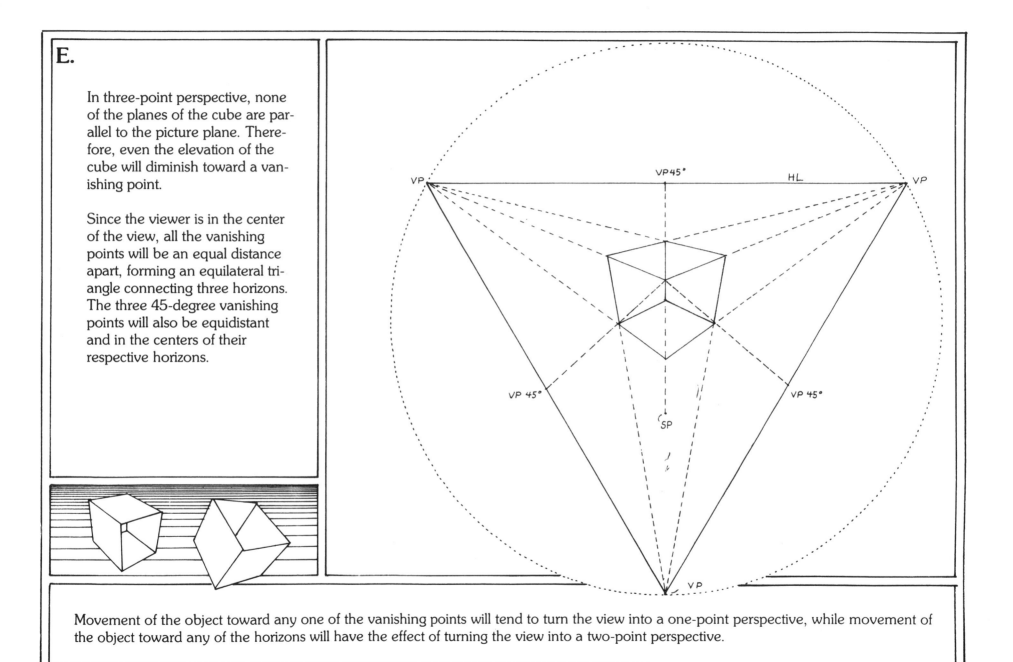

Movement of the object toward any one of the vanishing points will tend to turn the view into a one-point perspective, while movement of the object toward any of the horizons will have the effect of turning the view into a two-point perspective.

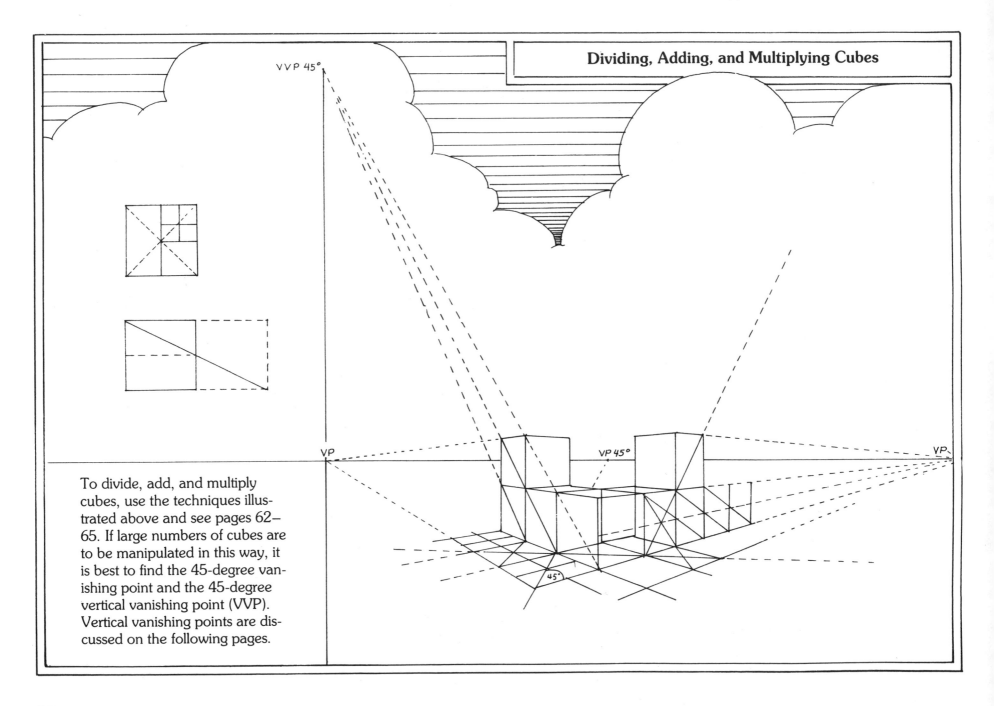

VVP 45°

Dividing, Adding, and Multiplying Cubes

VP

VP 45°

VP

45°

To divide, add, and multiply cubes, use the techniques illustrated above and see pages 62–65. If large numbers of cubes are to be manipulated in this way, it is best to find the 45-degree vanishing point and the 45-degree vertical vanishing point (VVP). Vertical vanishing points are discussed on the following pages.

Sloping Planes and Surfaces

6

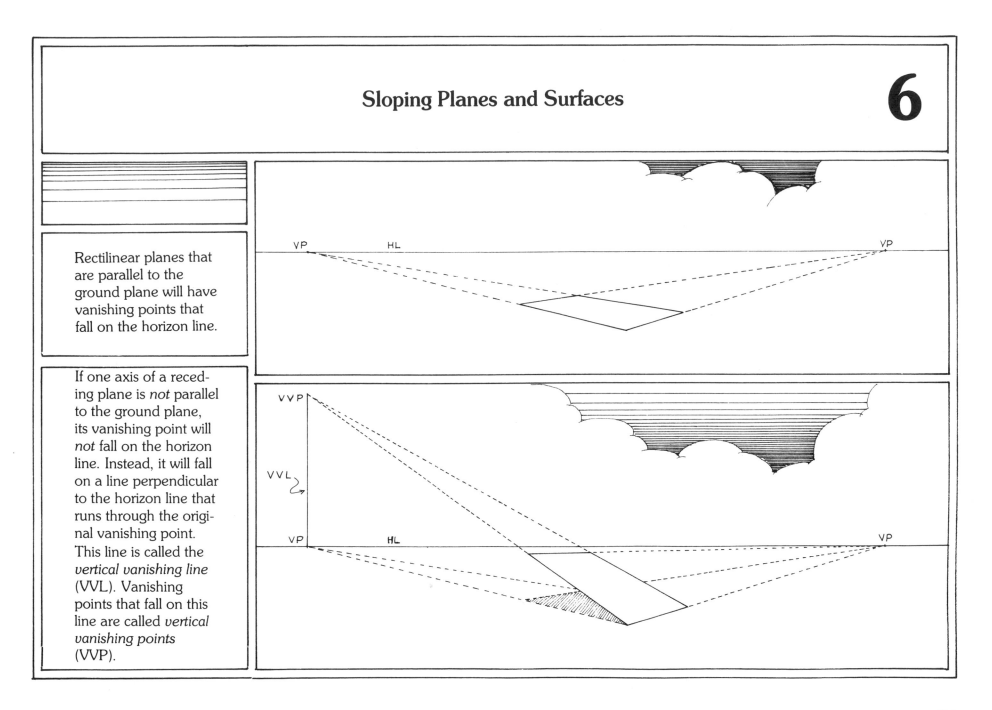

Rectilinear planes that are parallel to the ground plane will have vanishing points that fall on the horizon line.

If one axis of a receding plane is *not* parallel to the ground plane, its vanishing point will *not* fall on the horizon line. Instead, it will fall on a line perpendicular to the horizon line that runs through the original vanishing point. This line is called the *vertical vanishing line* (VVL). Vanishing points that fall on this line are called *vertical vanishing points* (VVP).

The steeper the angle of a plane's ascent or descent from the ground plane, the further up or down on the vertical vanishing line the points will fall.

It is important to realize that the vertical vanishing line operates just like the horizon line, except that it is perpendicular to the horizon.

Turn the page on end and note that the image becomes a three-point-perspective setup.

Note how the sloping planes diminish toward vanishing points below the horizon line after they have passed an angle 90 degrees to the ground plane.

VVP

If the other axis of these planes were sloping, a vertical vanishing line would run through this vanishing point.

HL

VP

VP

Vanishing point when the object is parallel to the ground plane.

VVP

The vanishing point for these lines is so far away that the lines appear to be parallel

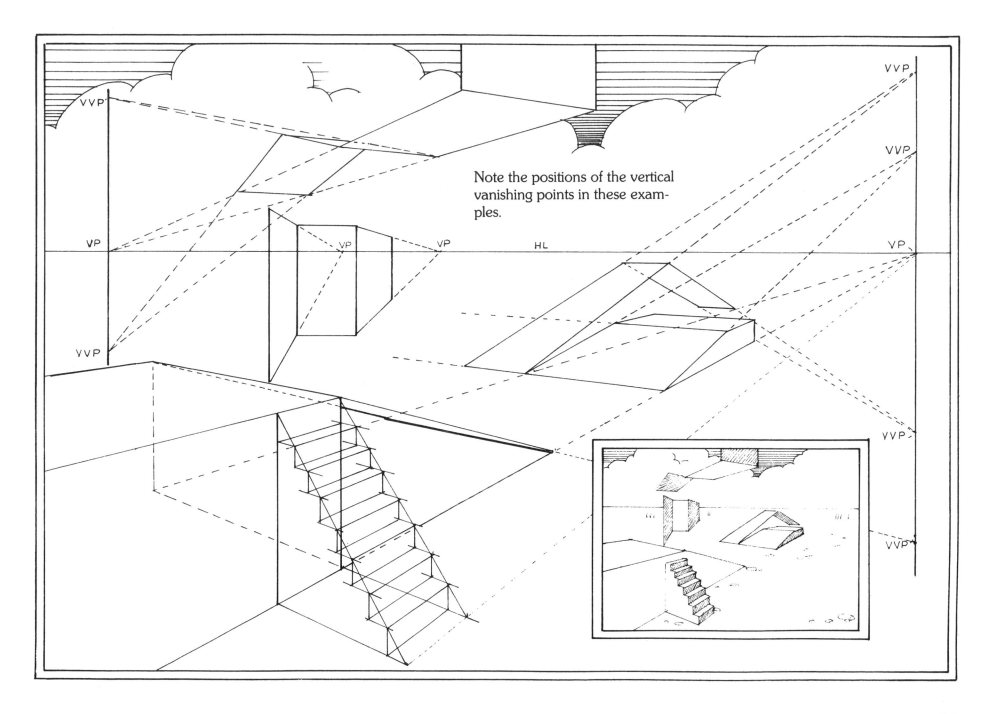

Note the positions of the vertical vanishing points in these examples.

VVP

VVP

VP   VP   VP   HL   VP

VVP

VVP

VVP

VVP

83

Drawing Slopes Off Rectangles

It is not always convenient or necessary to find the vanishing points for a sloped plane or angle.

If the base and the height of an angle are known, the angle can be drawn by connecting the two extremes with a diagonal line.

If the base is drawn in perspective, the sloping plane will automatically converge toward its vertical vanishing point. Thus, it is possible to plot complex angles and slopes by determining their base length and height.

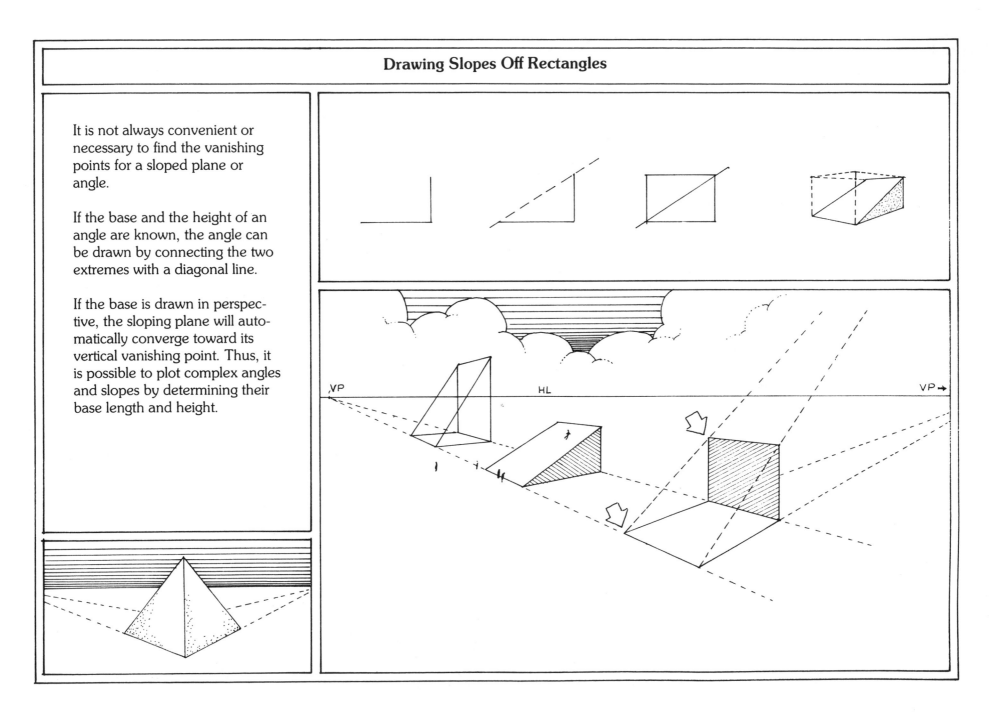

VP   HL   VP →

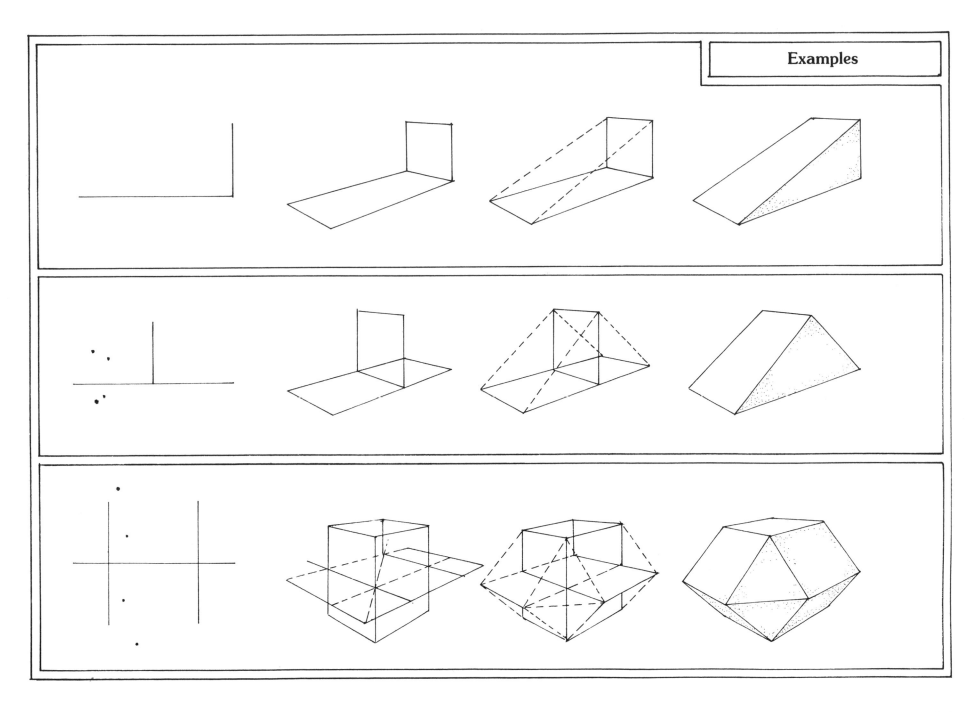

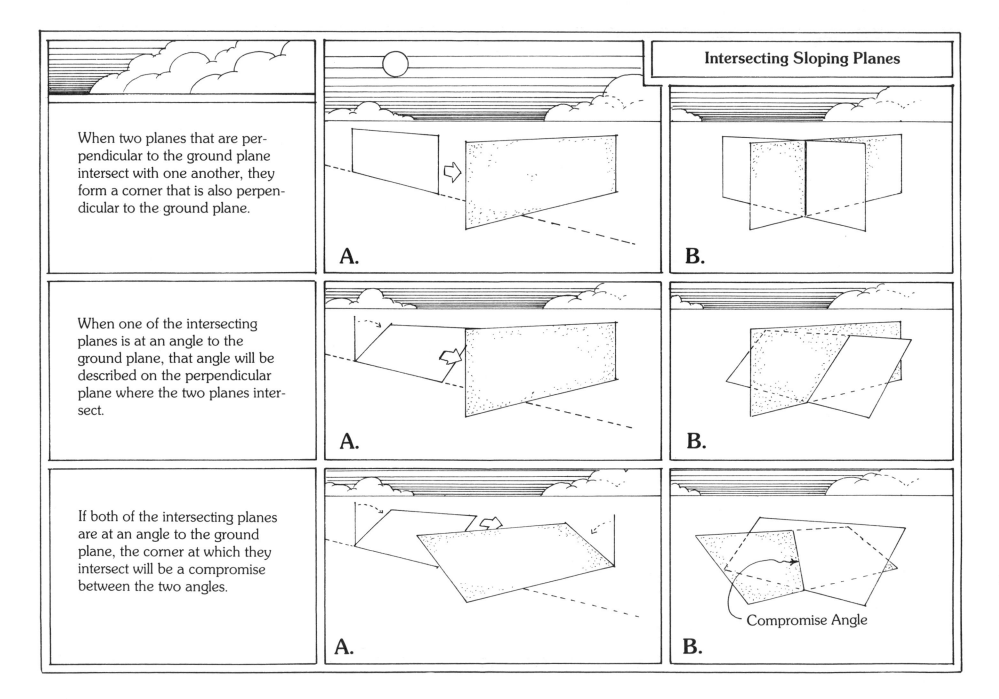

Intersecting Sloping Planes

When two planes that are perpendicular to the ground plane intersect with one another, they form a corner that is also perpendicular to the ground plane.

A.

B.

When one of the intersecting planes is at an angle to the ground plane, that angle will be described on the perpendicular plane where the two planes intersect.

A.

B.

If both of the intersecting planes are at an angle to the ground plane, the corner at which they intersect will be a compromise between the two angles.

A.

B.

Compromise Angle

86

If the tops of intersecting planes are the same height off the ground plane, the angle of the intersecting corner can be found by drawing a line between the points where the edges of the two planes meet.

However, if the intersecting planes are of different heights, it is necessary to find the point where the smaller plane enters the larger one before the position and angle of the corner can be drawn. (Directions follow.)

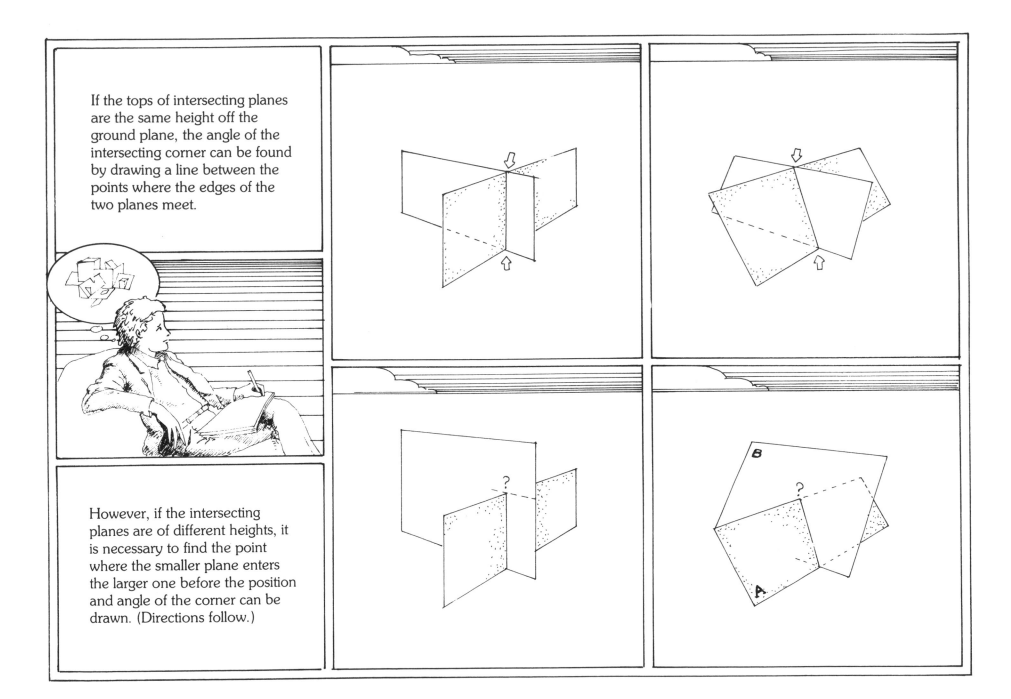

To find the point on the larger plane where the smaller one intersects it, mark the height of the smaller plane on the larger plane. This point marks the top of the intersecting corner.

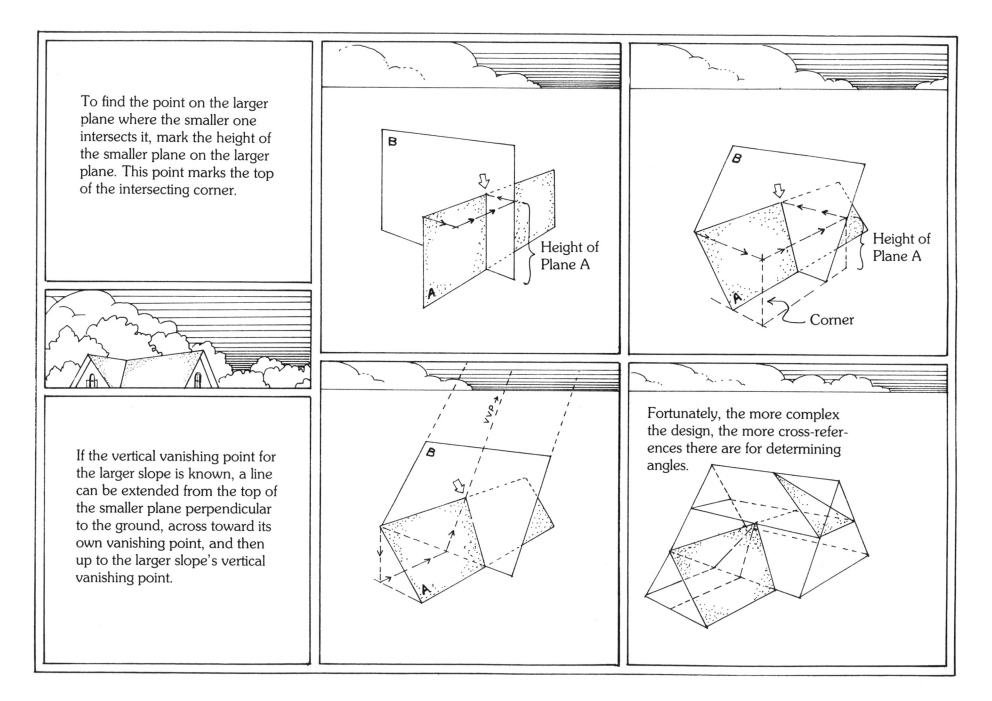

Height of Plane A

Height of Plane A

Corner

If the vertical vanishing point for the larger slope is known, a line can be extended from the top of the smaller plane perpendicular to the ground, across toward its own vanishing point, and then up to the larger slope's vertical vanishing point.

Fortunately, the more complex the design, the more cross-references there are for determining angles.

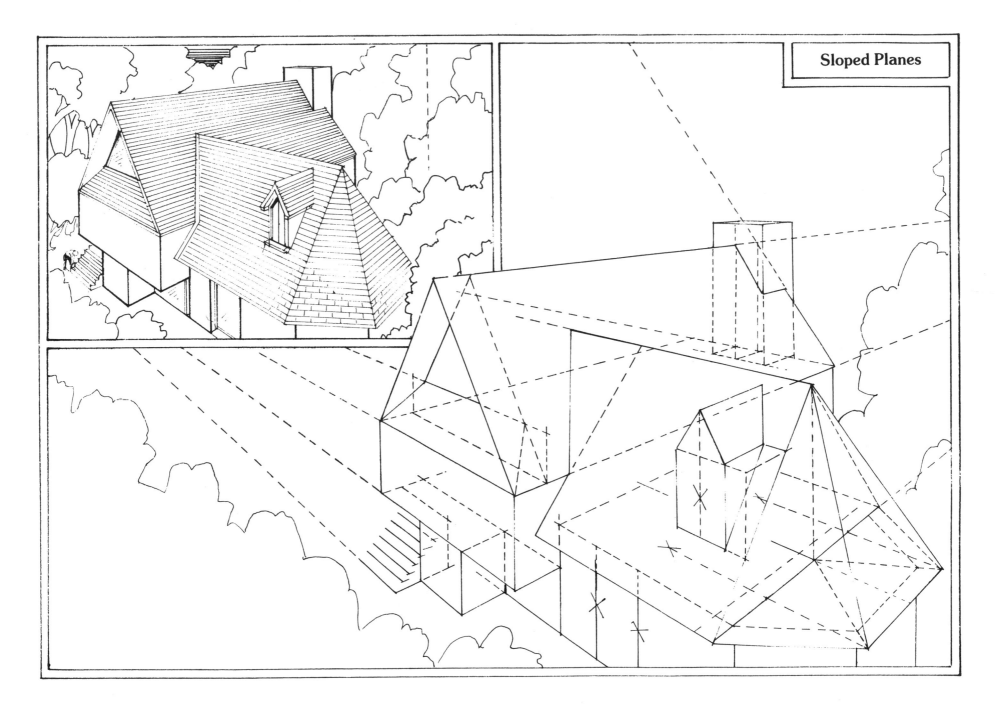

Drawing a Measured Angle in Perspective

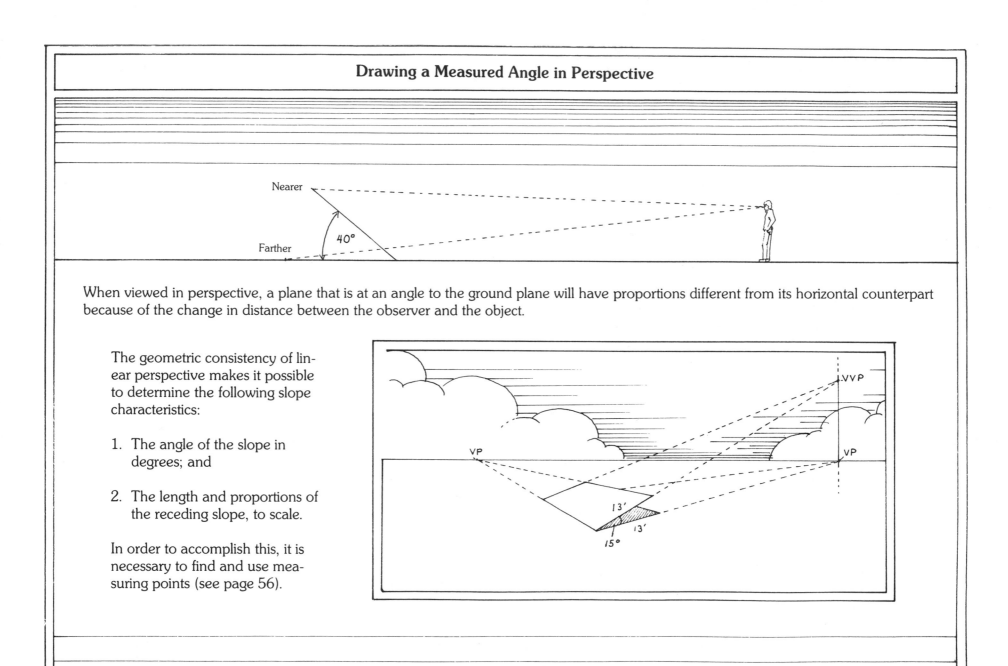

When viewed in perspective, a plane that is at an angle to the ground plane will have proportions different from its horizontal counterpart because of the change in distance between the observer and the object.

The geometric consistency of linear perspective makes it possible to determine the following slope characteristics:

1. The angle of the slope in degrees; and

2. The length and proportions of the receding slope, to scale.

In order to accomplish this, it is necessary to find and use measuring points (see page 56).

1.

Begin by finding the measuring point for the axis on which the angle will ascend and descend.

You will recall that the vanishing point to station point line is the same distance on the picture plane as the vanishing point to measuring point line (see page 56).

2.

Once you have transferred the vanishing points and measuring points to the horizon line, lay down a ground line and connect the base lines of the angle to their respective vanishing points.

With the measuring point as the axis, draw a line from the horizon line. The point at which this line strikes the vertical vanishing line marks the vertical vanishing point for the desired angle.

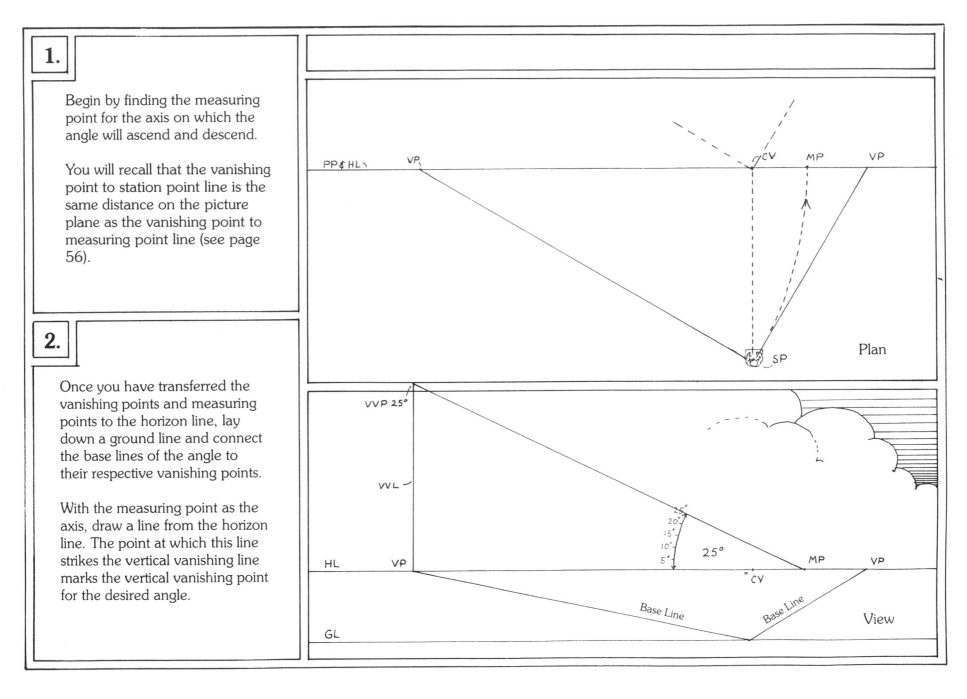

PP & HL   VP   CV   MP   VP

SP   Plan

VVP 25°

VVL

HL   VP   25°   20°   15°   10°   5°   25°   MP   VP

CV

Base Line   Base Line   View

GL

3.

The measuring point provides a side view (elevation) of the angle, so the angle can be scaled and measured with a protractor. Here, the angle is 25 degrees.

Note that all angled lines that strike the 25-degree vertical vanishing point are 25 degrees off the ground plane, no matter where they fall on the ground plane.

Since any angle can become the diagonal of a rectangle, the vanishing point of an angle can serve as a guide for multiplying and dividing rectangles of given proportions.

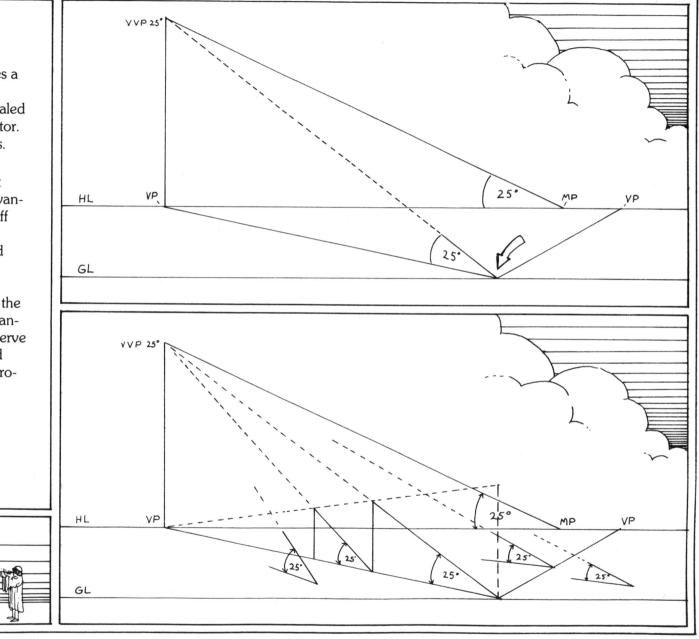

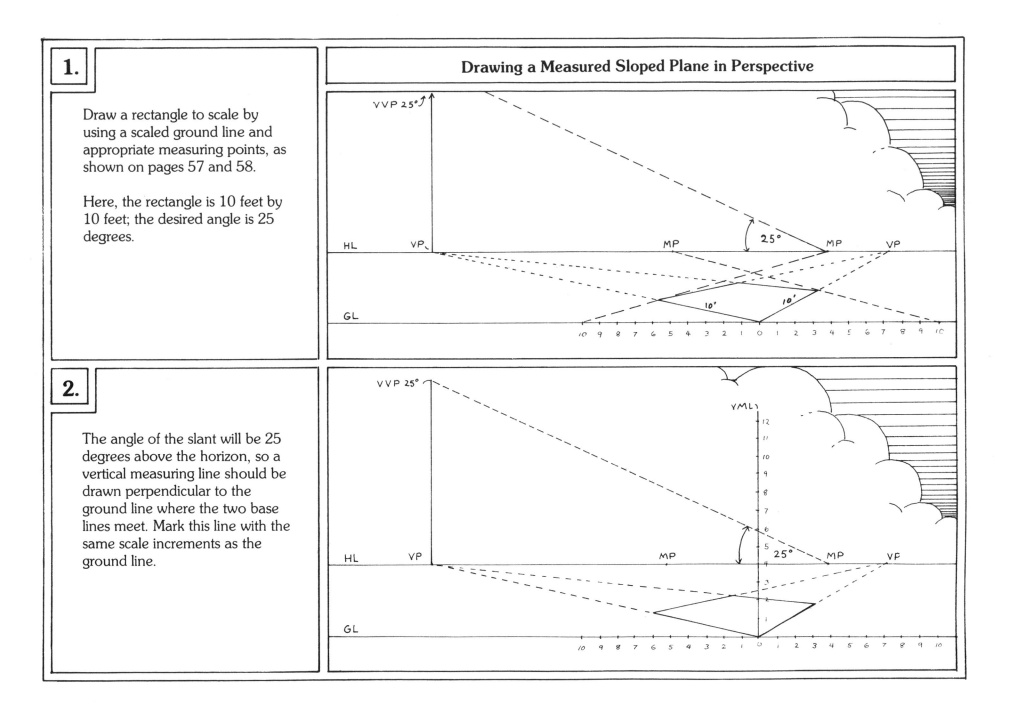

1.

Drawing a Measured Sloped Plane in Perspective

Draw a rectangle to scale by using a scaled ground line and appropriate measuring points, as shown on pages 57 and 58.

Here, the rectangle is 10 feet by 10 feet; the desired angle is 25 degrees.

VVP 25°

HL   VP   MP   25°   MP   VP

GL

10'   10'

10 9 8 7 6 5 4 3 2 1 0 1 2 3 4 5 6 7 8 9 10

2.

The angle of the slant will be 25 degrees above the horizon, so a vertical measuring line should be drawn perpendicular to the ground line where the two base lines meet. Mark this line with the same scale increments as the ground line.

VVP 25°

VML

12
11
10
9
8
7
6

HL   VP   MP   5   25°   MP   VP
4
3
2
GL   1

10 9 8 7 6 5 4 3 2 1 0 1 2 3 4 5 6 7 8 9 10

3.

Establish the sloping plane by connecting the right-hand corners of the rectangle to the 25-degree vertical vanishing point.

4.

In order to mark this slope to scale, you must find a measuring point on the vertical vanishing line. Draw a line from this point to the scaled vertical measuring line (VML) to mark the limit of the sloping plane.

Note that the vertical measuring point (VMP) is found by swinging an arc down from the measuring point on the horizon line, which has its axis at the 25-degree vanishing point.

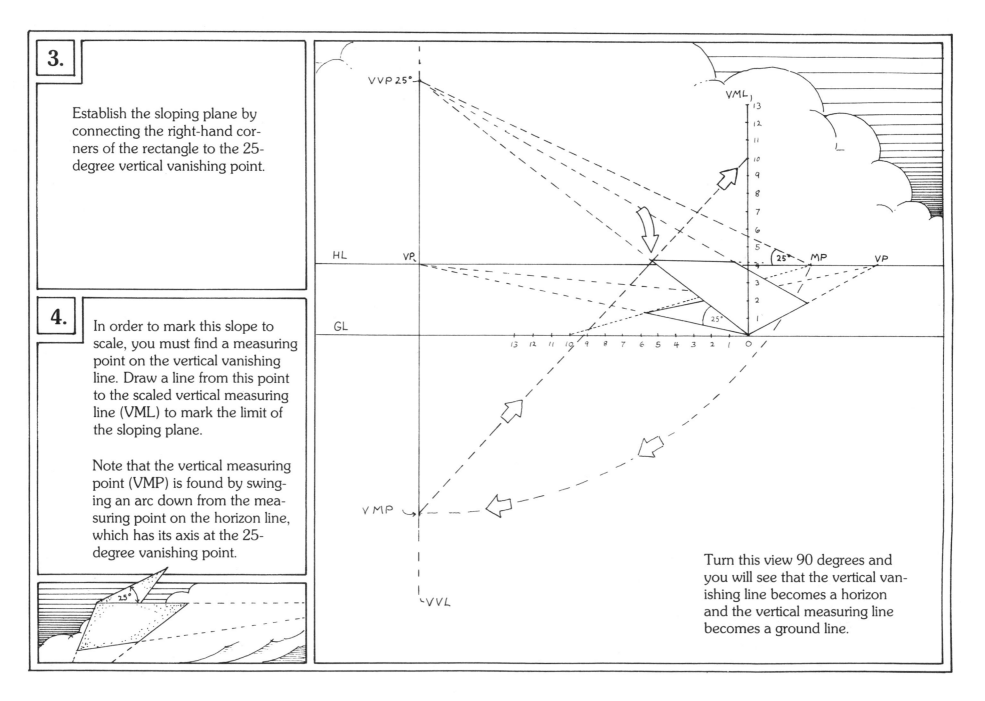

Turn this view 90 degrees and you will see that the vertical vanishing line becomes a horizon and the vertical measuring line becomes a ground line.

Circles and Curved Surfaces

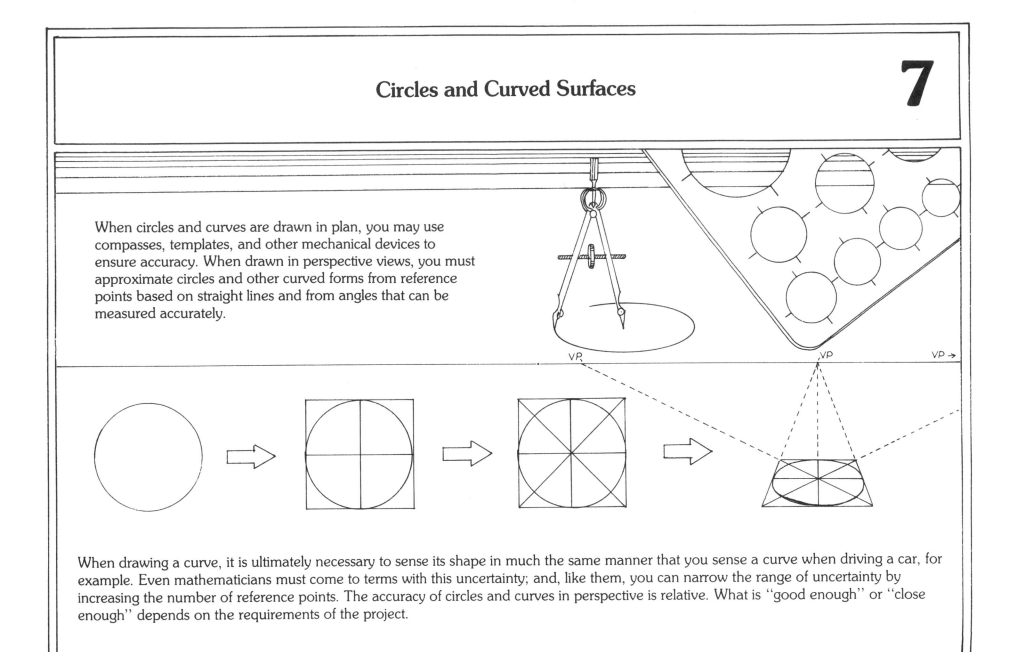

When circles and curves are drawn in plan, you may use compasses, templates, and other mechanical devices to ensure accuracy. When drawn in perspective views, you must approximate circles and other curved forms from reference points based on straight lines and from angles that can be measured accurately.

When drawing a curve, it is ultimately necessary to sense its shape in much the same manner that you sense a curve when driving a car, for example. Even mathematicians must come to terms with this uncertainty; and, like them, you can narrow the range of uncertainty by increasing the number of reference points. The accuracy of circles and curves in perspective is relative. What is "good enough" or "close enough" depends on the requirements of the project.

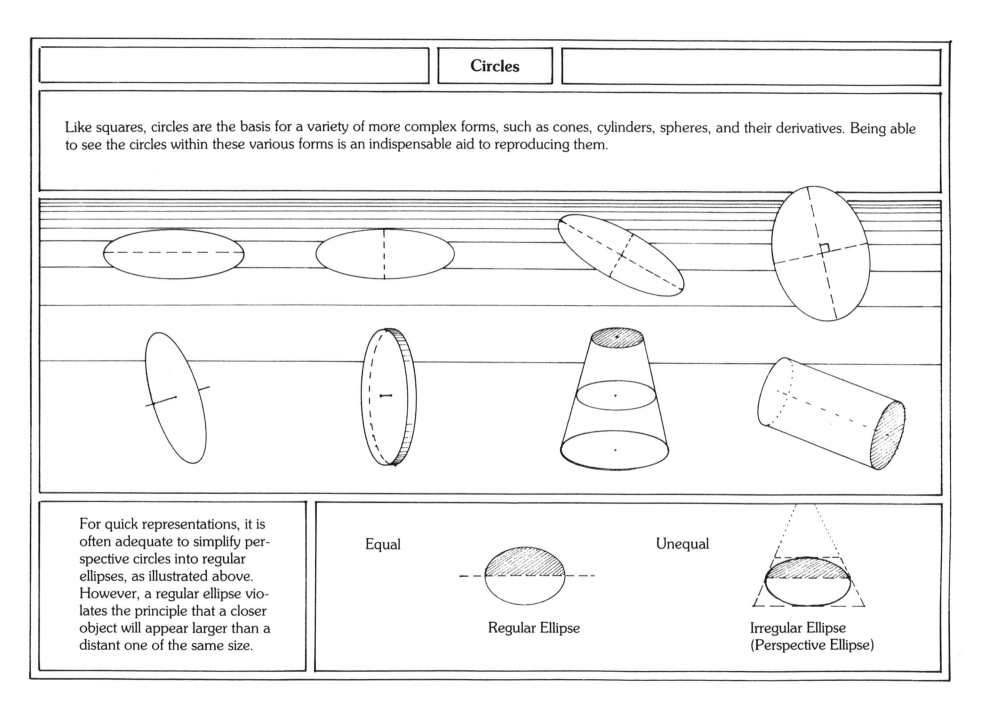

Circles

Like squares, circles are the basis for a variety of more complex forms, such as cones, cylinders, spheres, and their derivatives. Being able to see the circles within these various forms is an indispensable aid to reproducing them.

For quick representations, it is often adequate to simplify perspective circles into regular ellipses, as illustrated above. However, a regular ellipse violates the principle that a closer object will appear larger than a distant one of the same size.

Equal

Regular Ellipse

Unequal

Irregular Ellipse
(Perspective Ellipse)

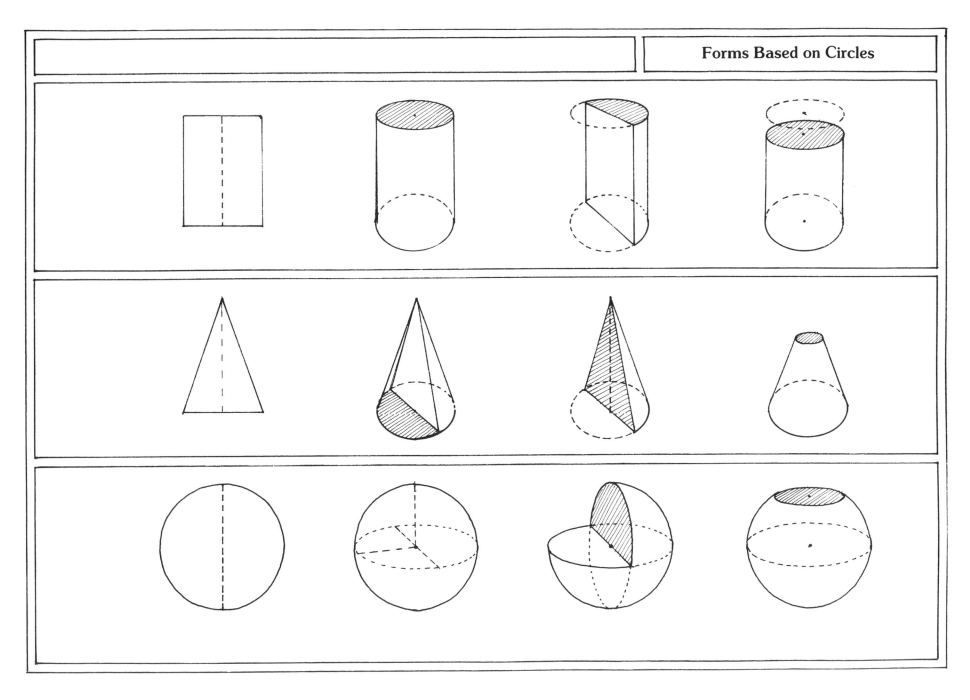

Forms Based on Circles

97

Drawing Circles Inside Squares

One of the most practical methods of drawing perspective circles is to draw them inside perspective squares. Perspective squares can be constructed easily and can supply the basic reference points needed for guiding the arcs of the circles.

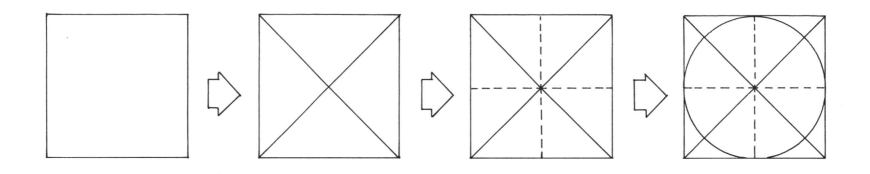

The arc of a circle touches the center of each side of the square that inscribes it. The arc also cuts across the diagonals at a little more than two-thirds distance from the center. By estimating the position of this point of intersection, the curve can be drawn, using three reference points.

Once the position of the arc is found on one quarter, the other three can be found by using the vanishing points and verticals.

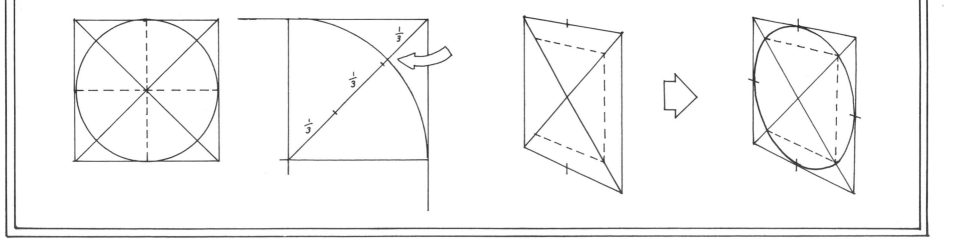

Another method of drawing a circle in perspective, which requires even less guesswork, is to transfer the circle from a plan to a perspective view, as demonstrated earlier with rectangles and squares.

In this method, points on the circle's arcs can be brought down to the ground line via the picture plane and marked off accurately in the view.

In this example, lines have been drawn through the points of intersection between the diagonals and the arc. When these same lines are taken back from the ground line to the vanishing point, they mark the diagonals in the view at the correct point.

Actually, only one such intersection need be found in the plan, since the others could be derived from the view.

If even greater accuracy is desired (that is, more reference points), additional lines can be dropped from the arc. The circle could even be gridded.

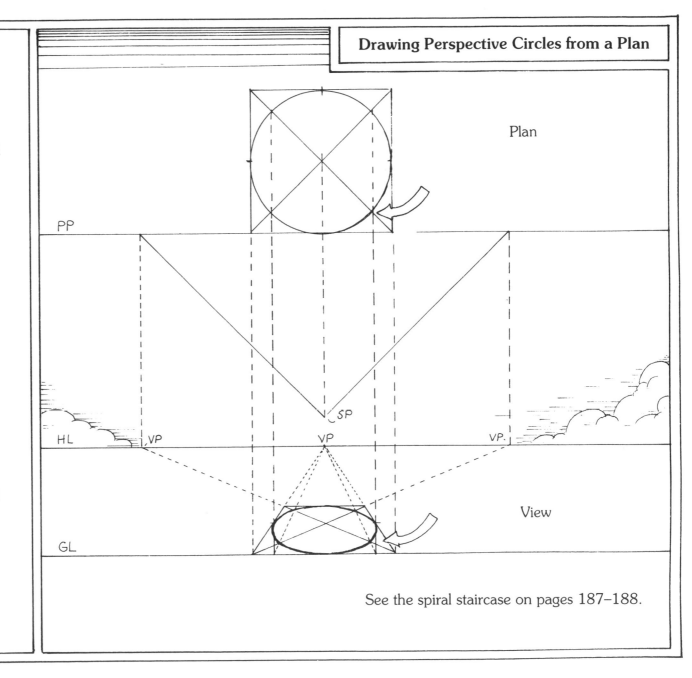

Drawing Perspective Circles from a Plan

Plan

PP

SP

HL   VP   VP   VP.

GL   View

See the spiral staircase on pages 187–188.

A third method of deriving a circle from a square again involves the identification of the point at which the diagonals of the square cross the arcs of the circle.

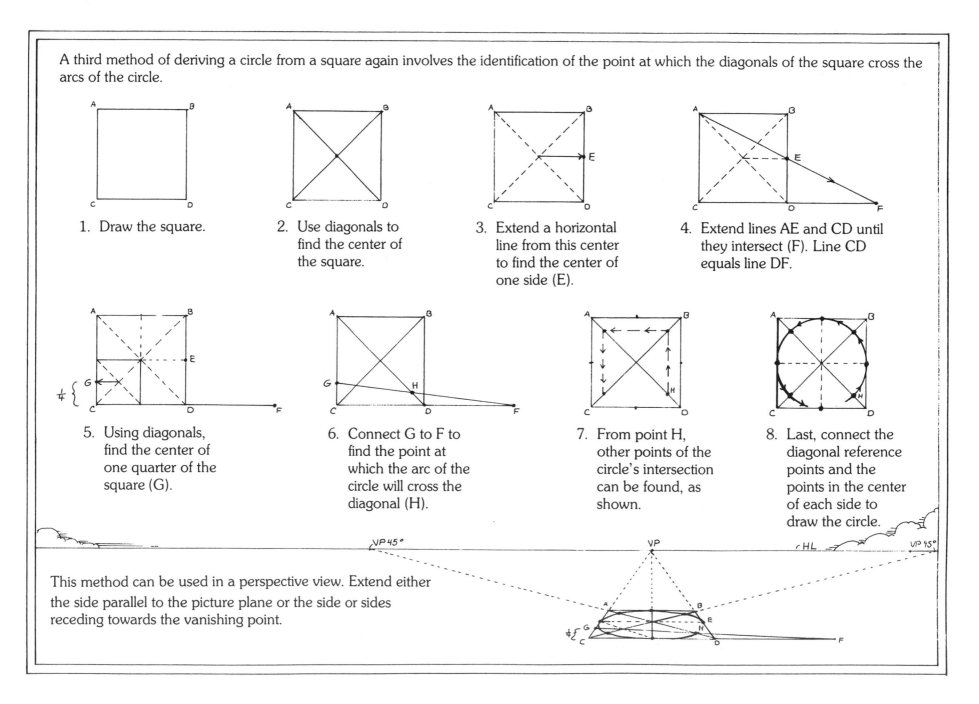

1. Draw the square.

2. Use diagonals to find the center of the square.

3. Extend a horizontal line from this center to find the center of one side (E).

4. Extend lines AE and CD until they intersect (F). Line CD equals line DF.

5. Using diagonals, find the center of one quarter of the square (G).

6. Connect G to F to find the point at which the arc of the circle will cross the diagonal (H).

7. From point H, other points of the circle's intersection can be found, as shown.

8. Last, connect the diagonal reference points and the points in the center of each side to draw the circle.

This method can be used in a perspective view. Extend either the side parallel to the picture plane or the side or sides receding towards the vanishing point.

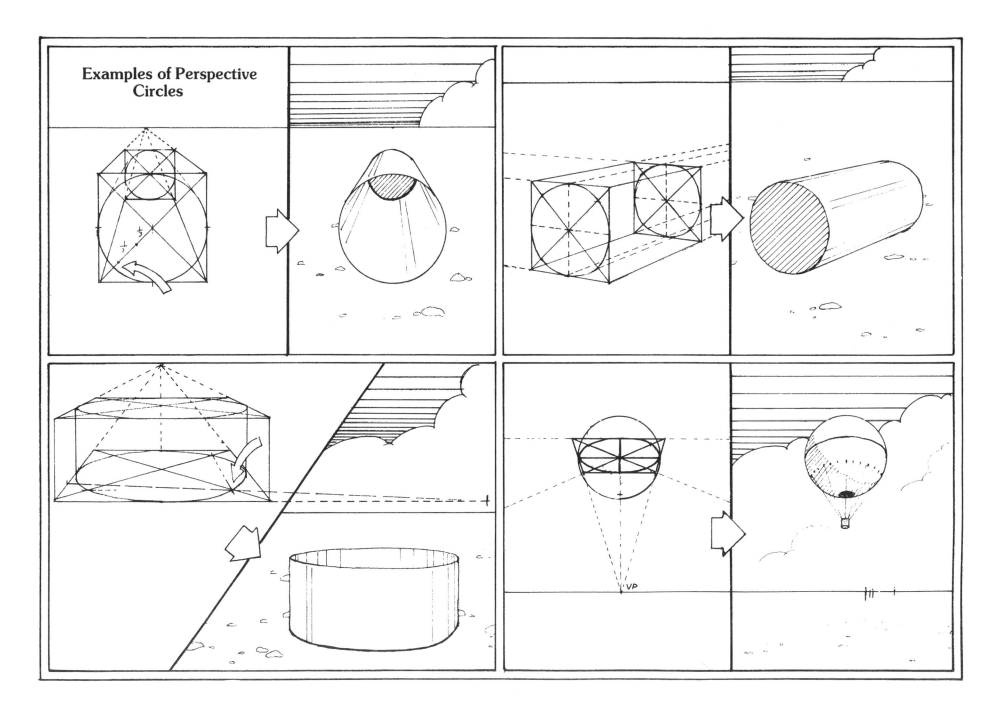

Examples of Perspective
Circles

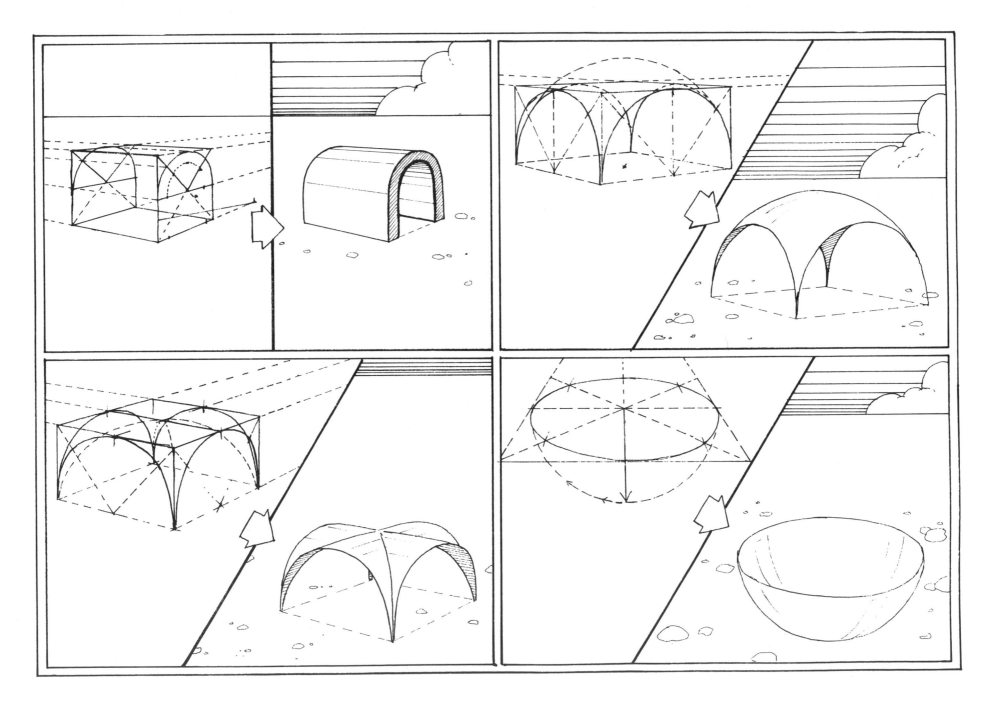

The key to drawing curved lines and surfaces in perspective is to plot significant apexes and other reference points by means of right-angle coordinates, which can be measured easily.

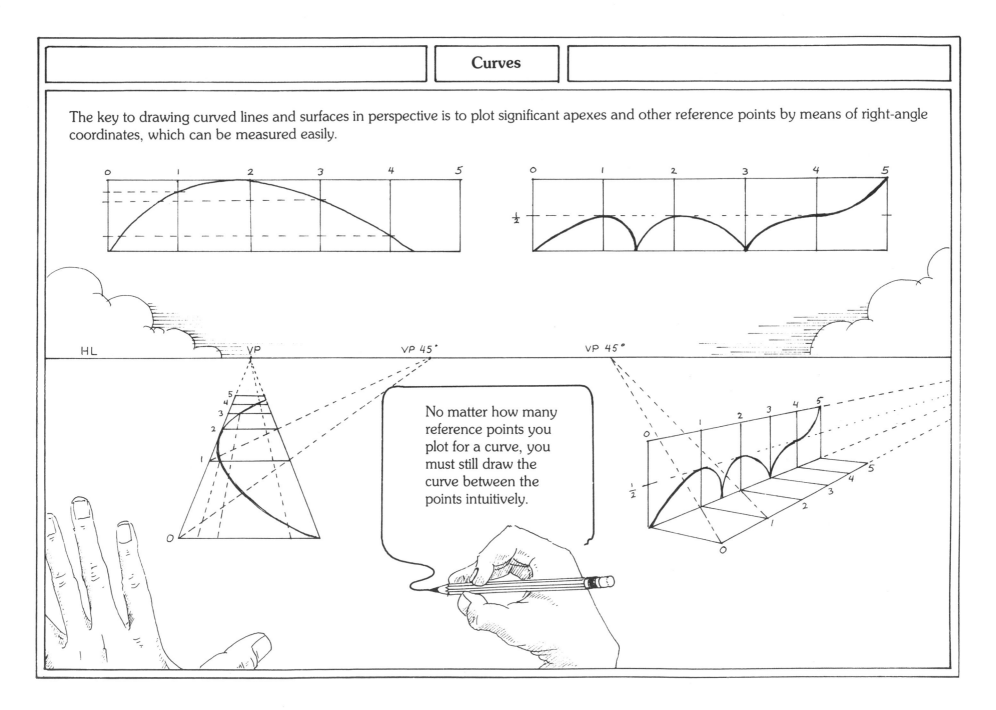

No matter how many reference points you plot for a curve, you must still draw the curve between the points intuitively.

The accuracy of a curve can be increased by plotting more reference points. While this is not always practical or possible, there are a number of techniques and tools that can help guide the curved line between known points.

On a very basic level, it is helpful to think about "driving" or "steering" a curve, much as we steer an automobile, i.e., it is important to anticipate the arcs of the turns.

It is also important to know and to anticipate the direction in which the line is traveling at the moment it passes through a given reference point.

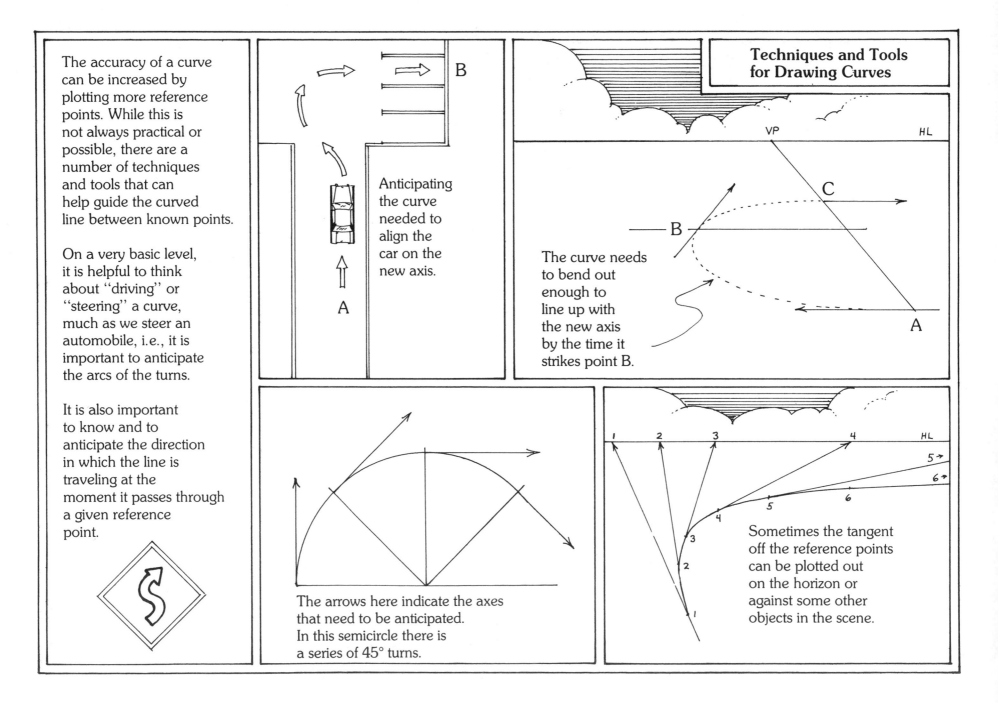

Anticipating the curve needed to align the car on the new axis.

Techniques and Tools for Drawing Curves

The curve needs to bend out enough to line up with the new axis by the time it strikes point B.

The arrows here indicate the axes that need to be anticipated. In this semicircle there is a series of 45° turns.

Sometimes the tangent off the reference points can be plotted out on the horizon or against some other objects in the scene.

104

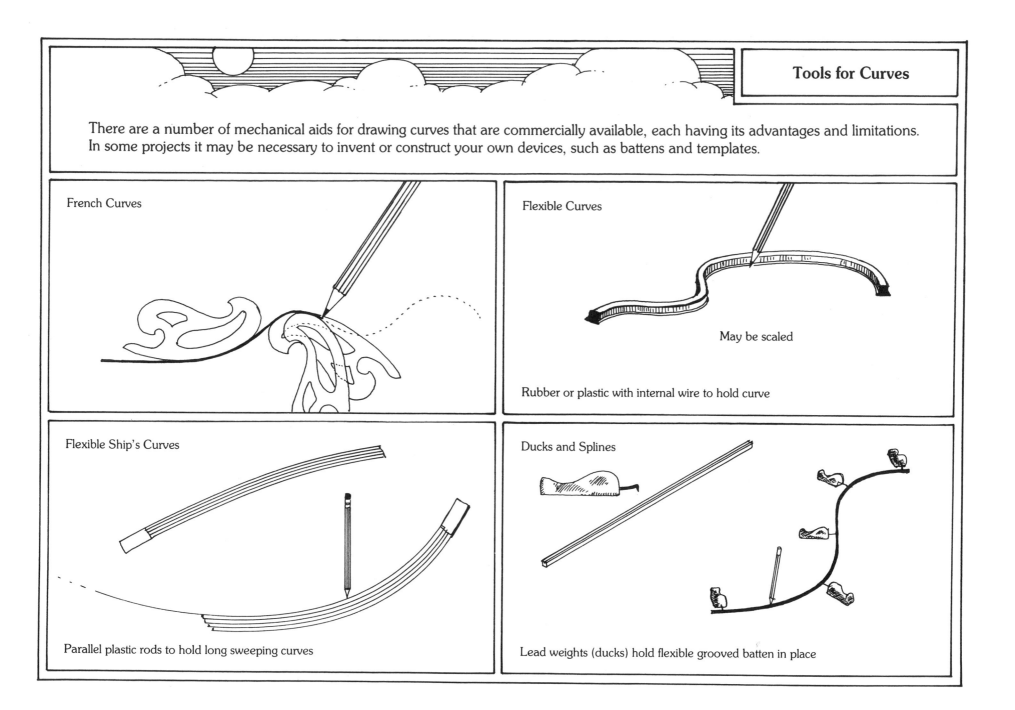

Tools for Curves

There are a number of mechanical aids for drawing curves that are commercially available, each having its advantages and limitations. In some projects it may be necessary to invent or construct your own devices, such as battens and templates.

French Curves

Flexible Curves

May be scaled

Rubber or plastic with internal wire to hold curve

Flexible Ship's Curves

Parallel plastic rods to hold long sweeping curves

Ducks and Splines

Lead weights (ducks) hold flexible grooved batten in place

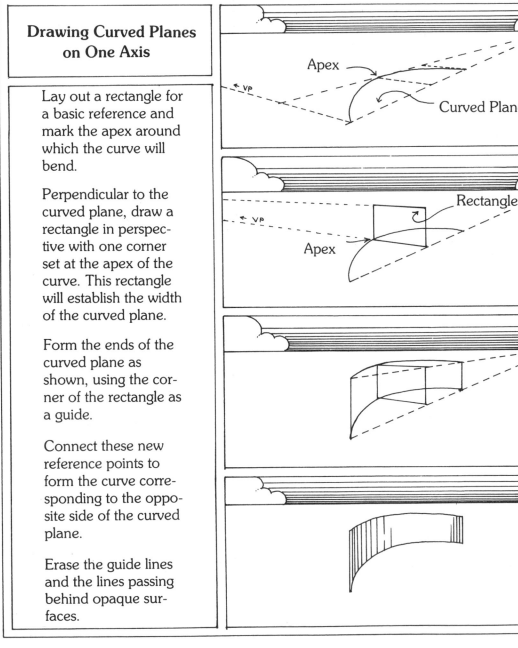

Drawing Curved Planes on One Axis

Lay out a rectangle for a basic reference and mark the apex around which the curve will bend.

Perpendicular to the curved plane, draw a rectangle in perspective with one corner set at the apex of the curve. This rectangle will establish the width of the curved plane.

Form the ends of the curved plane as shown, using the corner of the rectangle as a guide.

Connect these new reference points to form the curve corresponding to the opposite side of the curved plane.

Erase the guide lines and the lines passing behind opaque surfaces.

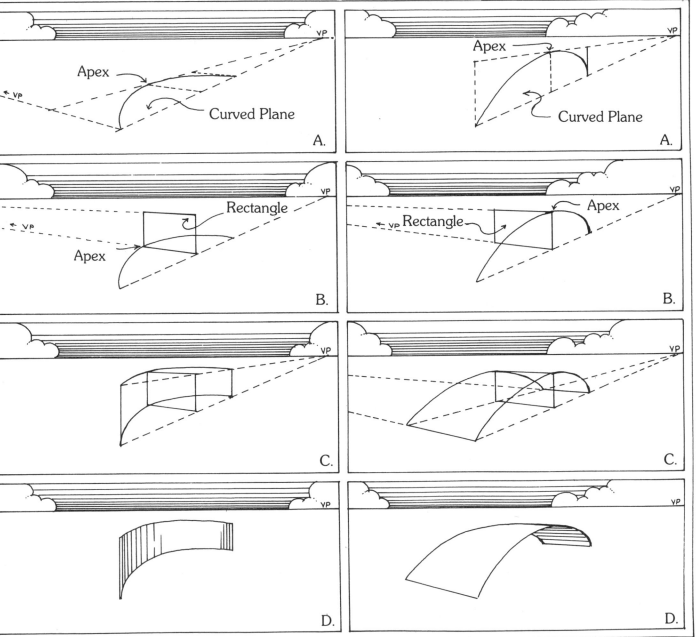

Drawing Curved Planes on Two Axes

Planes that curve along two axes can create additional

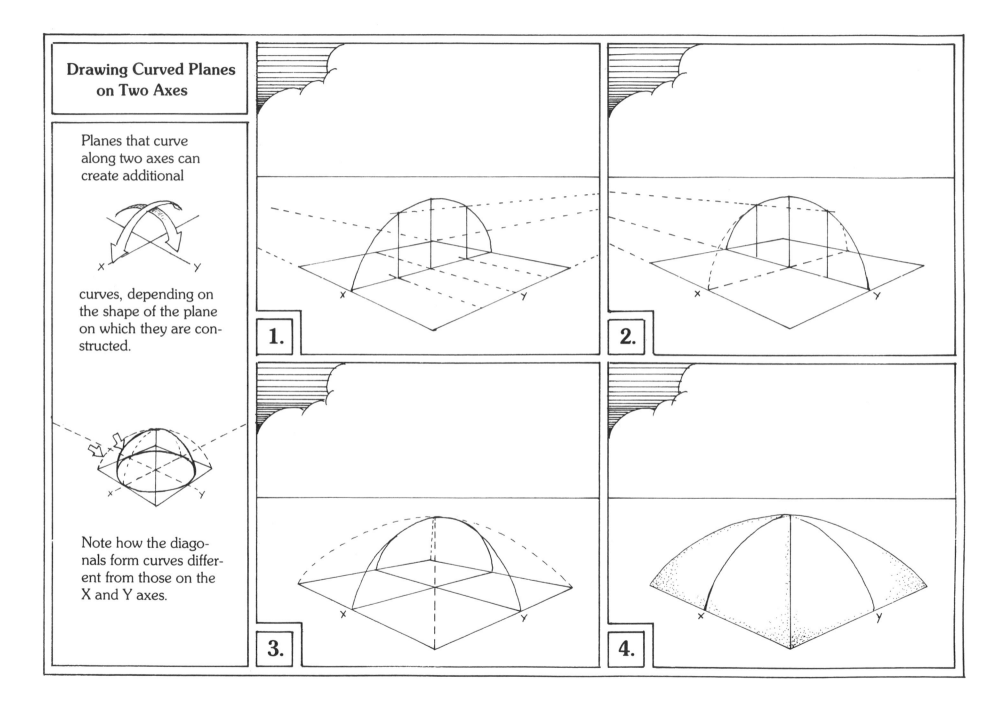

curves, depending on the shape of the plane on which they are constructed.

Note how the diagonals form curves different from those on the X and Y axes.

1.

2.

3.

4.

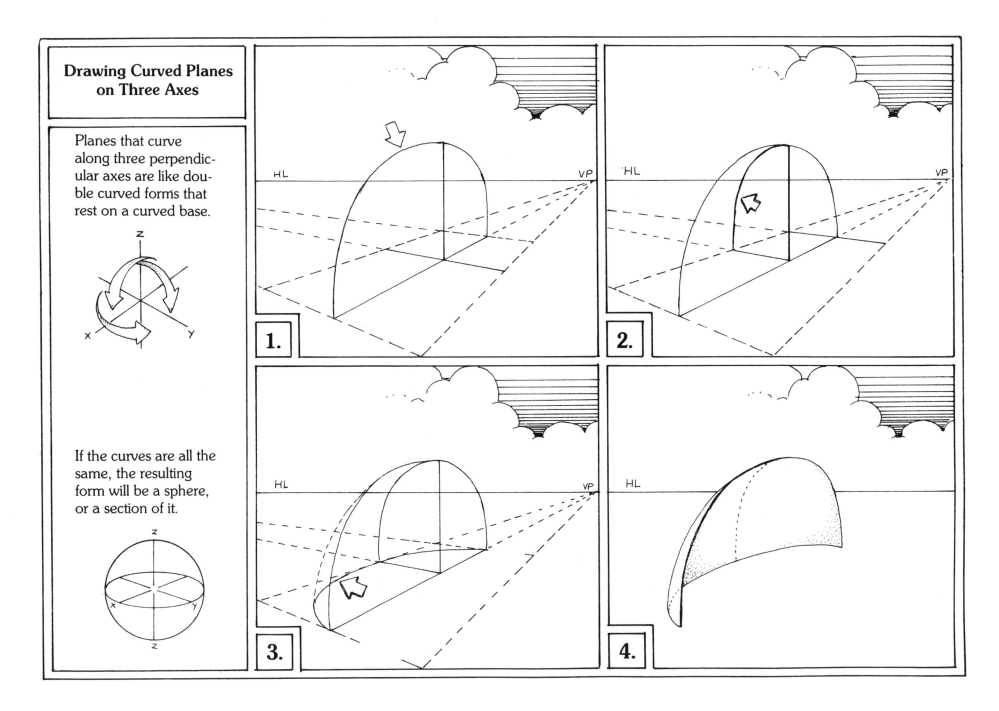

Drawing Curved Planes on Three Axes

Planes that curve along three perpendicular axes are like double curved forms that rest on a curved base.

If the curves are all the same, the resulting form will be a sphere, or a section of it.

1.

2.

3.

4.

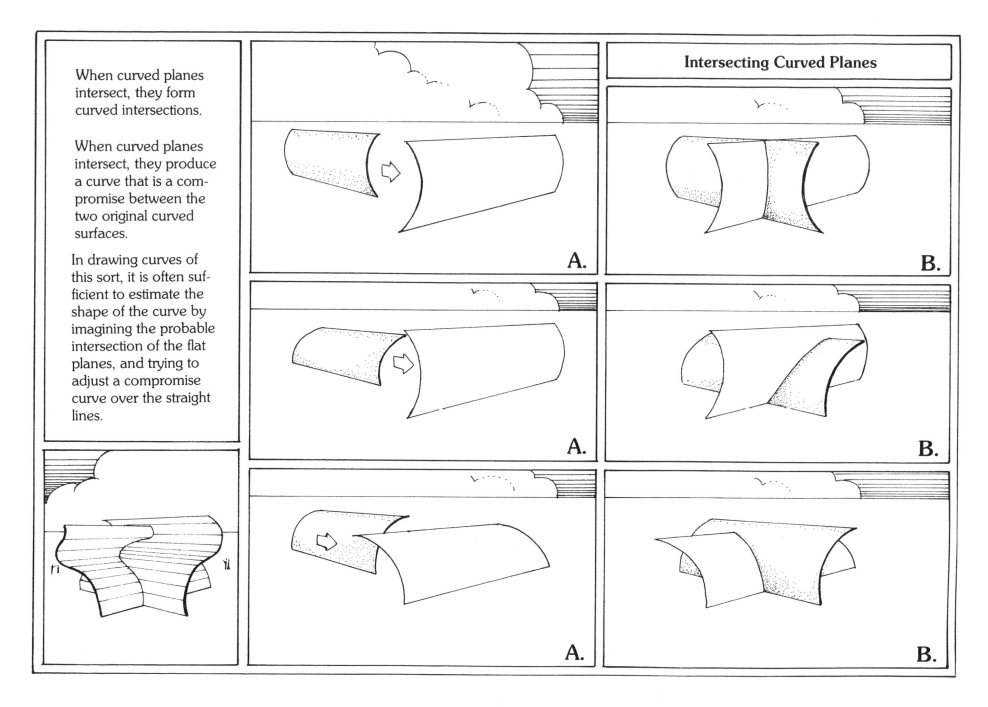

When curved planes intersect, they form curved intersections.

When curved planes intersect, they produce a curve that is a compromise between the two original curved surfaces.

In drawing curves of this sort, it is often sufficient to estimate the shape of the curve by imagining the probable intersection of the flat planes, and trying to adjust a compromise curve over the straight lines.

Intersecting Curved Planes

A.

B.

A.

B.

A.

B.

The most accurate way to plot the intersection of curved planes is to follow the method of transferring the height of the smaller plane to the larger one using a corner. See pages 80–84.

By marking reference points along the ends of either of the curves and repeating the process, guide points for the compromise curve can be plotted along the intersection.

Note how each reference point is actually the corner of a separate horizontal plane.

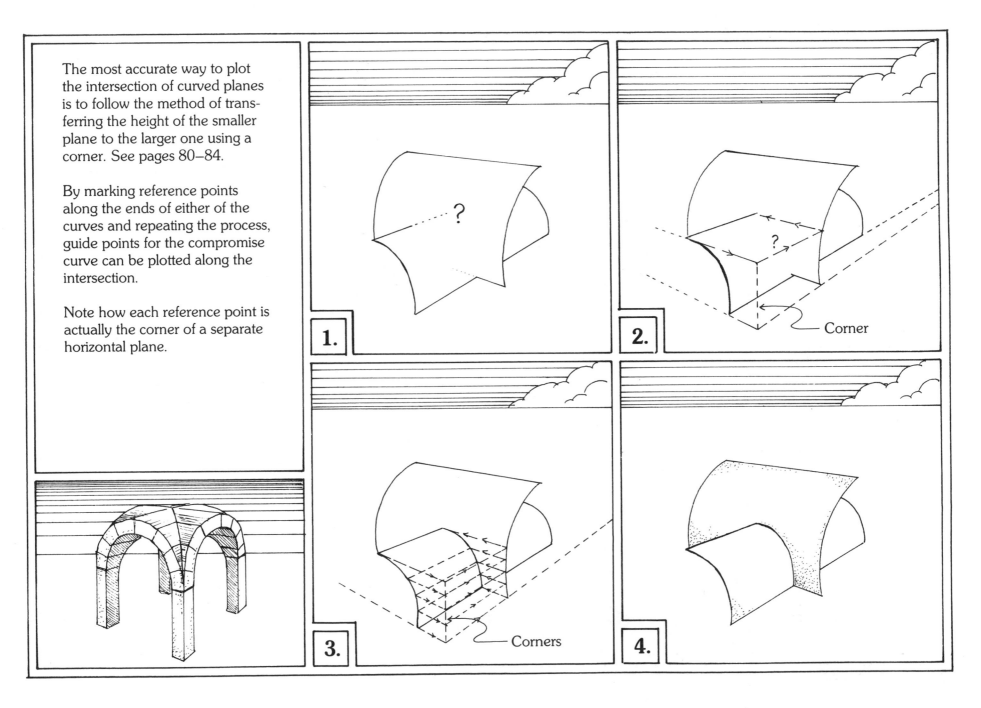

1.

2.

Corner

3.

Corners

4.

The stations that carry the points from one curved surface to the other need not be rectangles, as long as the lines that form them are connected to the proper vanishing points.

Here, for example, the two planes are not intersecting at right angles; thus, the base of each curved plane has its own set of vanishing points.

With complex surfaces like these, more reference points need to be plotted to guide the intersecting curve.

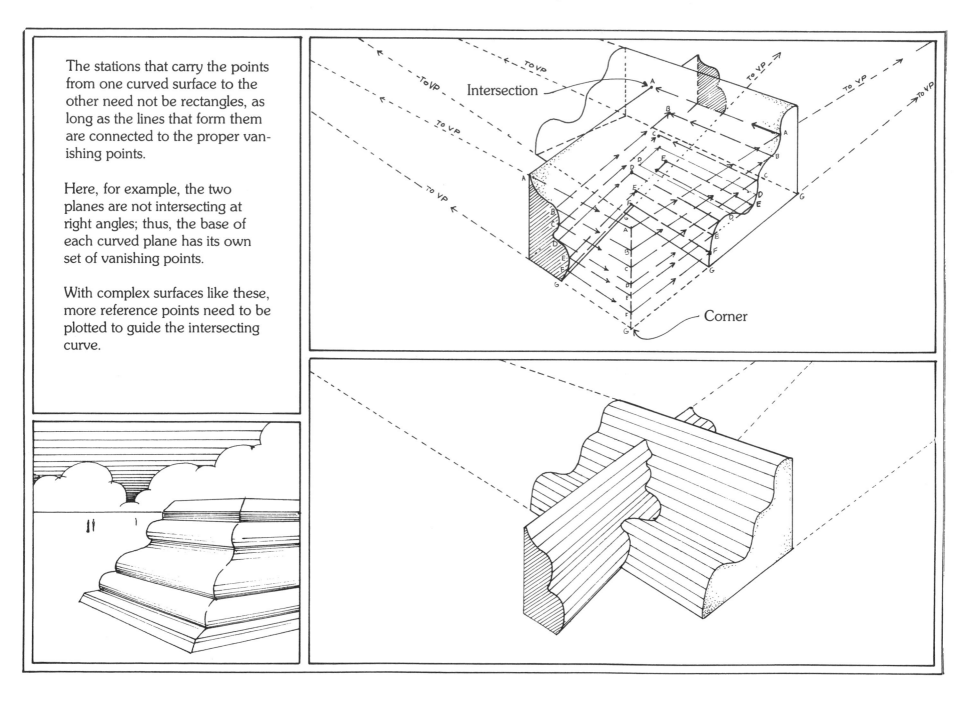

Intersection

Corner

111

Drawing Complex Curved Shapes in Perspective

There is no one way in which to approach the drawing of complex and multiple curved surfaces in perspective, for each project will present a certain number of unique problems that will require unique solutions. However, whether one is loosely sketching or trying to render an object to scale, the basic principle of progressing from the simple to the complex remains valid. In particular, this means moving from straight lines and right angle coordinates, which can be plotted with certainty in a perspective view, to complex curves, which ultimately must be sensed.

In the example at the lower right, note the way in which the final form, which has few straight lines, is built up from simple coordinates.

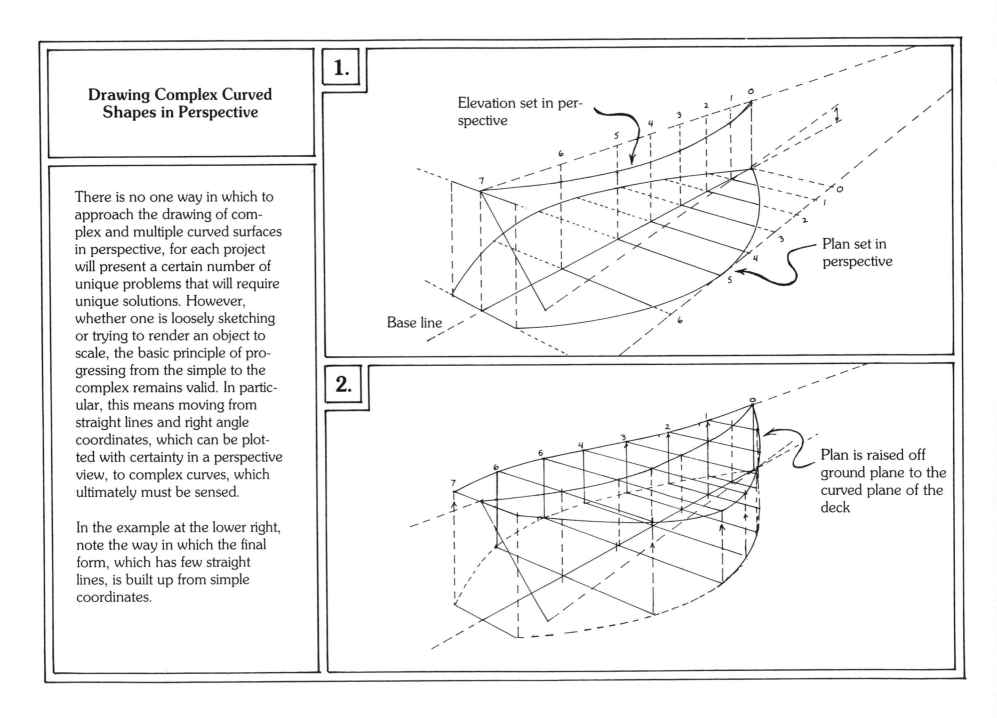

1.

Elevation set in perspective

Plan set in perspective

Base line

2.

Plan is raised off ground plane to the curved plane of the deck

112

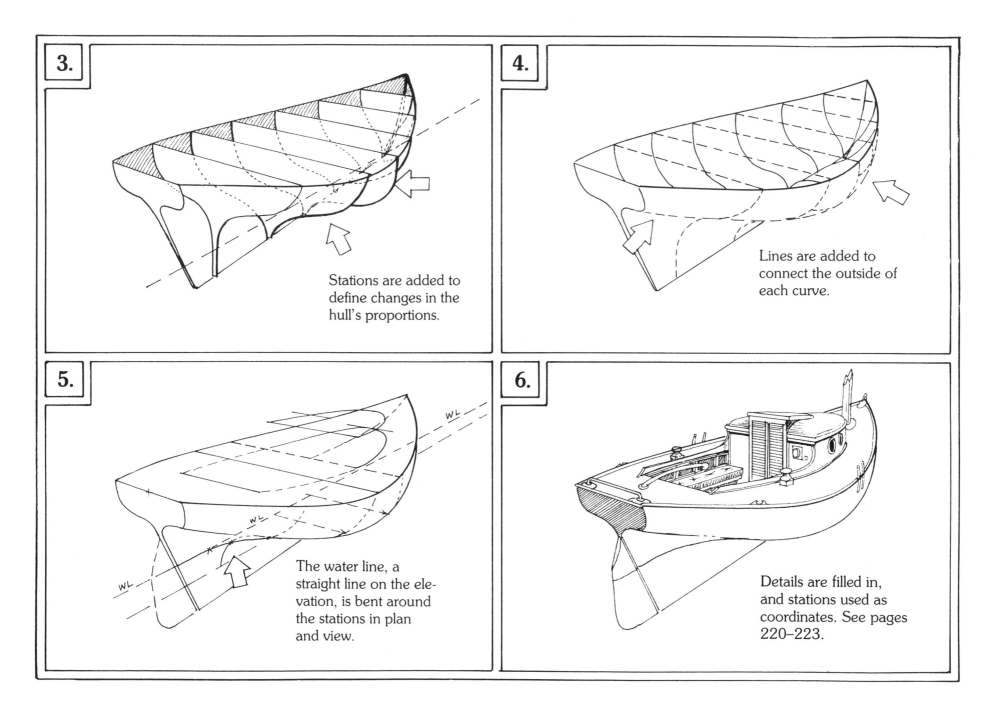

3. Stations are added to define changes in the hull's proportions.

4. Lines are added to connect the outside of each curve.

5. The water line, a straight line on the elevation, is bent around the stations in plan and view.

WL

WL

WL

6. Details are filled in, and stations used as coordinates. See pages 220–223.

113

Constructing Grids on Curved Surfaces

Knowing how to construct grids on curved surfaces makes it possible for you to plot complex designs on curves and transfer designs from plans and elevations. For freehand sketching, it is often enough to have a general mental picture of the curving grid plane. For greater accuracy, however, a grid can be drawn in and subdivided.

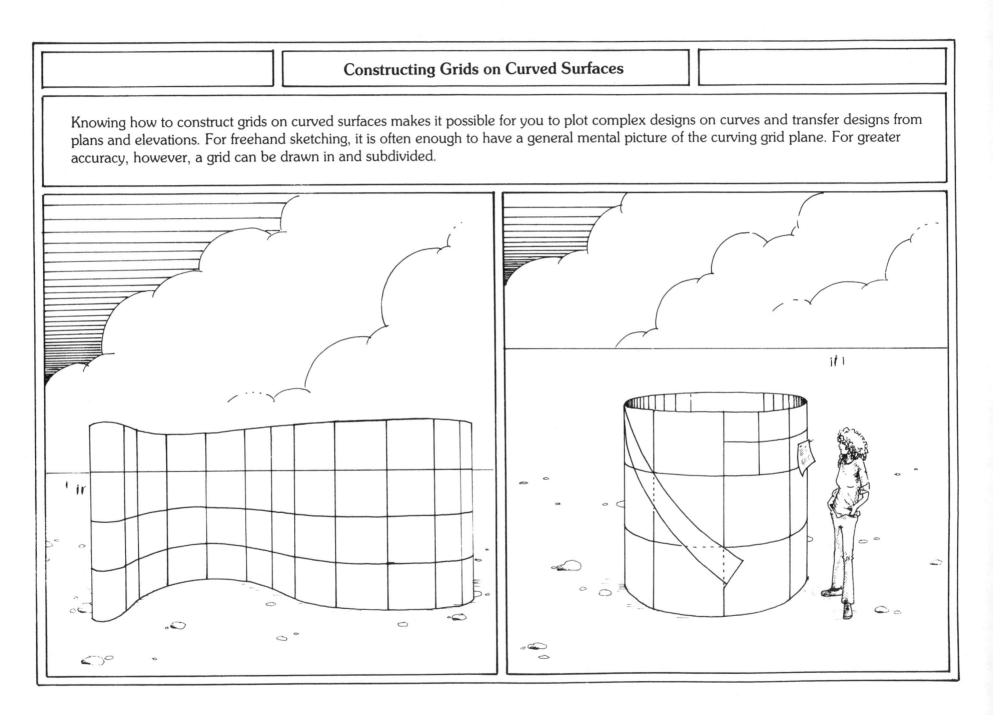

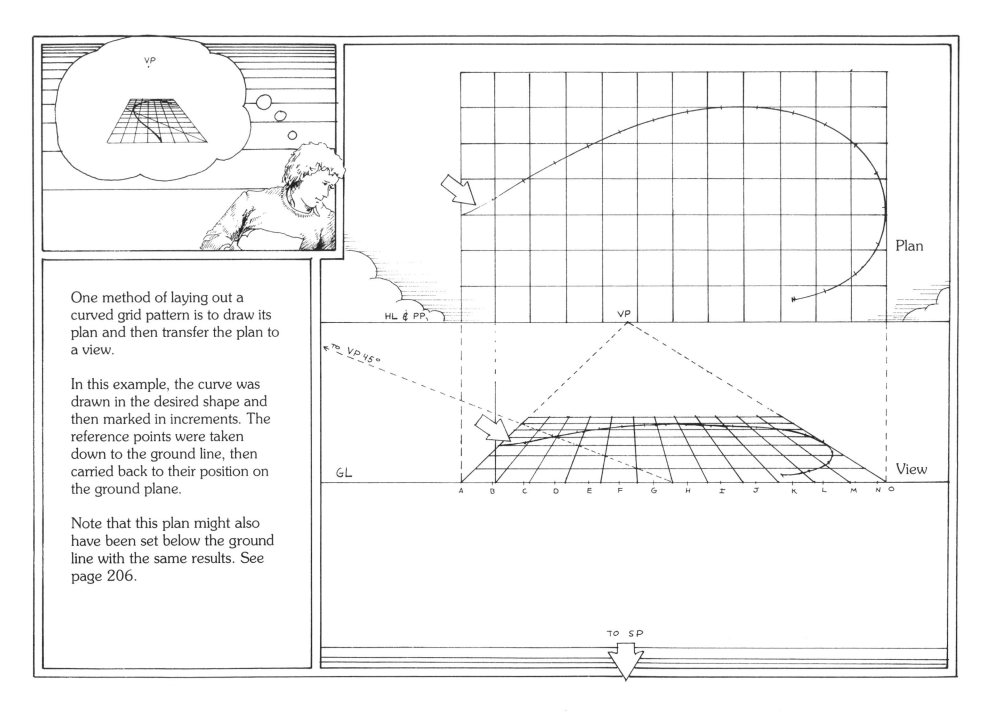

One method of laying out a curved grid pattern is to draw its plan and then transfer the plan to a view.

In this example, the curve was drawn in the desired shape and then marked in increments. The reference points were taken down to the ground line, then carried back to their position on the ground plane.

Note that this plan might also have been set below the ground line with the same results. See page 206.

Once you have laid the base curve out on the ground plane, add verticals perpendicular to the incremental marks on the curve. These are the vertical lines of the grid. Note that the space between them differs, depending on their distance from the picture plane.

Now, on a vertical measuring line, mark the increments of the horizontal lines of the grid and connect them back to the curve. In theory, each vertical of the grid will have to be marked off separately from a line at the picture plane. However, a few judiciously placed marks may be enough to guide the whole line.

Curved diagonals can be set up across the curved squares to check accuracy.

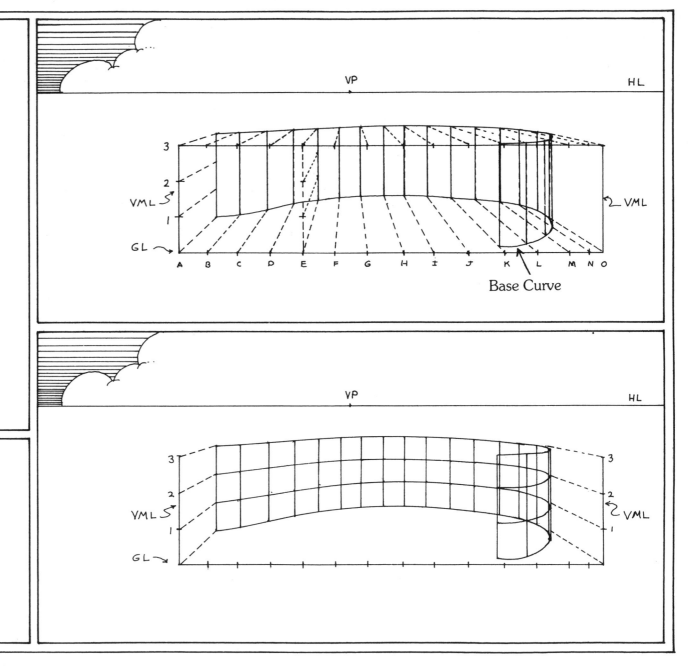

Base Curve

Perspective Grids Based on Circles

Cylinders, cones, and spheres are the primary curved forms based on circles. From these forms, a great variety of shapes and combinations can be derived.

Notice in these examples that the lateral divisions of the grid patterns are circles or, in perspective, ellipses.

When drawing these forms the circles (ellipses) can be treated like stations. Designs can also be drawn on the flattened plan of the form and then "rolled" into perspective view.

In order to move back and forth between plan and view, it is important to understand something about the relationship between the diameter and circumference of a circle.

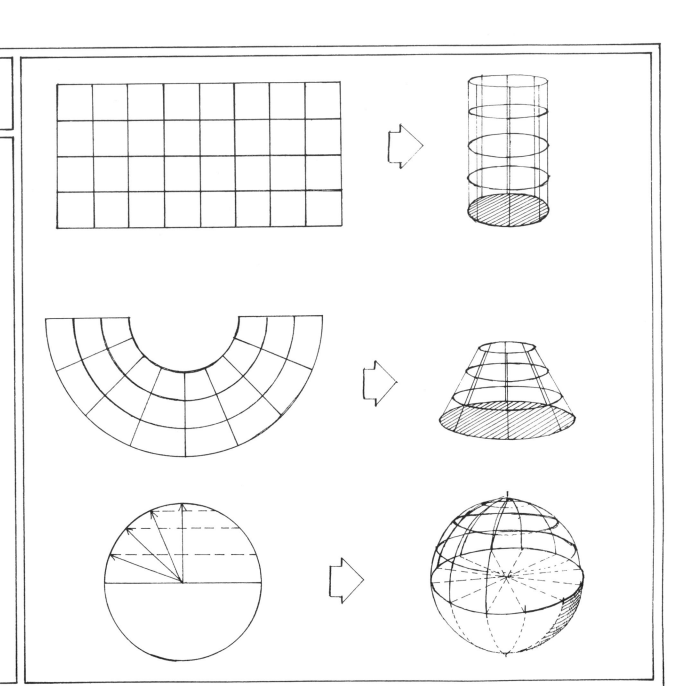

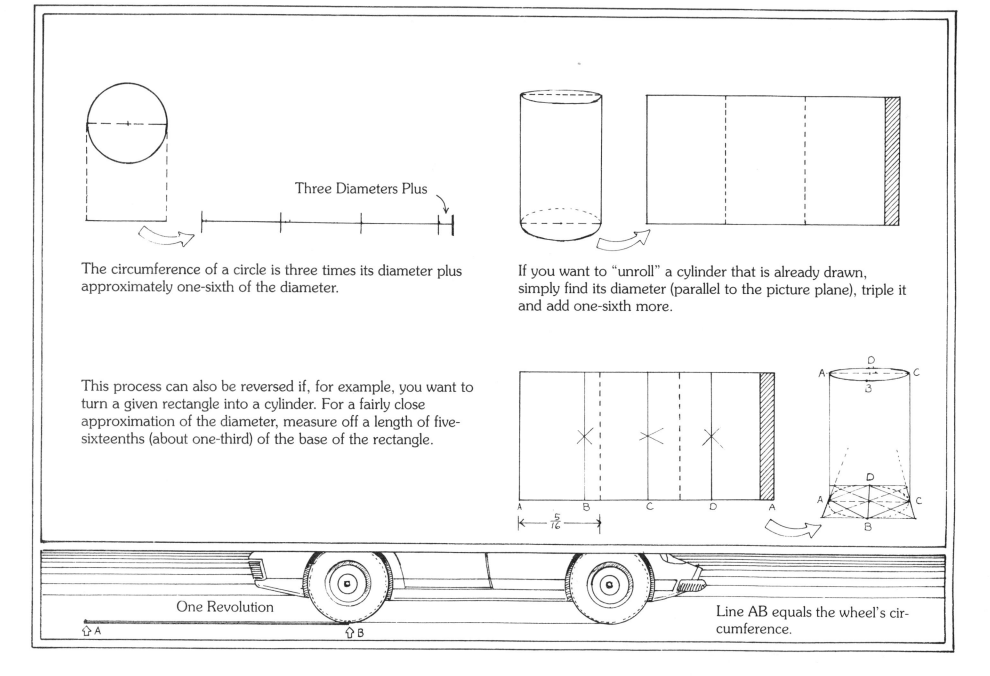

Three Diameters Plus

The circumference of a circle is three times its diameter plus approximately one-sixth of the diameter.

If you want to "unroll" a cylinder that is already drawn, simply find its diameter (parallel to the picture plane), triple it and add one-sixth more.

This process can also be reversed if, for example, you want to turn a given rectangle into a cylinder. For a fairly close approximation of the diameter, measure off a length of five-sixteenths (about one-third) of the base of the rectangle.

One Revolution

Line AB equals the wheel's circumference.

118

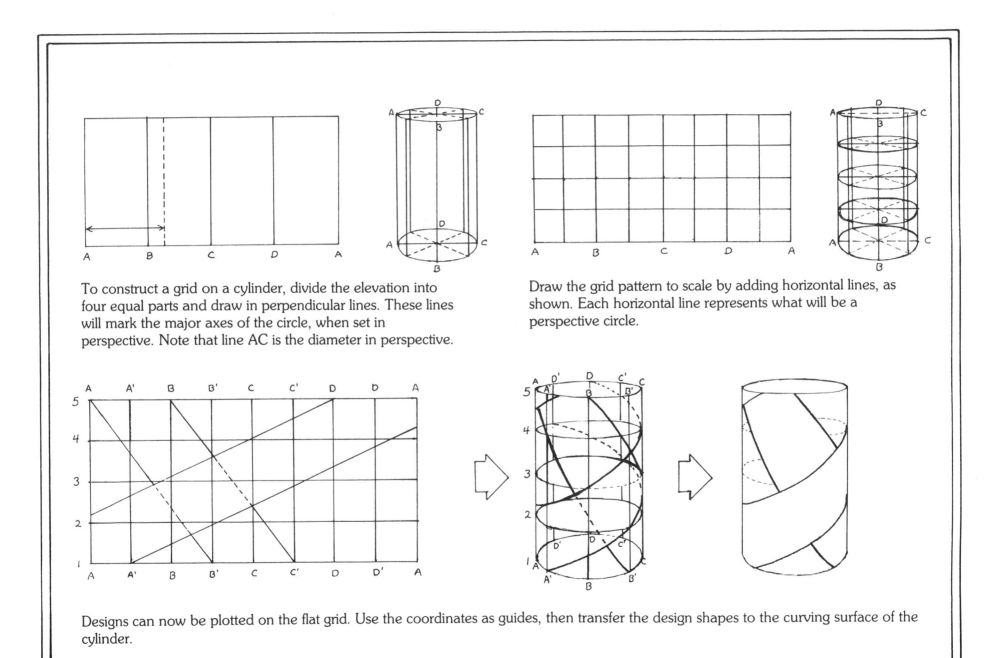

To construct a grid on a cylinder, divide the elevation into four equal parts and draw in perpendicular lines. These lines will mark the major axes of the circle, when set in perspective. Note that line AC is the diameter in perspective.

Draw the grid pattern to scale by adding horizontal lines, as shown. Each horizontal line represents what will be a perspective circle.

Designs can now be plotted on the flat grid. Use the coordinates as guides, then transfer the design shapes to the curving surface of the cylinder.

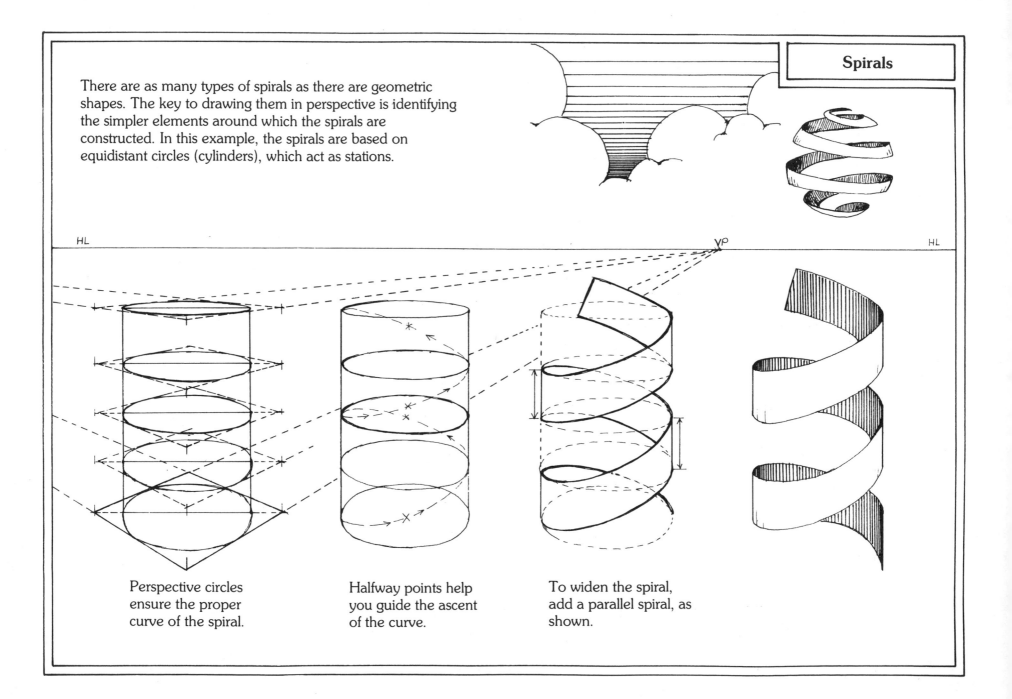

There are as many types of spirals as there are geometric shapes. The key to drawing them in perspective is identifying the simpler elements around which the spirals are constructed. In this example, the spirals are based on equidistant circles (cylinders), which act as stations.

HL   VP   HL

Perspective circles ensure the proper curve of the spiral.

Halfway points help you guide the ascent of the curve.

To widen the spiral, add a parallel spiral, as shown.

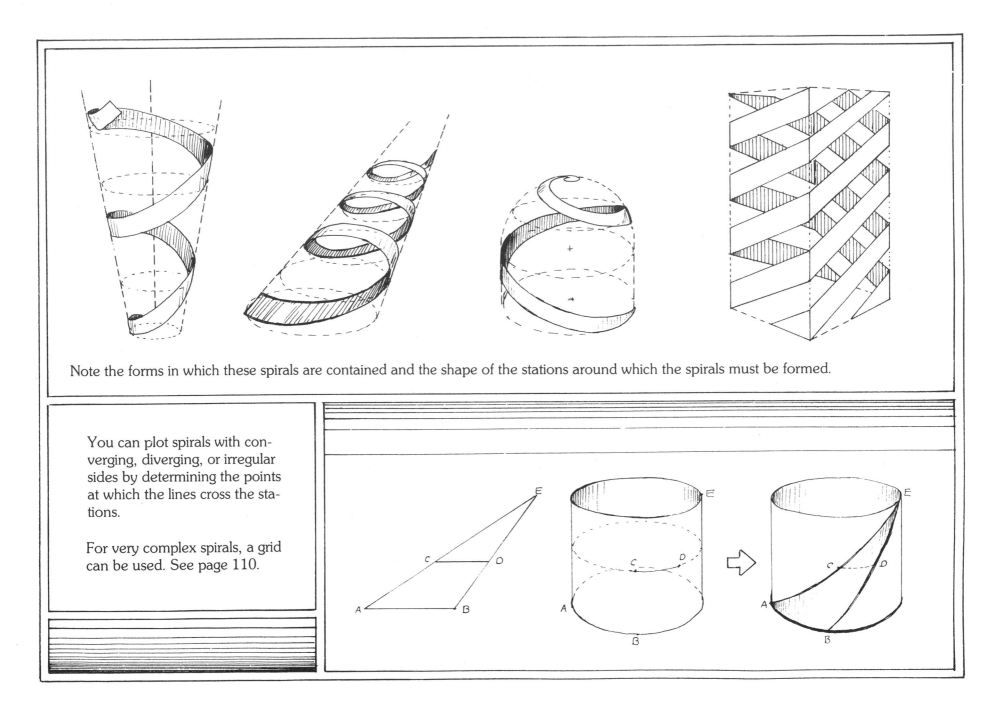

Note the forms in which these spirals are contained and the shape of the stations around which the spirals must be formed.

You can plot spirals with converging, diverging, or irregular sides by determining the points at which the lines cross the stations.

For very complex spirals, a grid can be used. See page 110.

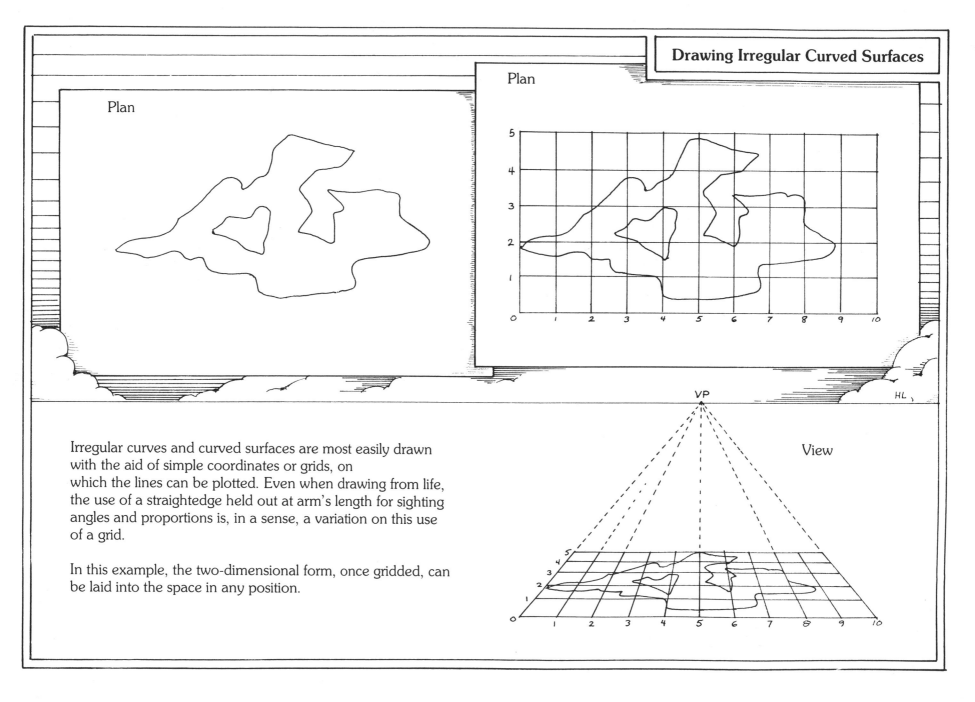

Plan

Plan

View

VP

HL

Irregular curves and curved surfaces are most easily drawn with the aid of simple coordinates or grids, on which the lines can be plotted. Even when drawing from life, the use of a straightedge held out at arm's length for sighting angles and proportions is, in a sense, a variation on this use of a grid.

In this example, the two-dimensional form, once gridded, can be laid into the space in any position.

122

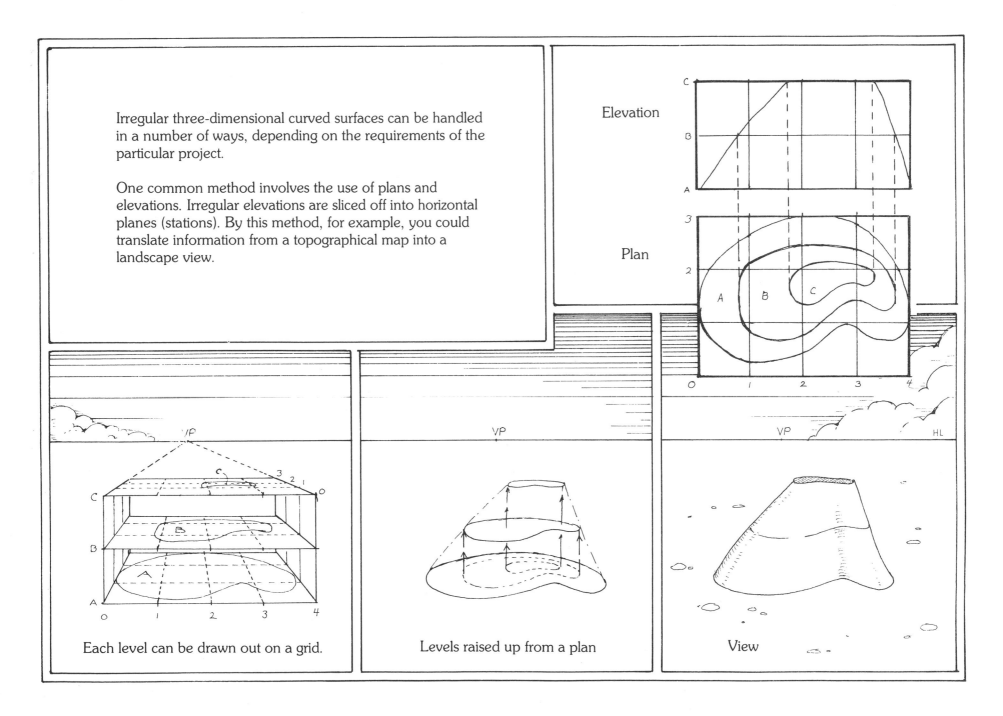

Irregular three-dimensional curved surfaces can be handled in a number of ways, depending on the requirements of the particular project.

One common method involves the use of plans and elevations. Irregular elevations are sliced off into horizontal planes (stations). By this method, for example, you could translate information from a topographical map into a landscape view.

Elevation

Plan

Each level can be drawn out on a grid.

Levels raised up from a plan

View

123

Another method for plotting irregular curved surfaces is to use a base grid on which perpendicular lines are set at various heights to mark significant coordinates.

This method is really the same as the one described on the previous page, except that here, the information has been sliced vertically rather than horizontally.

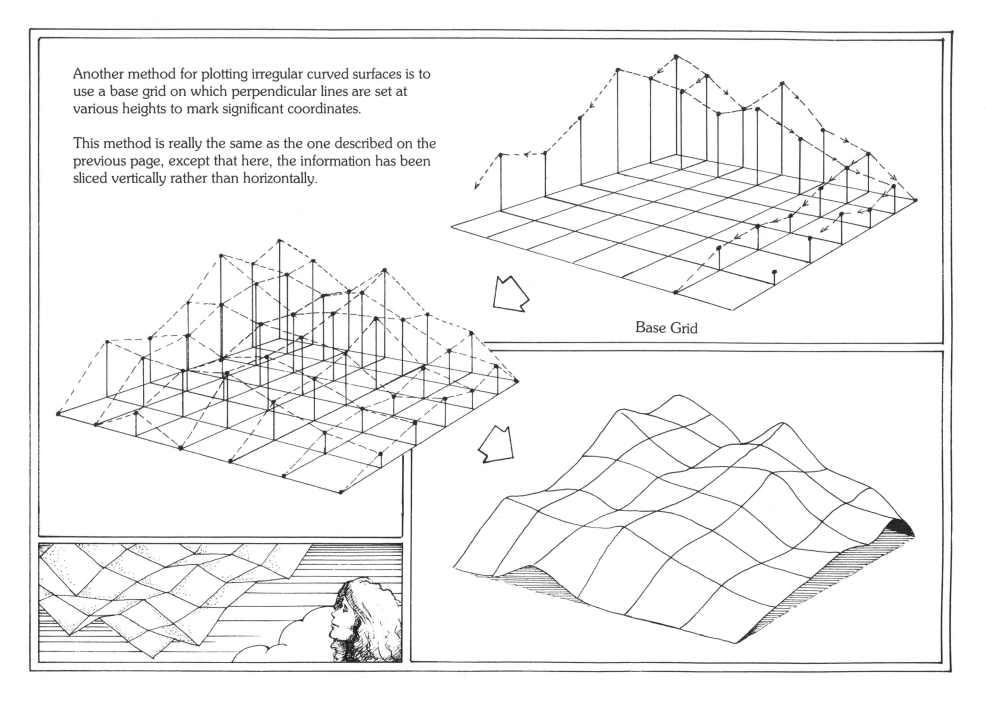

Base Grid

Shadows and Reflections

8

Despite their initial appearance of complexity, shadows and reflections obey the same immutable rules of perspective illustrated in the preceding sections of this book.

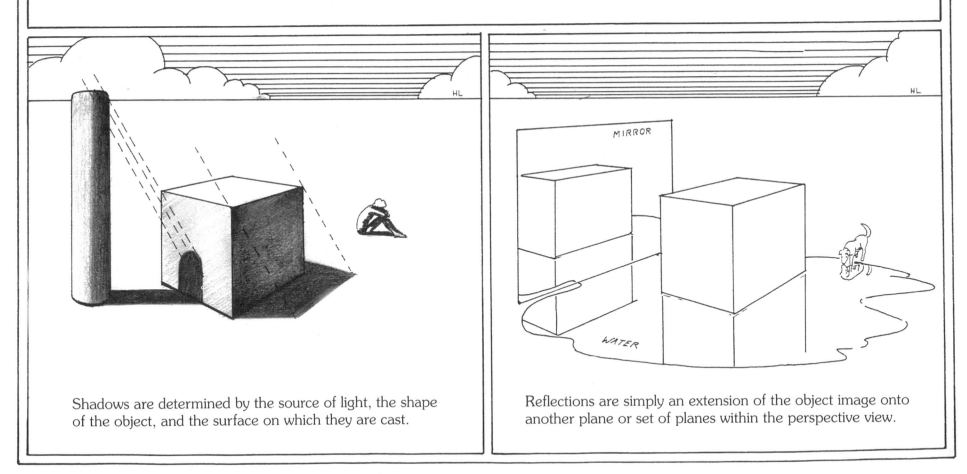

Shadows are determined by the source of light, the shape of the object, and the surface on which they are cast.

Reflections are simply an extension of the object image onto another plane or set of planes within the perspective view.

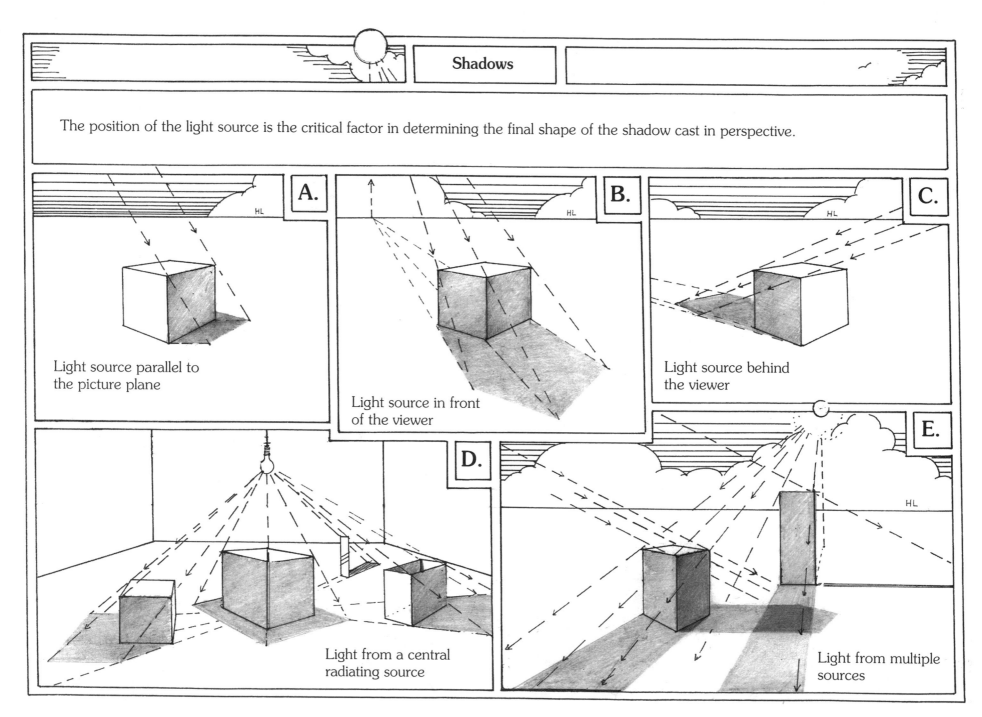

Shadows

The position of the light source is the critical factor in determining the final shape of the shadow cast in perspective.

A. Light source parallel to the picture plane

B. Light source in front of the viewer

C. Light source behind the viewer

D. Light from a central radiating source

E. Light from multiple sources

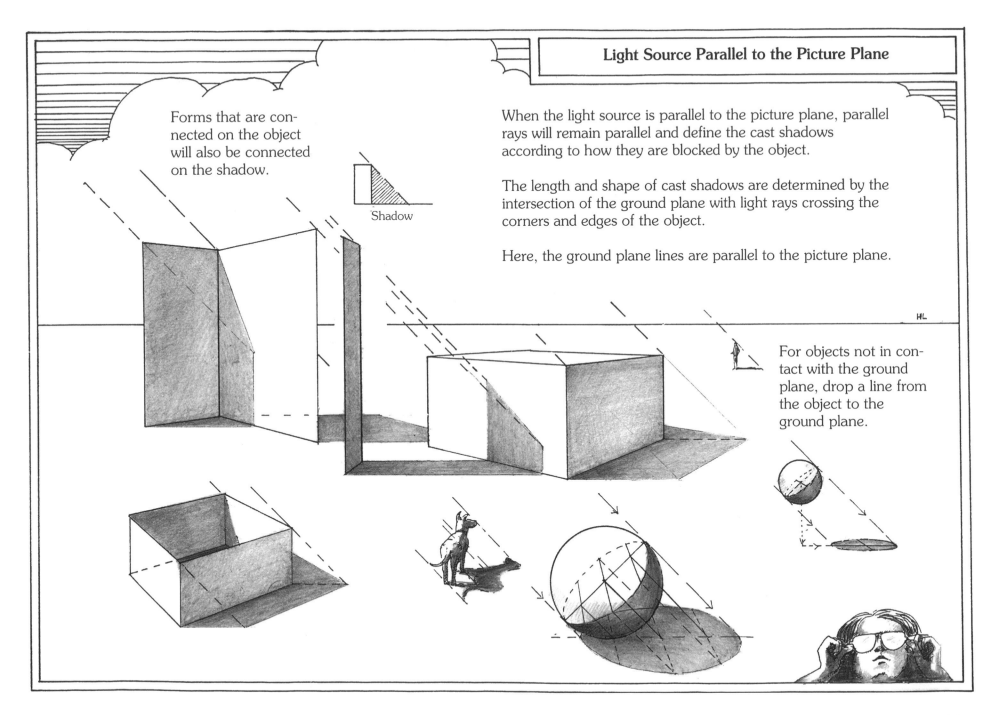

Forms that are connected on the object will also be connected on the shadow.

Shadow

When the light source is parallel to the picture plane, parallel rays will remain parallel and define the cast shadows according to how they are blocked by the object.

The length and shape of cast shadows are determined by the intersection of the ground plane with light rays crossing the corners and edges of the object.

Here, the ground plane lines are parallel to the picture plane.

For objects not in contact with the ground plane, drop a line from the object to the ground plane.

HL

127

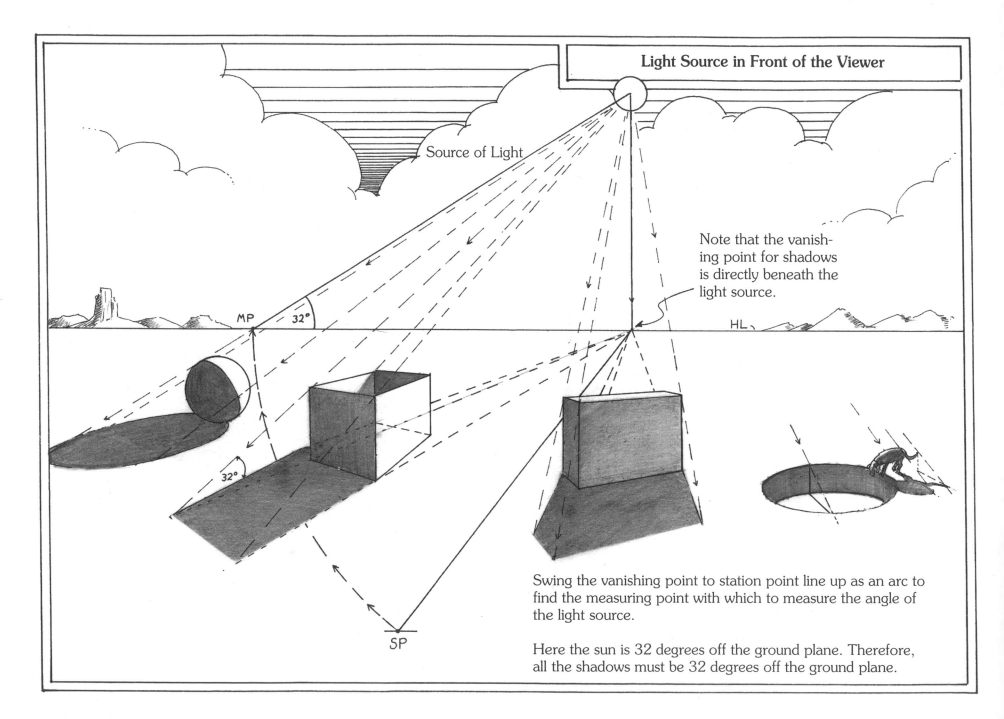

Light Source in Front of the Viewer

Source of Light

Note that the vanishing point for shadows is directly beneath the light source.

MP 32°

HL

32°

SP

Swing the vanishing point to station point line up as an arc to find the measuring point with which to measure the angle of the light source.

Here the sun is 32 degrees off the ground plane. Therefore, all the shadows must be 32 degrees off the ground plane.

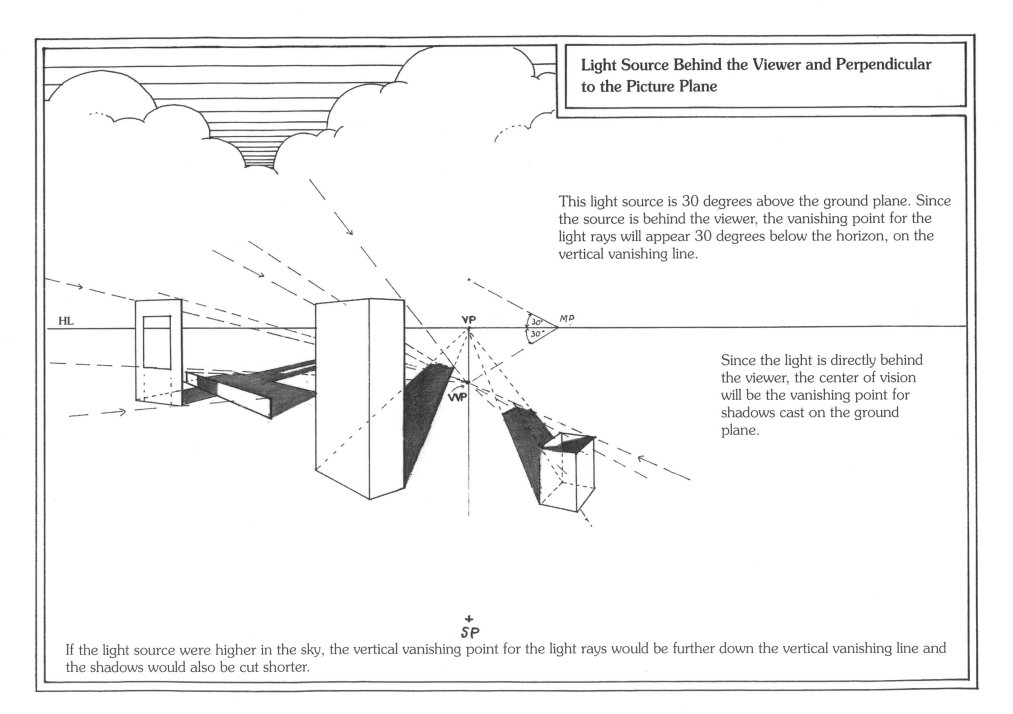

Light Source Behind the Viewer and Perpendicular to the Picture Plane

This light source is 30 degrees above the ground plane. Since the source is behind the viewer, the vanishing point for the light rays will appear 30 degrees below the horizon, on the vertical vanishing line.

Since the light is directly behind the viewer, the center of vision will be the vanishing point for shadows cast on the ground plane.

HL

VP

MP

30°
30°

VVP

+
SP

If the light source were higher in the sky, the vertical vanishing point for the light rays would be further down the vertical vanishing line and the shadows would also be cut shorter.

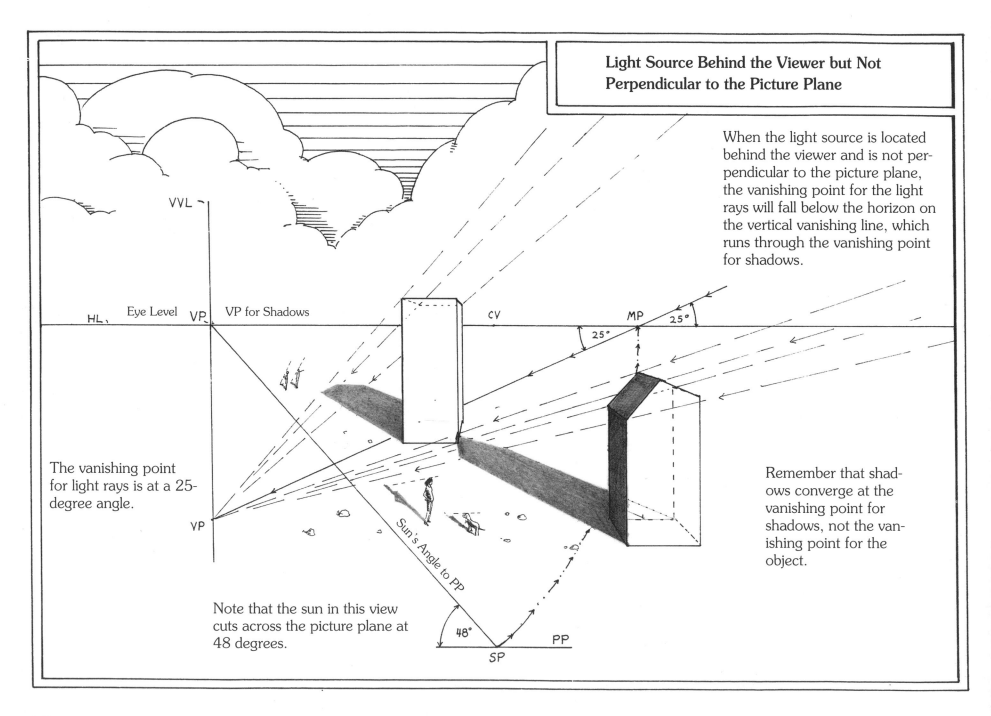

Light Source Behind the Viewer but Not Perpendicular to the Picture Plane

When the light source is located behind the viewer and is not perpendicular to the picture plane, the vanishing point for the light rays will fall below the horizon on the vertical vanishing line, which runs through the vanishing point for shadows.

VVL

HL、   Eye Level   VP   VP for Shadows   CV   MP   25°

25°

The vanishing point for light rays is at a 25-degree angle.

VP

Sun's Angle to PP

Remember that shadows converge at the vanishing point for shadows, not the vanishing point for the object.

Note that the sun in this view cuts across the picture plane at 48 degrees.

48°

SP   PP

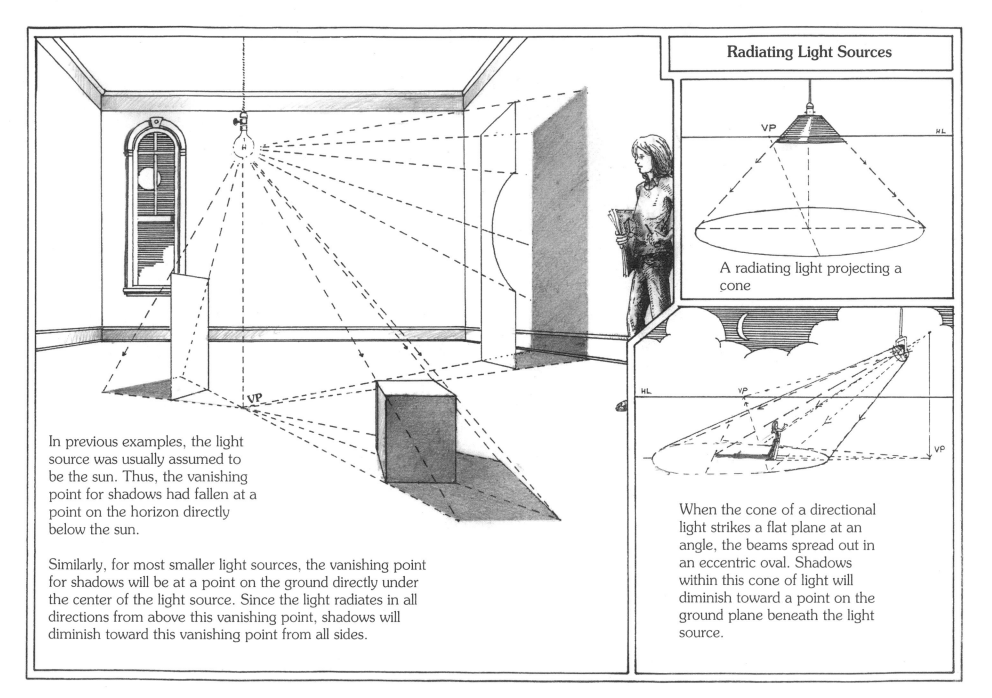

A radiating light projecting a cone

In previous examples, the light source was usually assumed to be the sun. Thus, the vanishing point for shadows had fallen at a point on the horizon directly below the sun.

Similarly, for most smaller light sources, the vanishing point for shadows will be at a point on the ground directly under the center of the light source. Since the light radiates in all directions from above this vanishing point, shadows will diminish toward this vanishing point from all sides.

When the cone of a directional light strikes a flat plane at an angle, the beams spread out in an eccentric oval. Shadows within this cone of light will diminish toward a point on the ground plane beneath the light source.

131

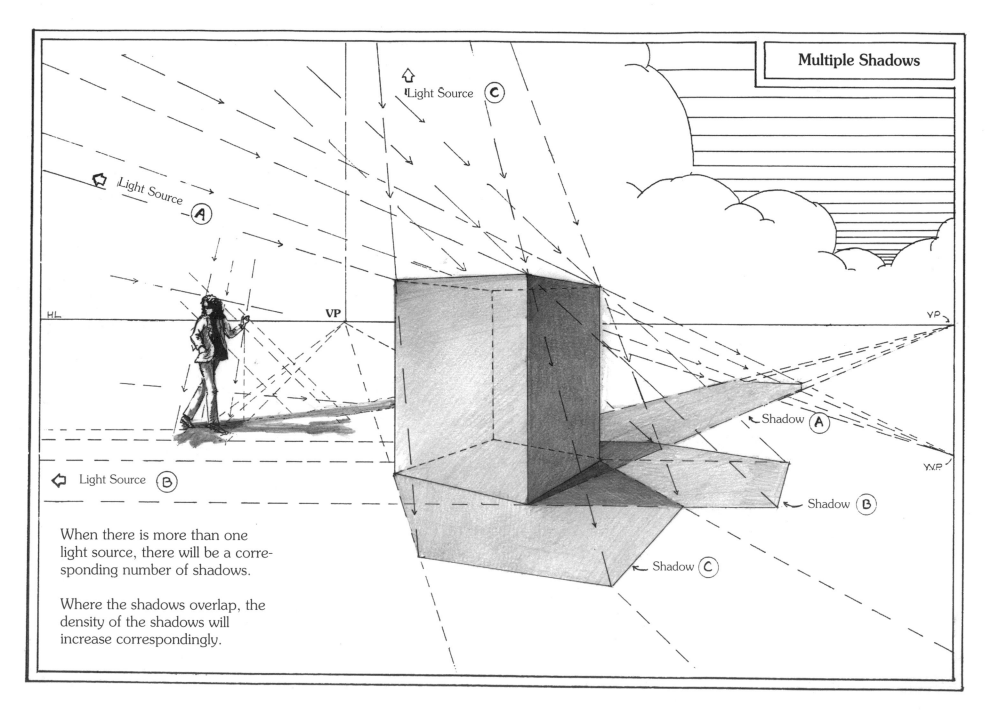

Light Source Ⓒ

Light Source Ⓐ

HL

VP

VP

V.P.

Light Source Ⓑ

← Shadow Ⓐ

← Shadow Ⓑ

← Shadow Ⓒ

When there is more than one light source, there will be a corresponding number of shadows.

Where the shadows overlap, the density of the shadows will increase correspondingly.

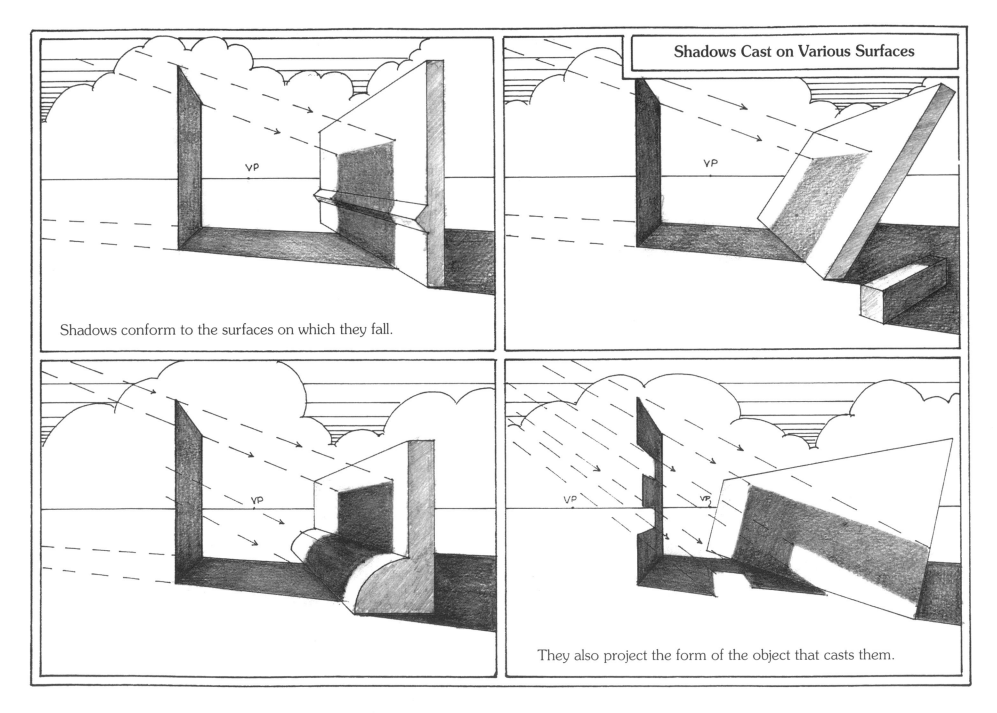

Shadows Cast on Various Surfaces

Shadows conform to the surfaces on which they fall.

They also project the form of the object that casts them.

133

Reflections

A reflection is simply the mirror image, or equal and opposite extension of, the original object and its perspective system. Drawing parallel reflections requires only a simple extension of the object through the reflecting surface, while angular reflections require more complicated calculations.

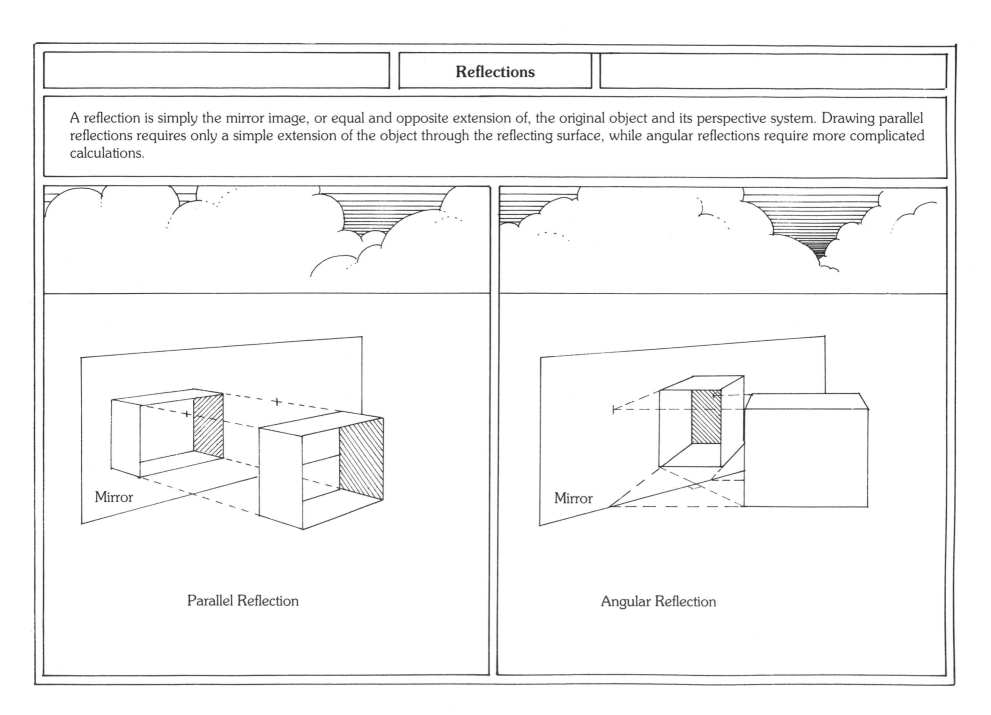

Parallel Reflection

Angular Reflection

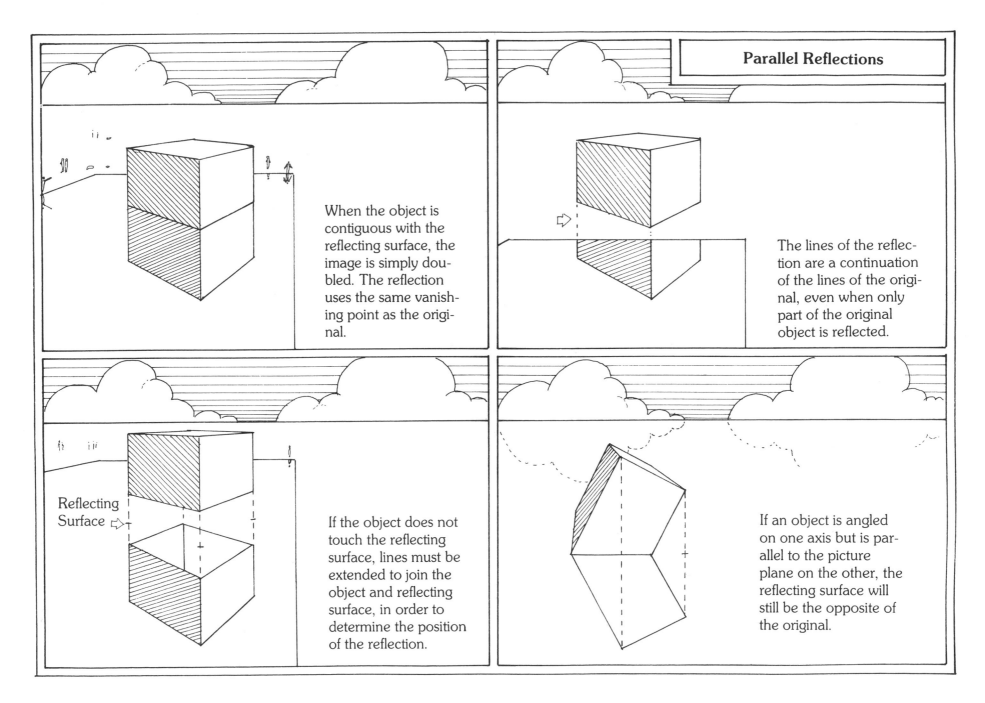

When the object is contiguous with the reflecting surface, the image is simply doubled. The reflection uses the same vanishing point as the original.

The lines of the reflection are a continuation of the lines of the original, even when only part of the original object is reflected.

Reflecting Surface ⇨

If the object does not touch the reflecting surface, lines must be extended to join the object and reflecting surface, in order to determine the position of the reflection.

If an object is angled on one axis but is parallel to the picture plane on the other, the reflecting surface will still be the opposite of the original.

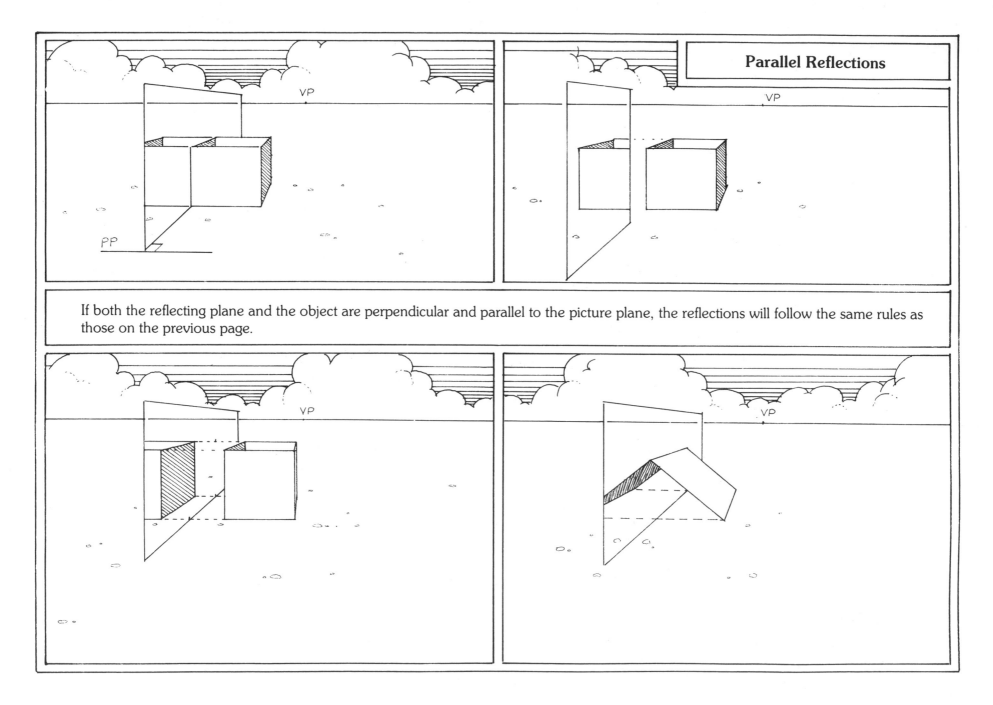

Parallel Reflections

If both the reflecting plane and the object are perpendicular and parallel to the picture plane, the reflections will follow the same rules as those on the previous page.

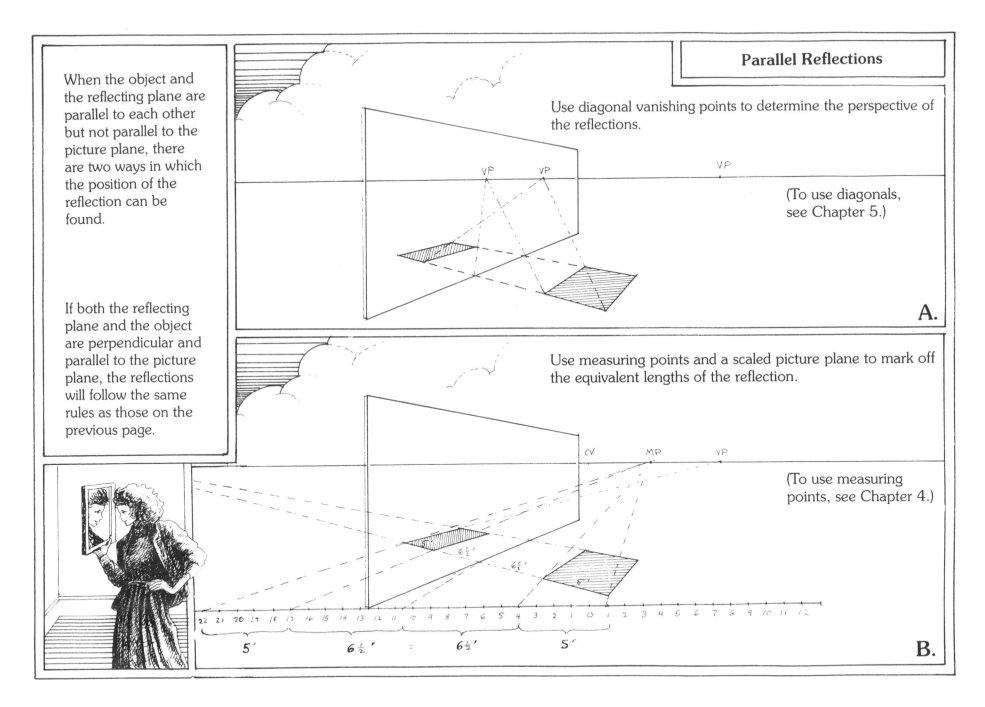

When the object and the reflecting plane are parallel to each other but not parallel to the picture plane, there are two ways in which the position of the reflection can be found.

If both the reflecting plane and the object are perpendicular and parallel to the picture plane, the reflections will follow the same rules as those on the previous page.

Use diagonal vanishing points to determine the perspective of the reflections.

(To use diagonals, see Chapter 5.)

VP   VP   VP

A.

Use measuring points and a scaled picture plane to mark off the equivalent lengths of the reflection.

(To use measuring points, see Chapter 4.)

CV   MP   VP

6 1/2'   6 1/2'   5'

22 21 20 19 18 17 16 15 14 13 12 11 10 9 8 7 6 5 4 3 2 1 0 1 2 3 4 5 6 7 8 9 10 11 12

5'   6 1/2' = 6 1/2'   5'

B.

It is a relatively simple matter to find the reflection when the object and reflective surface are parallel to each other, as shown in A and B. However, when the object and reflecting surface are at anything other than 90 degrees or 45 degrees to each other, the vanishing point of the reflection will be different from that of the object or its diagonals, as in C.

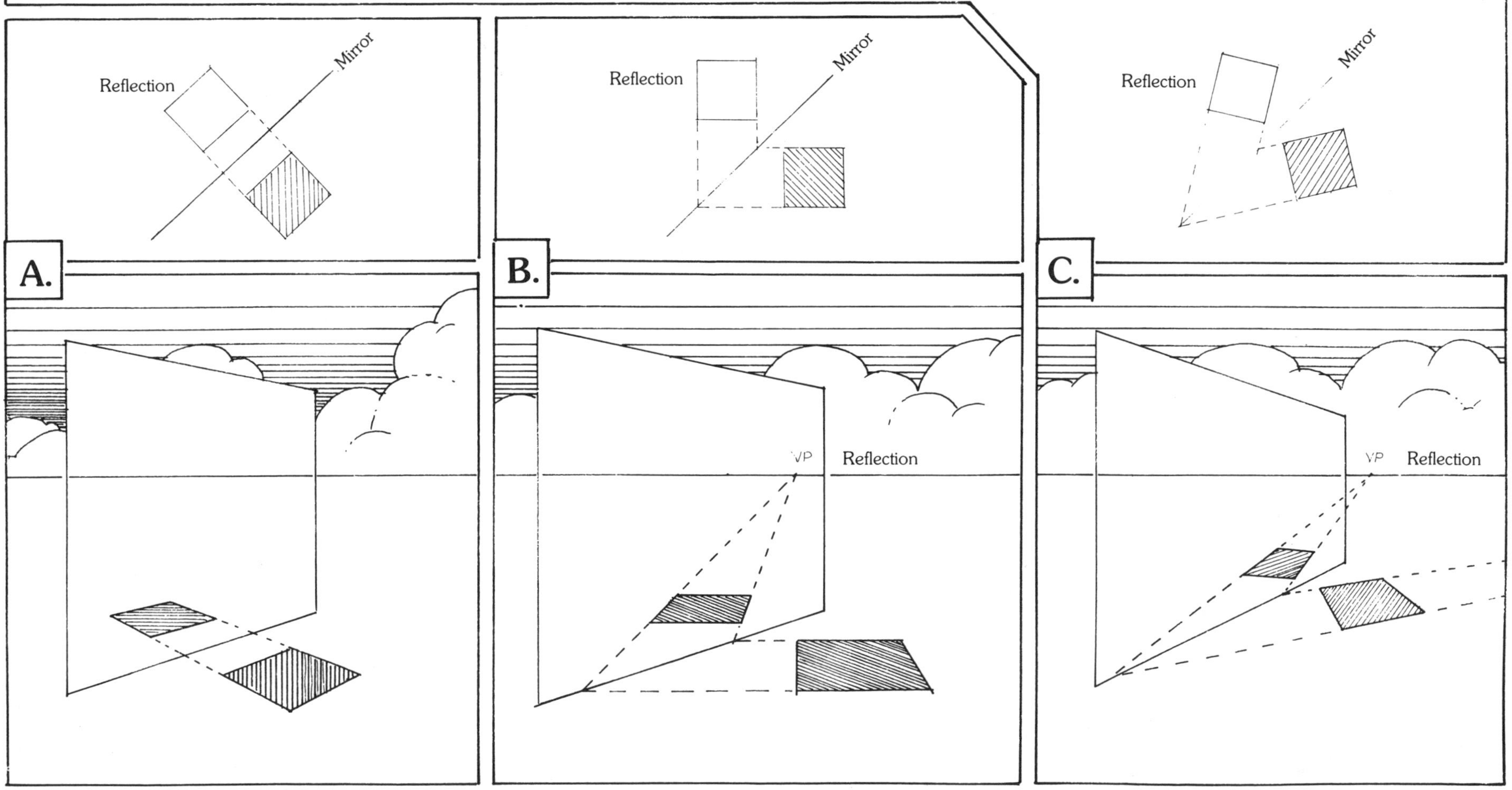

A.

B.

C.

Reflection   Mirror

Reflection   Mirror

Reflection   Mirror

VP   Reflection

VP   Reflection

138

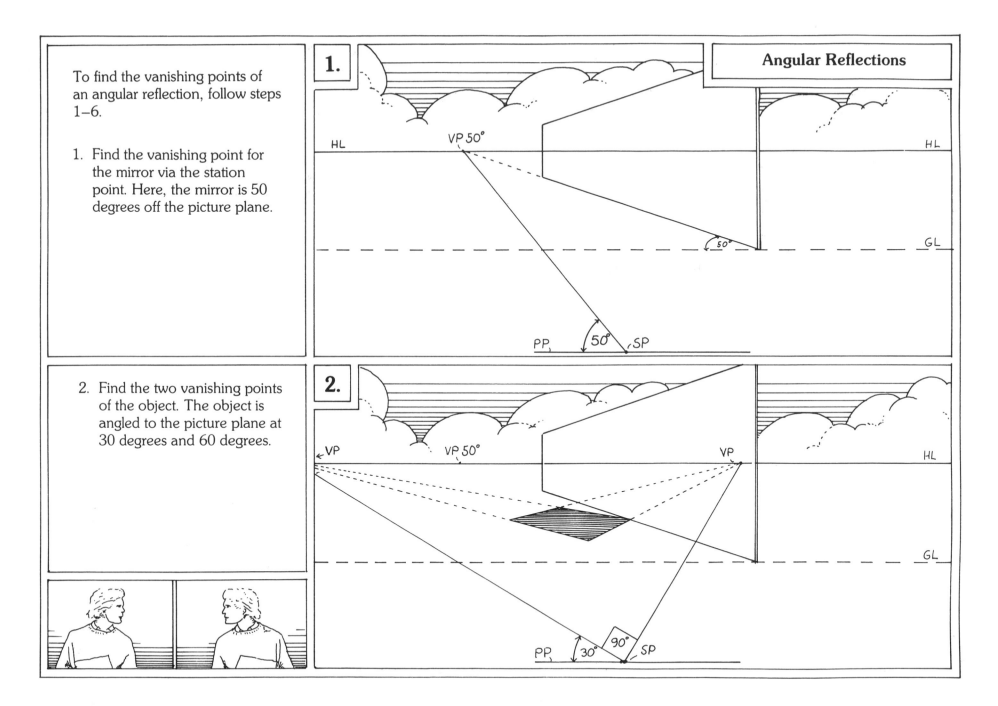

To find the vanishing points of an angular reflection, follow steps 1–6.

1. Find the vanishing point for the mirror via the station point. Here, the mirror is 50 degrees off the picture plane.

1.

Angular Reflections

HL

VP 50°

HL

GL

50°

PP 50° SP

2. Find the two vanishing points of the object. The object is angled to the picture plane at 30 degrees and 60 degrees.

2.

VP

VP 50°

VP

HL

GL

PP 30° 90° SP

139

3. Find the angle of the object to the mirror by subtracting the 30-degree angle of the object from the 50-degree angle of the mirror; this new angle is 20 degrees.

4. Find the vanishing point of the reflection by doubling the 20-degree angle of the object to the mirror.

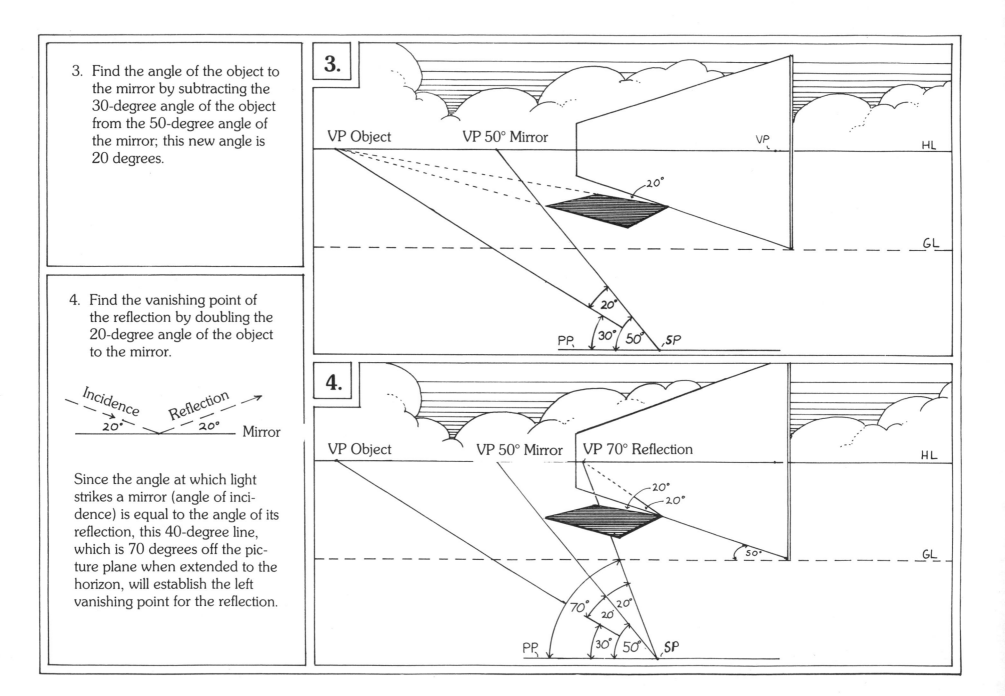

Since the angle at which light strikes a mirror (angle of incidence) is equal to the angle of its reflection, this 40-degree line, which is 70 degrees off the picture plane when extended to the horizon, will establish the left vanishing point for the reflection.

140

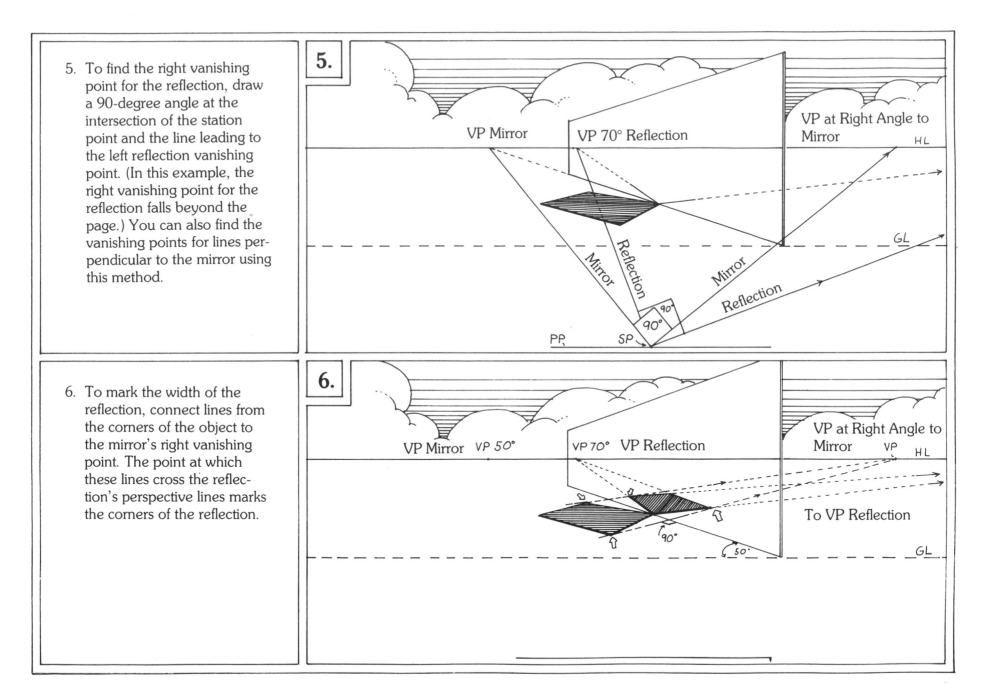

5. To find the right vanishing point for the reflection, draw a 90-degree angle at the intersection of the station point and the line leading to the left reflection vanishing point. (In this example, the right vanishing point for the reflection falls beyond the page.) You can also find the vanishing points for lines perpendicular to the mirror using this method.

6. To mark the width of the reflection, connect lines from the corners of the object to the mirror's right vanishing point. The point at which these lines cross the reflection's perspective lines marks the corners of the reflection.

5.

VP Mirror   VP 70° Reflection   VP at Right Angle to Mirror   HL

GL

Mirror   Reflection   Mirror   Reflection

90°   90°

PP   SP

6.

VP Mirror   VP 50°   VP 70°   VP Reflection   VP at Right Angle to Mirror   VP   HL

To VP Reflection

90°   50°

GL

141

1. Draw the plan above the picture plane. Here, the picture plane doubles as the horizon line. In laying out the plan, make sure the angle of the object and the angle of the reflection are equal and opposite.

2. Establish the distance from object to observer by setting the station point.

3. Establish the height of the observer from the ground line.

4. To find the mirror's vanishing point, set the 65-degree angle for the mirror at the station point.

5. Connect the lines between the station point and the key corners of the plan. Mark the points where these lines of sight cross the picture plane, then drop lines down into the view to mark off the proportions of receding planes.

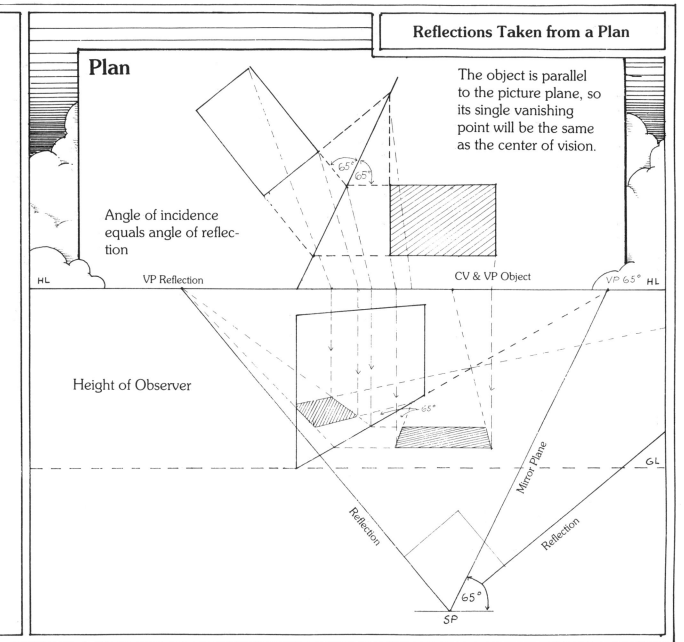

Plan

The object is parallel to the picture plane, so its single vanishing point will be the same as the center of vision.

65°
65°

Angle of incidence equals angle of reflection

HL   VP Reflection   CV & VP Object   VP 65° HL

Height of Observer

65°

Mirror Plane   GL

Reflection

Reflection

65°

SP

142

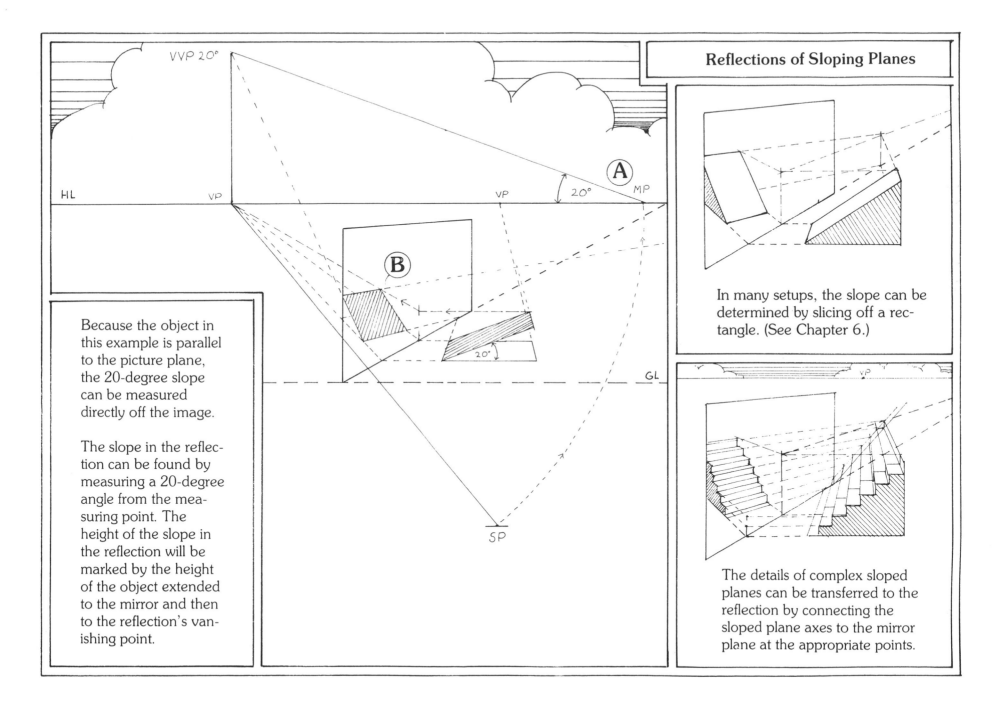

Reflections of Sloping Planes

Because the object in this example is parallel to the picture plane, the 20-degree slope can be measured directly off the image.

The slope in the reflection can be found by measuring a 20-degree angle from the measuring point. The height of the slope in the reflection will be marked by the height of the object extended to the mirror and then to the reflection's vanishing point.

In many setups, the slope can be determined by slicing off a rectangle. (See Chapter 6.)

The details of complex sloped planes can be transferred to the reflection by connecting the sloped plane axes to the mirror plane at the appropriate points.

VVP 20°

HL   VP   VP   20° MP
                                              A
                    B
                         20°
                                         GL

SP

143

1. Set up the vanishing points for the mirror by establishing its right and left vanishing points on the horizon.

2. Using the measuring point, find the vertical vanishing point for the tilt of the mirror. Here, the angle is 70 degrees.

3. Draw the object. Note that it is 90 degrees off the ground plane, angling it 20 degrees off the tilted mirror.

4. To find the angles of the reflection's vertical lines, add another 20-degree angle to the angle of the mirror at the measuring point. This establishes the vanishing point for reflections on the vertical vanishing line.

5. Adding a 90-degree angle to this reflection angle will give you the vertical vanishing point below the horizon for the perpendicular angles of the reflection.

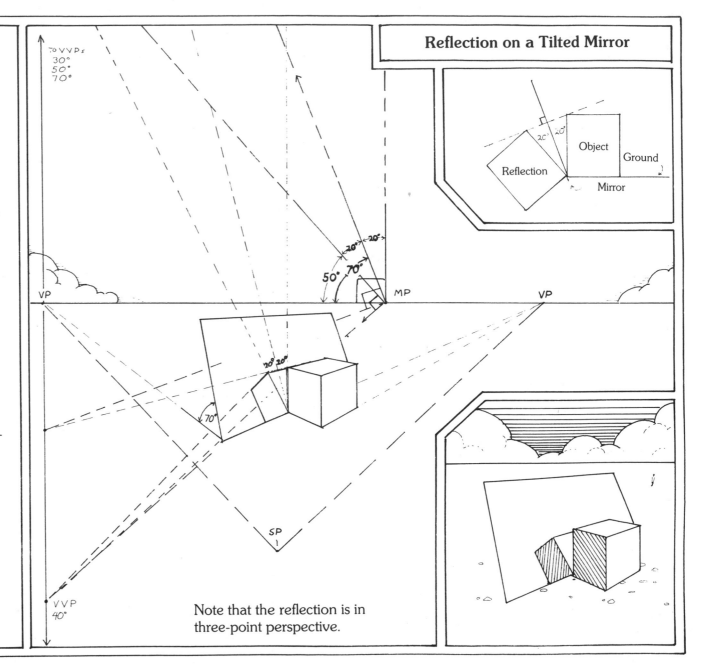

Reflection on a Tilted Mirror

TO VVPs
30°
50°
70°

Note that the reflection is in three-point perspective.

144

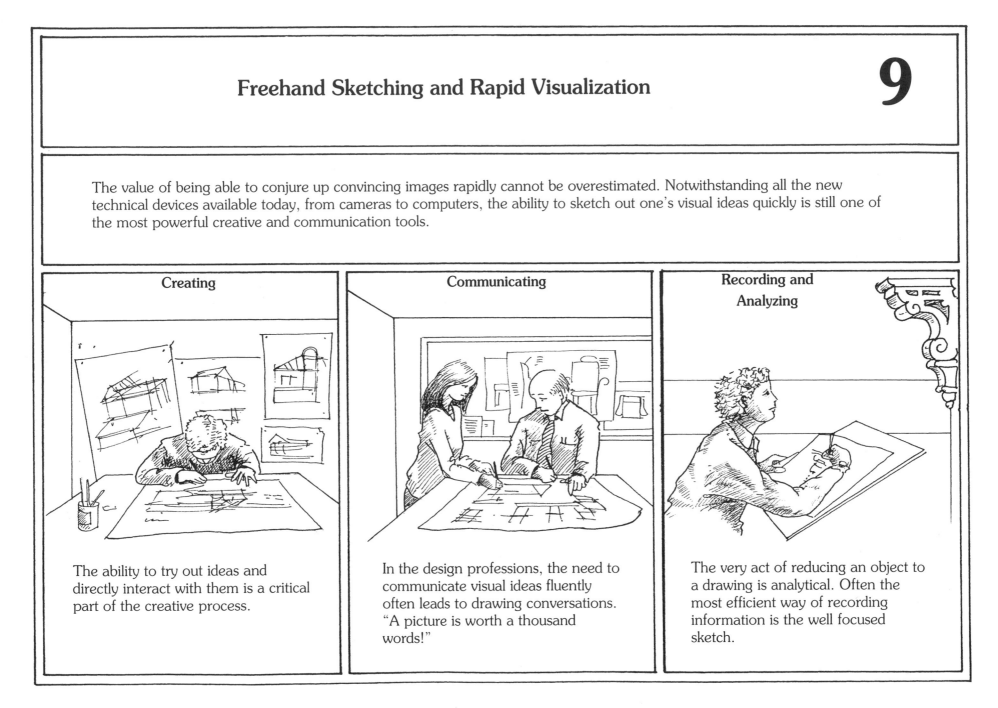

Freehand Sketching and Rapid Visualization

9

The value of being able to conjure up convincing images rapidly cannot be overestimated. Notwithstanding all the new technical devices available today, from cameras to computers, the ability to sketch out one's visual ideas quickly is still one of the most powerful creative and communication tools.

Creating

The ability to try out ideas and directly interact with them is a critical part of the creative process.

Communicating

In the design professions, the need to communicate visual ideas fluently often leads to drawing conversations. "A picture is worth a thousand words!"

Recording and Analyzing

The very act of reducing an object to a drawing is analytical. Often the most efficient way of recording information is the well focused sketch.

Here are some basic procedures and techniques for controlling a drawing without the aid, or encumbrance, of drafting tools. With practice and experience, one can develop tremendous natural freehand skill and speed and still produce convincing images.

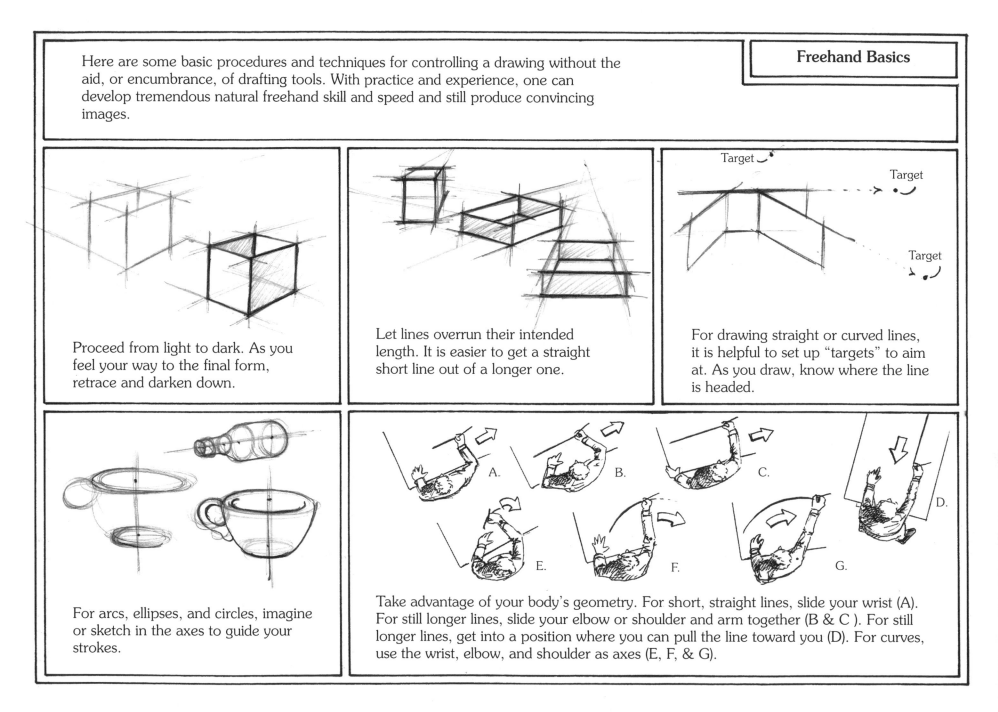

Proceed from light to dark. As you feel your way to the final form, retrace and darken down.

Let lines overrun their intended length. It is easier to get a straight short line out of a longer one.

For drawing straight or curved lines, it is helpful to set up "targets" to aim at. As you draw, know where the line is headed.

For arcs, ellipses, and circles, imagine or sketch in the axes to guide your strokes.

Take advantage of your body's geometry. For short, straight lines, slide your wrist (A). For still longer lines, slide your elbow or shoulder and arm together (B & C). For still longer lines, get into a position where you can pull the line toward you (D). For curves, use the wrist, elbow, and shoulder as axes (E, F, & G).

When rapidity of execution is a major concern, it is even more important than ever to proceed from the general to the specific—from the overall outlines to the details.

By "fitting" the new lines and forms inside of what has already been drawn, you can keep all the parts in proportion.

Lay out the shape of the space or environment first. Even if you don't actually draw them, have an idea of where the horizon and vanishing points lie.

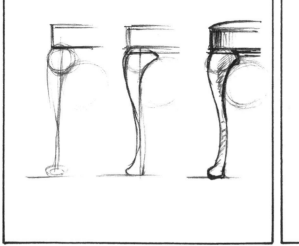

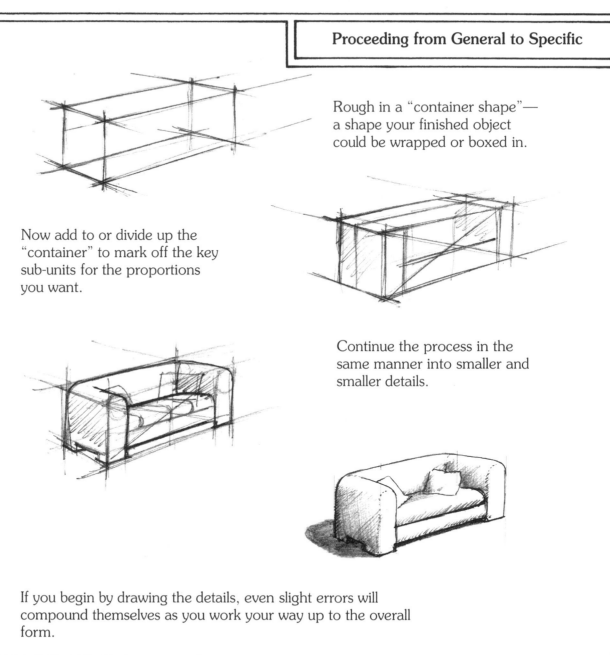

Rough in a "container shape"— a shape your finished object could be wrapped or boxed in.

Now add to or divide up the "container" to mark off the key sub-units for the proportions you want.

Continue the process in the same manner into smaller and smaller details.

If you begin by drawing the details, even slight errors will compound themselves as you work your way up to the overall form.

147

If there is no critical need to show something from a specific optical point of view, it is often most convenient to show the object by one of the paraline methods (See Chapter 3).

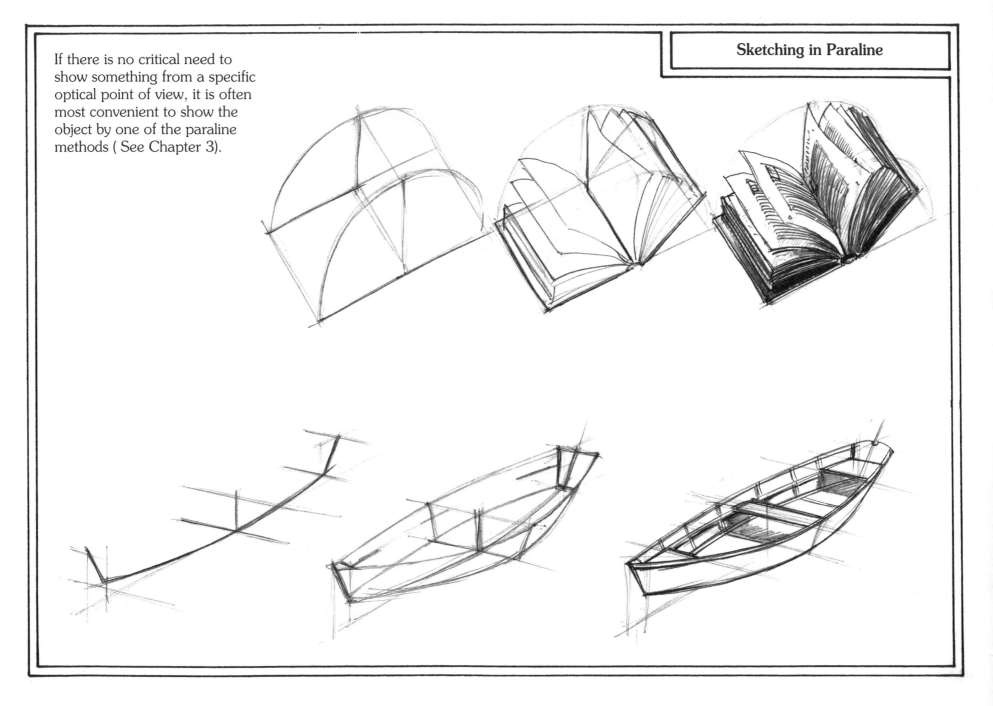

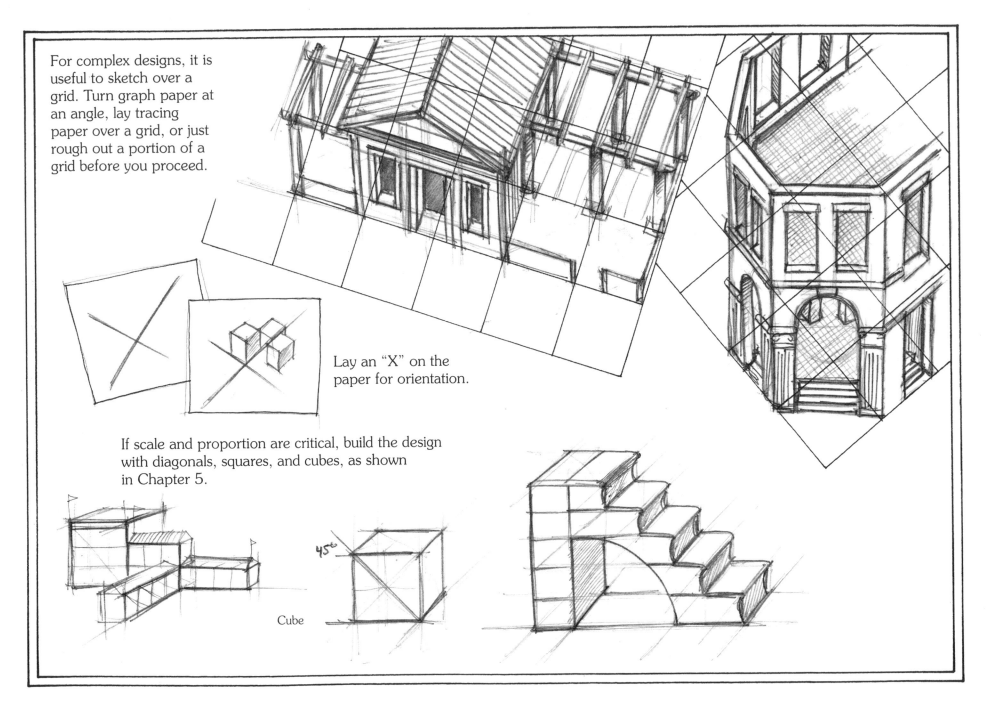

For complex designs, it is useful to sketch over a grid. Turn graph paper at an angle, lay tracing paper over a grid, or just rough out a portion of a grid before you proceed.

Lay an "X" on the paper for orientation.

If scale and proportion are critical, build the design with diagonals, squares, and cubes, as shown in Chapter 5.

45°

Cube

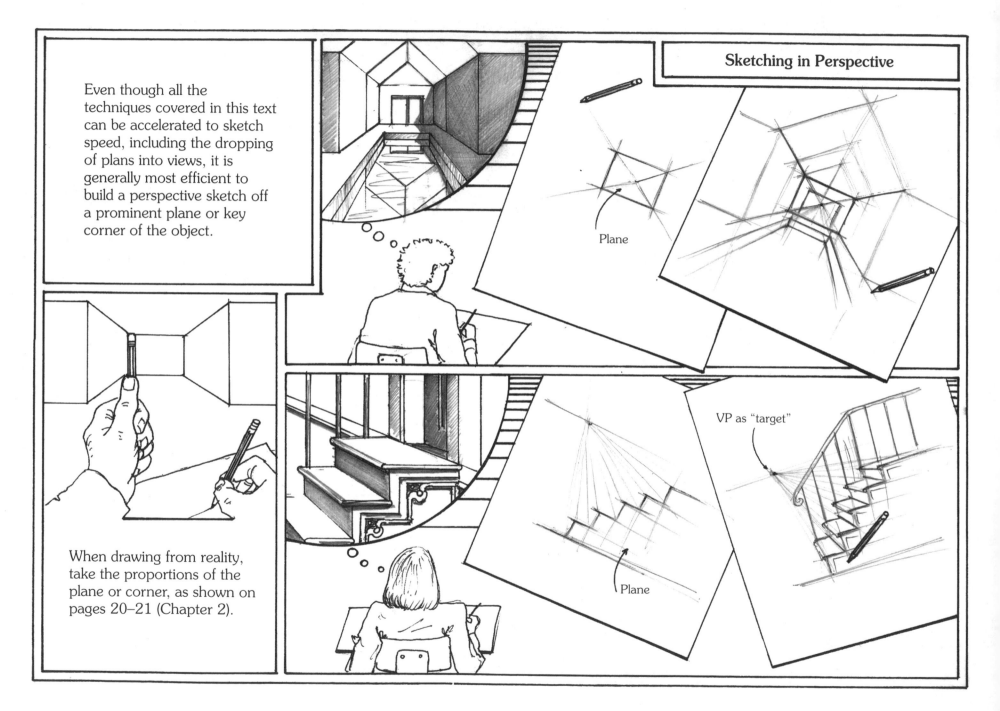

Even though all the techniques covered in this text can be accelerated to sketch speed, including the dropping of plans into views, it is generally most efficient to build a perspective sketch off a prominent plane or key corner of the object.

When drawing from reality, take the proportions of the plane or corner, as shown on pages 20–21 (Chapter 2).

Plane

Plane

VP as "target"

Imagined corner of "container."

Many objects lend themselves to being constructed from simple geometric primitives, such as cubes, prisms, cylinders etc.

At the "box" or "container" stage, proportions can be adjusted and corrected before moving on.

Squares and cubes, as already shown with paraline drawings, can help control difficult proportions when necessary and also act as building blocks.

Having a sense of where the 45-degree vanishing point is gives yet an extra degree of control over quickly sketching squares and cubes.

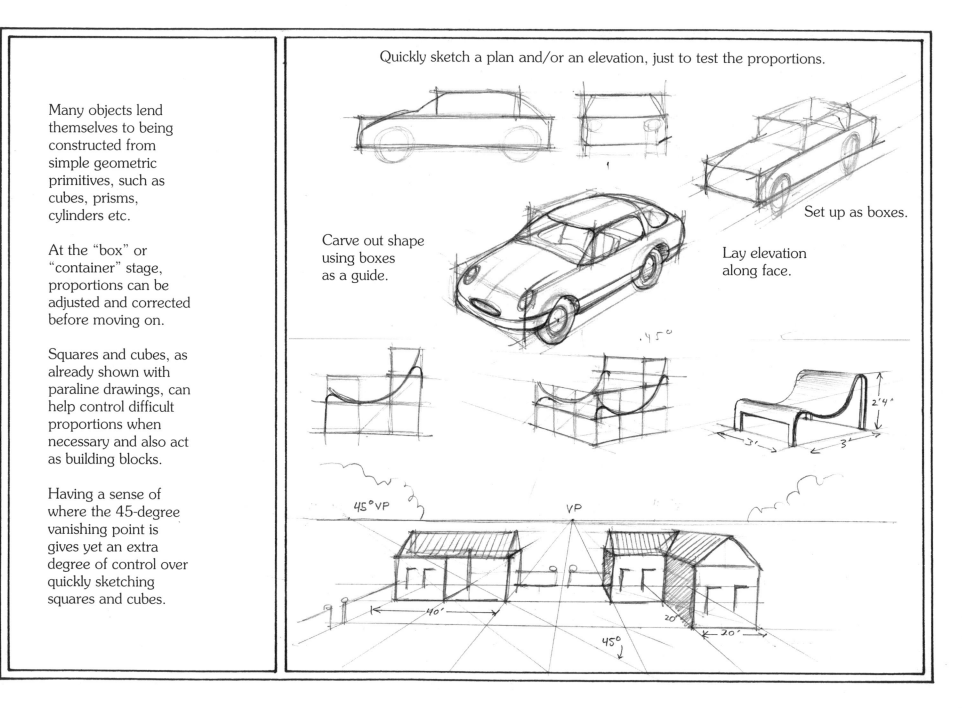

Quickly sketch a plan and/or an elevation, just to test the proportions.

Set up as boxes.

Carve out shape using boxes as a guide.

Lay elevation along face.

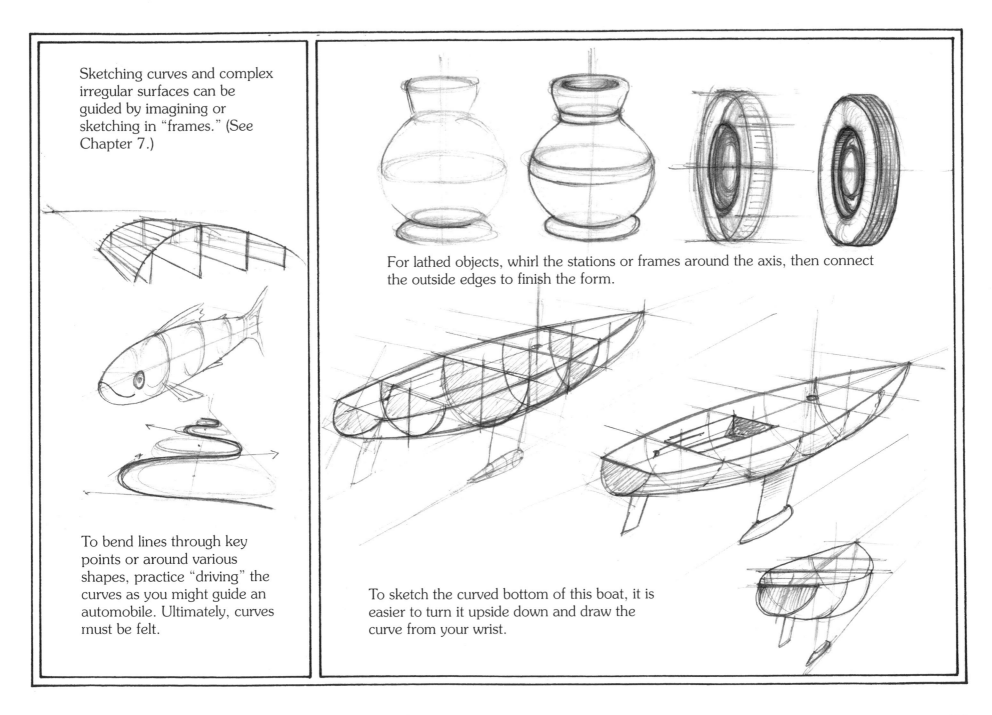

Sketching curves and complex irregular surfaces can be guided by imagining or sketching in "frames." (See Chapter 7.)

To bend lines through key points or around various shapes, practice "driving" the curves as you might guide an automobile. Ultimately, curves must be felt.

For lathed objects, whirl the stations or frames around the axis, then connect the outside edges to finish the form.

To sketch the curved bottom of this boat, it is easier to turn it upside down and draw the curve from your wrist.

153

154

The Figure in Perspective

10

It is worthwhile developing a basic understanding of the human figure in perspective drawing, for even if figures are not the focus of the drawing, they can add scale, depth, and interest to objects and spaces around them. For human figures to inhabit three-dimensional perspective space credibly, they obviously must obey all the same optical laws. If they do not, they can easily destroy an otherwise perfectly rendered scene.

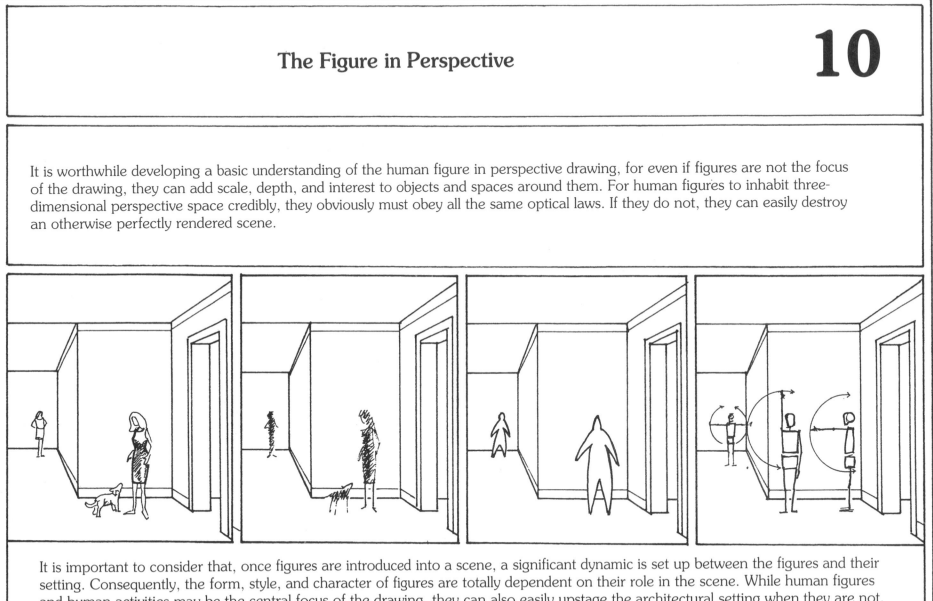

It is important to consider that, once figures are introduced into a scene, a significant dynamic is set up between the figures and their setting. Consequently, the form, style, and character of figures are totally dependent on their role in the scene. While human figures and human activities may be the central focus of the drawing, they can also easily upstage the architectural setting when they are not. The key is to find the figure forms, types, and styles that are appropriate. Sometimes this may mean that figures are intentionally set in stark contrast to their setting.

Basic Human Proportions

The proportions of the human figure have been a subject of study for thousands of years, reflecting everything from scientific measurement to aesthetic and spiritual values. For our purposes, the science of anatomy is grossly oversimplified but at the same time very serviceable. What is presented here is a practical foundation for figure drawing that can be refined later with practice and observation.

To construct a "normal" figure, begin by dividing a height into thirds. These units (divisions) represent the height of the figure from the breast to the ankles, with divisions at the hips and knees. Shoulders are just under 1/2 unit above the breasts. Notice that the fingers touch the middle of the thighs, while the elbows mark off the waist (navel). Notice that the width of the head is a little shorter than 1/3 the width of the shoulders.

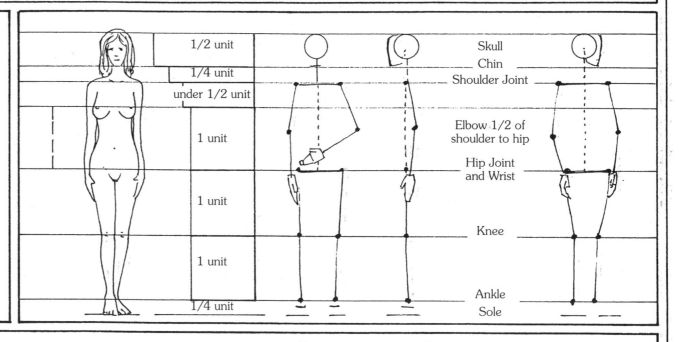

1/2 unit
1/4 unit
under 1/2 unit
1 unit
1 unit
1 unit
1/4 unit

Skull
Chin
Shoulder Joint

Elbow 1/2 of shoulder to hip

Hip Joint and Wrist

Knee

Ankle
Sole

There is considerable variety among individuals, of course, but basically we all share similar skeletal proportions. The only real exceptions reflect differences in physical maturity.

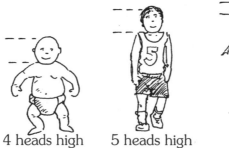

4 heads high   5 heads high

8 heads high

A mature adult usually stands between 7 and 8 heads high

Before proceeding to develop the full figure, it's useful to practice manipulating simple proportional models like those to the right. Understanding the geometry of these simple figures, their possible postures, attitudes, and movements, is essential for fitting them into a perspective environment.

Hips, elbows, shoulders, knees, and linear bones all form lines that must conform to perspective space.

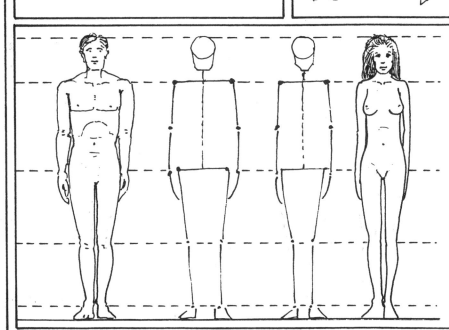

In general, male and female proportions differ in their relative breadth of shoulders and hips.

Male Torso

Female Torso

VP

Fleshing Out

There are many practical techniques for fleshing out the figure. Some use boxes, cylinders, and other geometric primitives, while others build the figure around a fairly complete skeleton.

The technique shown here builds on the key joints and lines already shown, with the idea that these underlying forms will guide the laying up of the surface skin.

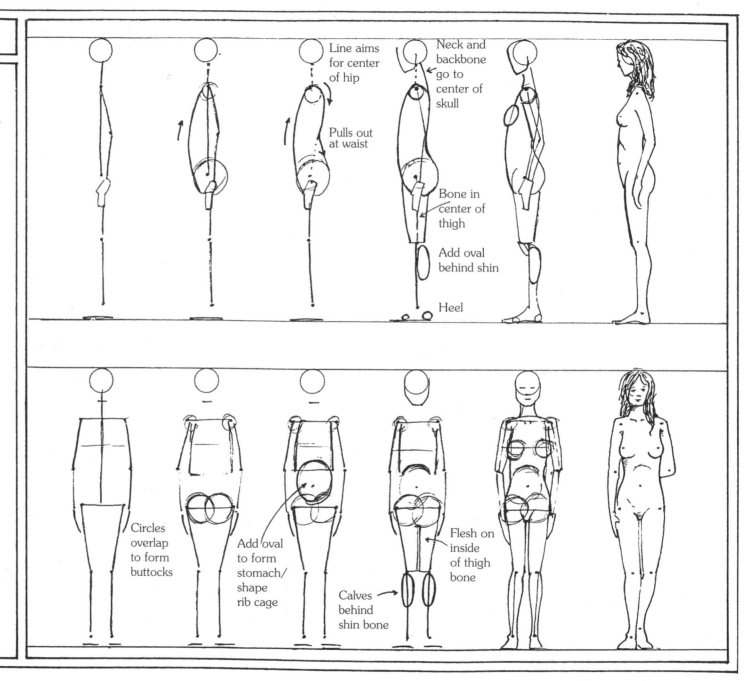

Line aims for center of hip

Pulls out at waist

Neck and backbone go to center of skull

Bone in center of thigh

Add oval behind shin

Heel

Circles overlap to form buttocks

Add oval to form stomach/ shape rib cage

Flesh on inside of thigh bone

Calves behind shin bone

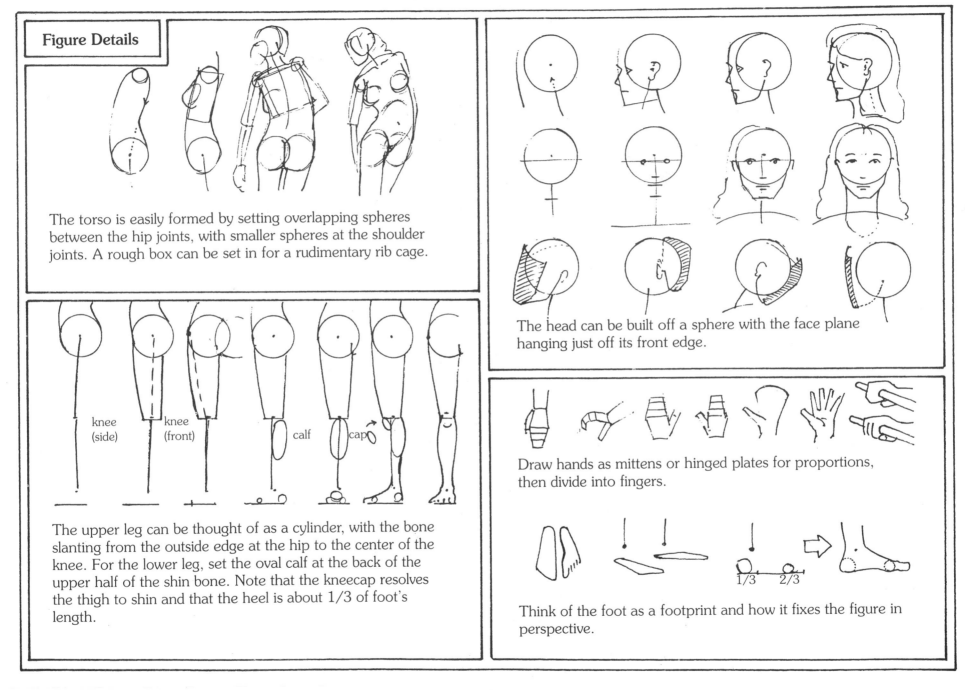

Figure Details

The torso is easily formed by setting overlapping spheres between the hip joints, with smaller spheres at the shoulder joints. A rough box can be set in for a rudimentary rib cage.

knee (side)

knee (front)

calf

cap

The upper leg can be thought of as a cylinder, with the bone slanting from the outside edge at the hip to the center of the knee. For the lower leg, set the oval calf at the back of the upper half of the shin bone. Note that the kneecap resolves the thigh to shin and that the heel is about 1/3 of foot's length.

The head can be built off a sphere with the face plane hanging just off its front edge.

Draw hands as mittens or hinged plates for proportions, then divide into fingers.

1/3   2/3

Think of the foot as a footprint and how it fixes the figure in perspective.

While we all share the same basic skeletal geometry, as noted, a wide variety of figure types are possible:

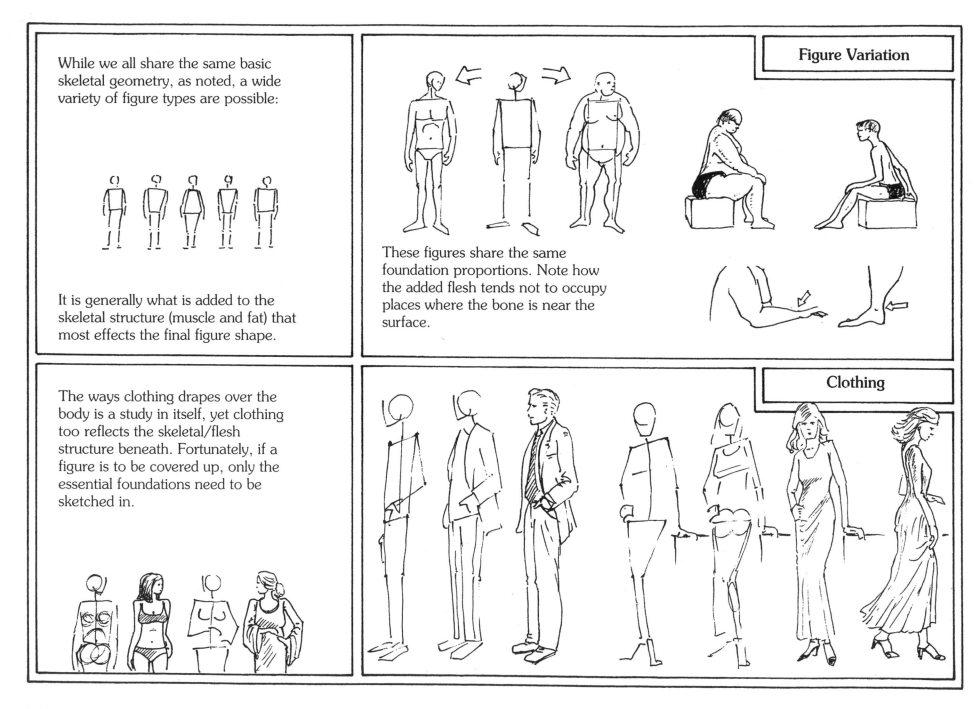

It is generally what is added to the skeletal structure (muscle and fat) that most effects the final figure shape.

Figure Variation

These figures share the same foundation proportions. Note how the added flesh tends not to occupy places where the bone is near the surface.

The ways clothing drapes over the body is a study in itself, yet clothing too reflects the skeletal/flesh structure beneath. Fortunately, if a figure is to be covered up, only the essential foundations need to be sketched in.

Clothing

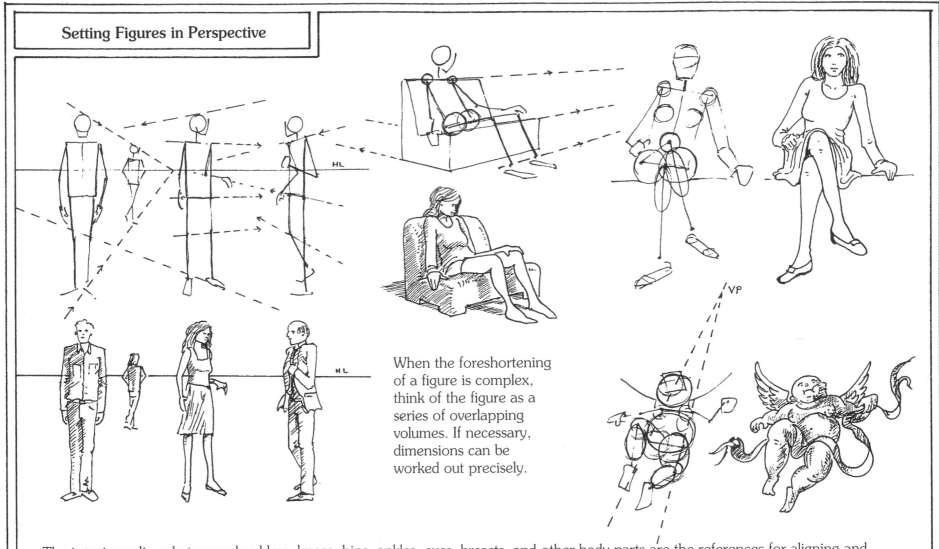

When the foreshortening of a figure is complex, think of the figure as a series of overlapping volumes. If necessary, dimensions can be worked out precisely.

The imaginary lines between shoulders, knees, hips, ankles, eyes, breasts, and other body parts are the references for aligning and arranging figures in space. Once the correct proportions and positions have been set, the figures can be fleshed out or clothed, as shown here and on the following page.

161

What we interpret as lines in optical reality are actually the contrasts between and among surfaces and tonal differences, as illustrated to the right.

The methods and styles for shading in surfaces can range from the lightest gestural suggestions to all the details and gradations of photo-realistic rendering, and with everything in between.

The choice of how one shades or renders these surfaces is ultimately a matter of fitness to purpose, style, and creativity.

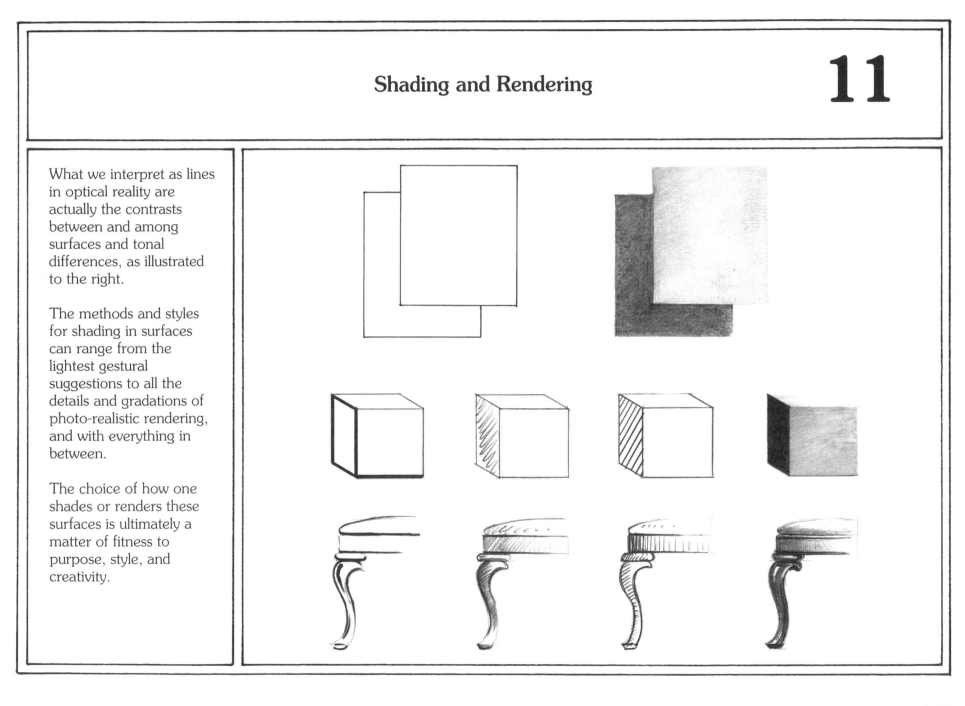

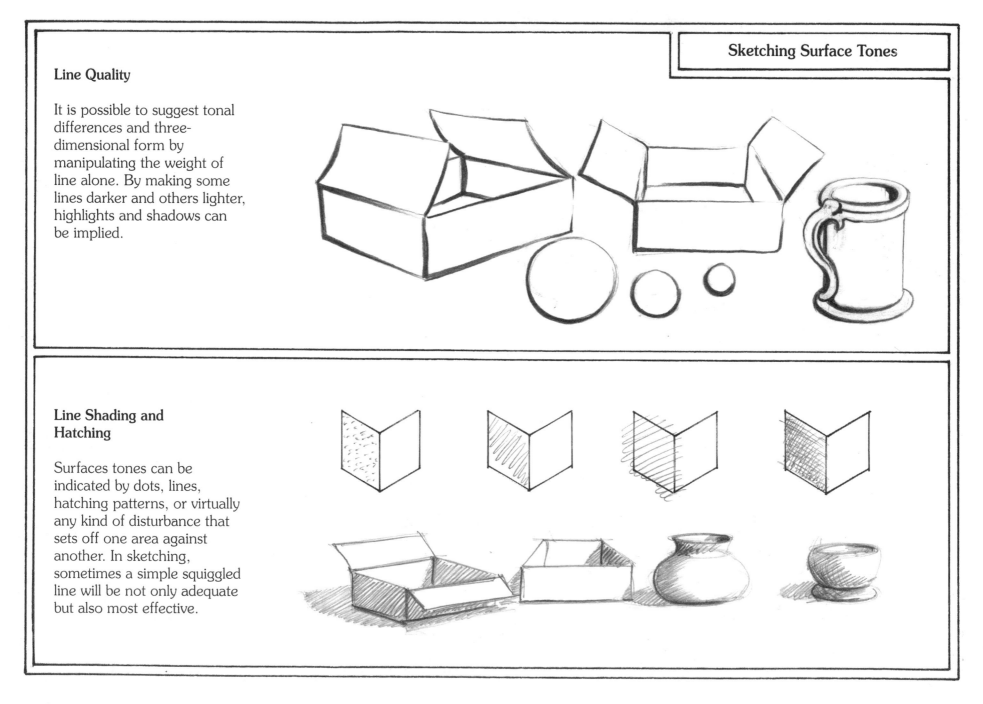

Line Quality

It is possible to suggest tonal differences and three-dimensional form by manipulating the weight of line alone. By making some lines darker and others lighter, highlights and shadows can be implied.

Line Shading and Hatching

Surfaces tones can be indicated by dots, lines, hatching patterns, or virtually any kind of disturbance that sets off one area against another. In sketching, sometimes a simple squiggled line will be not only adequate but also most *effective*.

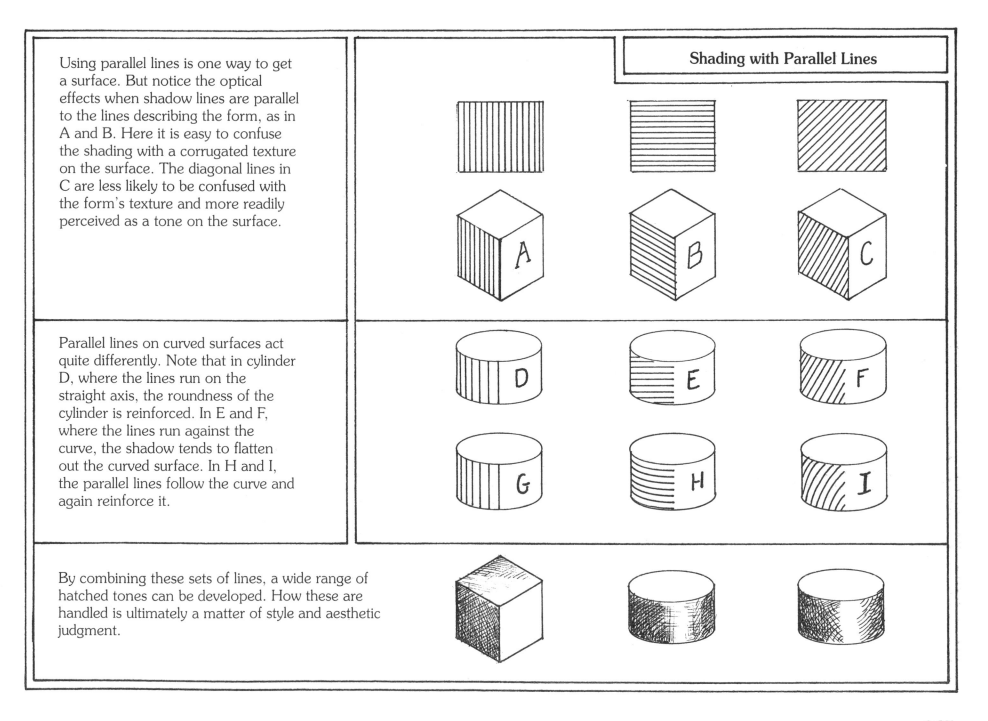

Using parallel lines is one way to get a surface. But notice the optical *effects* when shadow lines are parallel to the lines describing the form, as in A and B. Here it is easy to confuse the shading with a corrugated texture on the surface. The diagonal lines in C are less likely to be confused with the form's texture and more readily perceived as a tone on the surface.

Shading with Parallel Lines

Parallel lines on curved surfaces act quite differently. Note that in cylinder D, where the lines run on the straight axis, the roundness of the cylinder is reinforced. In E and F, where the lines run against the curve, the shadow tends to flatten out the curved surface. In H and I, the parallel lines follow the curve and again reinforce it.

By combining these sets of lines, a wide range of hatched tones can be developed. How these are handled is ultimately a matter of style and aesthetic judgment.

There are many ways to fill in a surface. Pens, pencils, markers, brushes, and computer commands all demand their own procedures. Here is a general suggestion for shading in a continuous tone with pencils and similar sharp tools.

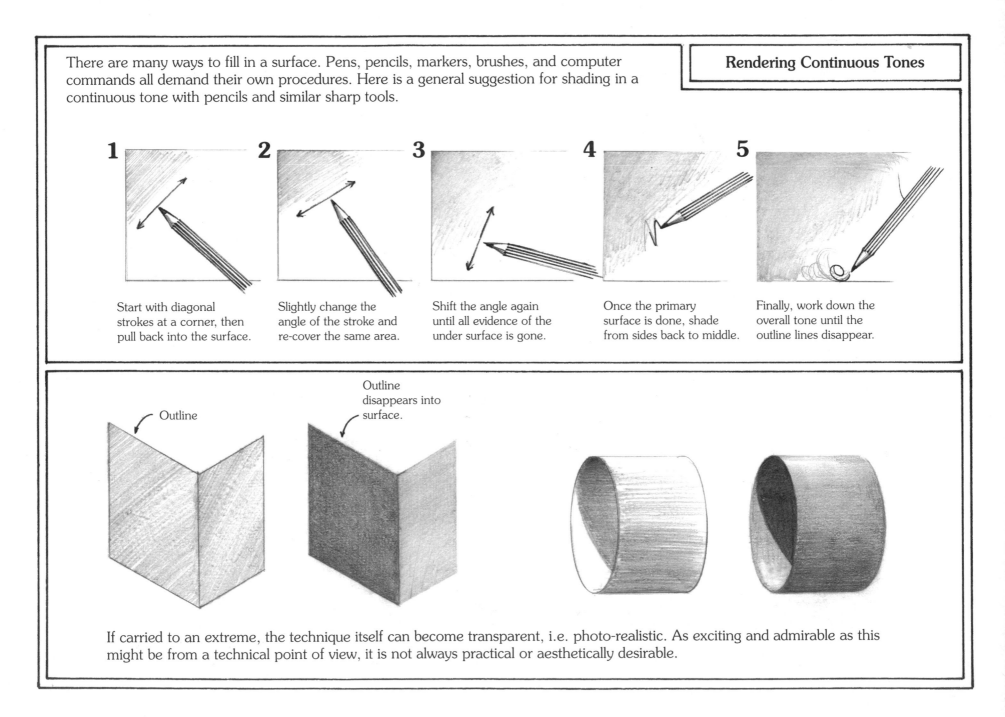

1 Start with diagonal strokes at a corner, then pull back into the surface.

2 Slightly change the angle of the stroke and re-cover the same area.

3 Shift the angle again until all evidence of the under surface is gone.

4 Once the primary surface is done, shade from sides back to middle.

5 Finally, work down the overall tone until the outline lines disappear.

Outline

Outline disappears into surface.

If carried to an extreme, the technique itself can become transparent, i.e. photo-realistic. As exciting and admirable as this might be from a technical point of view, it is not always practical or aesthetically desirable.

166

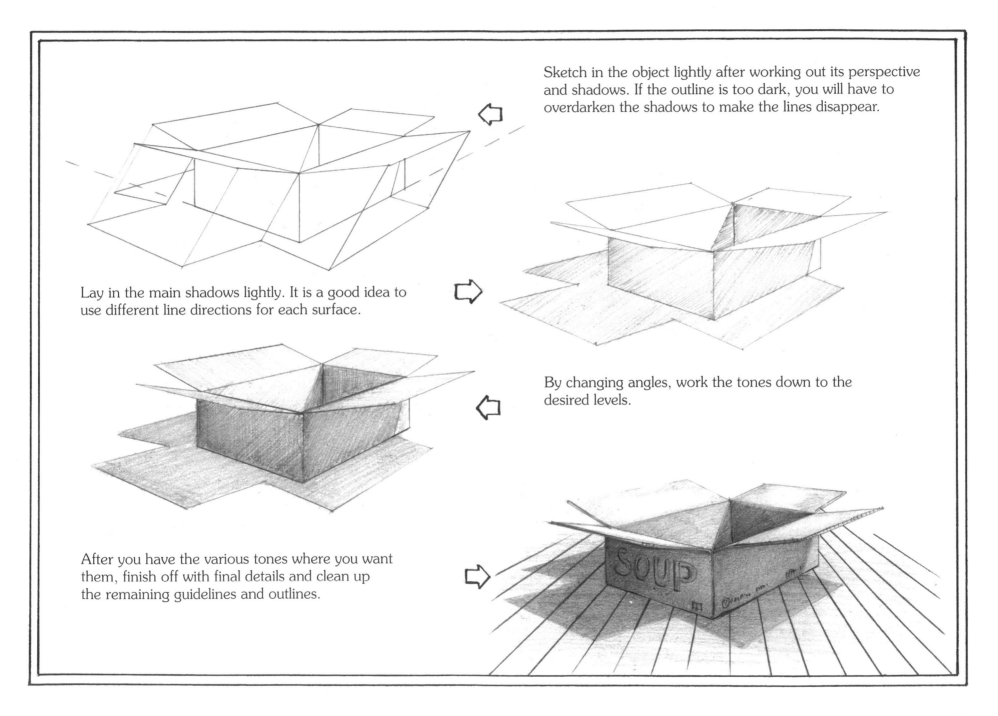

Sketch in the object lightly after working out its perspective and shadows. If the outline is too dark, you will have to overdarken the shadows to make the lines disappear.

Lay in the main shadows lightly. It is a good idea to use different line directions for each surface.

By changing angles, work the tones down to the desired levels.

After you have the various tones where you want them, finish off with final details and clean up the remaining guidelines and outlines.

167

Shading Rigid Surfaces

Cloth paper and other flexible materials pose special problems in rendering due to the complexity of possible forms. Nevertheless, there is order underlying these seemingly endlessly variations.

The character of folds reflects the nature of the material.

paper

cloth

Most folds result from material being crushed or pulled.

Most folds reveal some internal or external point of support.

supported

free-floating

Shading Flexible Surfaces

Pull shadows out and away from the lines of the overlaps and crevices.

pull

crush

Note the results of the crush and pull of the fabric.

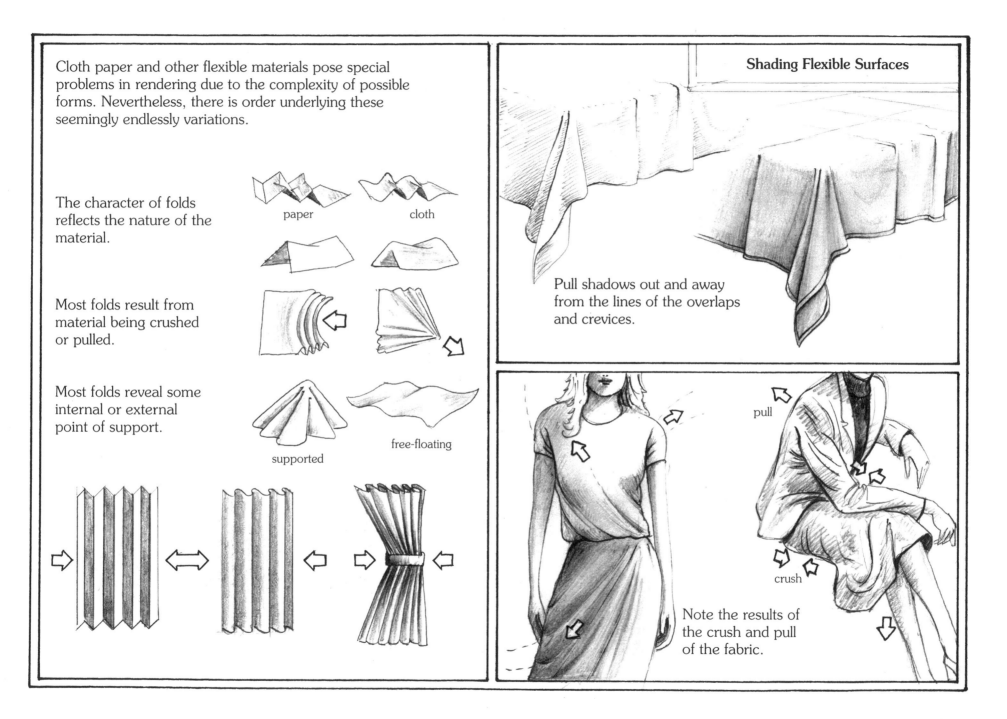

Variations in light, shade, and color can result from an object's distance from the viewer, the amount of light falling on it, and the atmosphere through which it is observed.

Objects set closer to the viewer tend to be sharper, more detailed, with harder edges and more distinct colors than objects further away, seen through the atmosphere.

Aerial perspective is most notable in landscapes and smoke-filled rooms, but it can also be used effectively as a means of focusing on an object by suppressing its background.

The intensity and clarity of the shadows and colors can be worked out in a consistent system so that the characteristics of an object can be determined for a given distance in a given atmosphere. Unlike linear perspective, aerial perspective is ultimately more intuitive and more forgiving, if not scientifically correct.

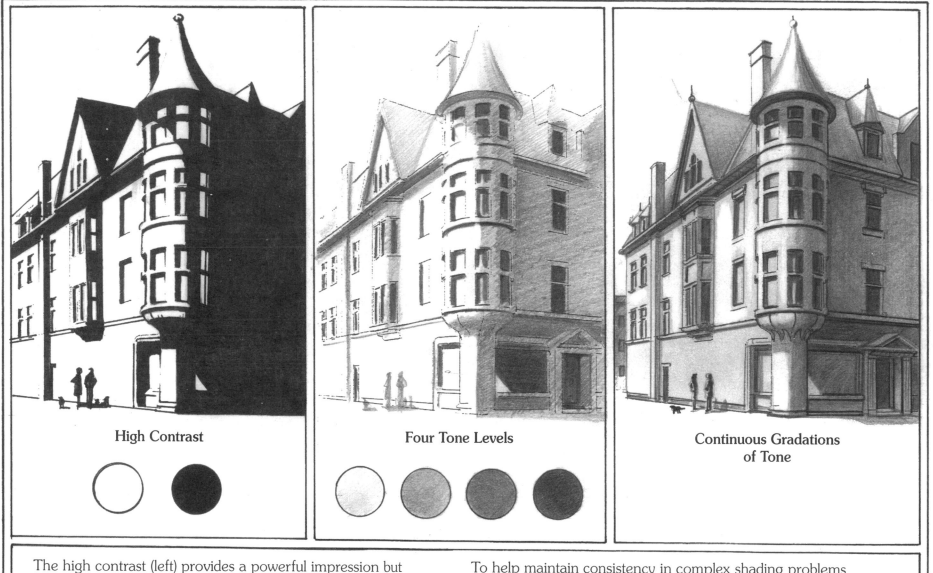

High Contrast

Four Tone Levels

Continuous Gradations of Tone

The high contrast (left) provides a powerful impression but gives little detail, while the continuous gradations of tones (right) allow for more subtlety.

To help maintain consistency in complex shading problems (center), it is a good idea to start by dividing the range of shadows into four or five discrete tones, then proceed to fill in the in-between tones.

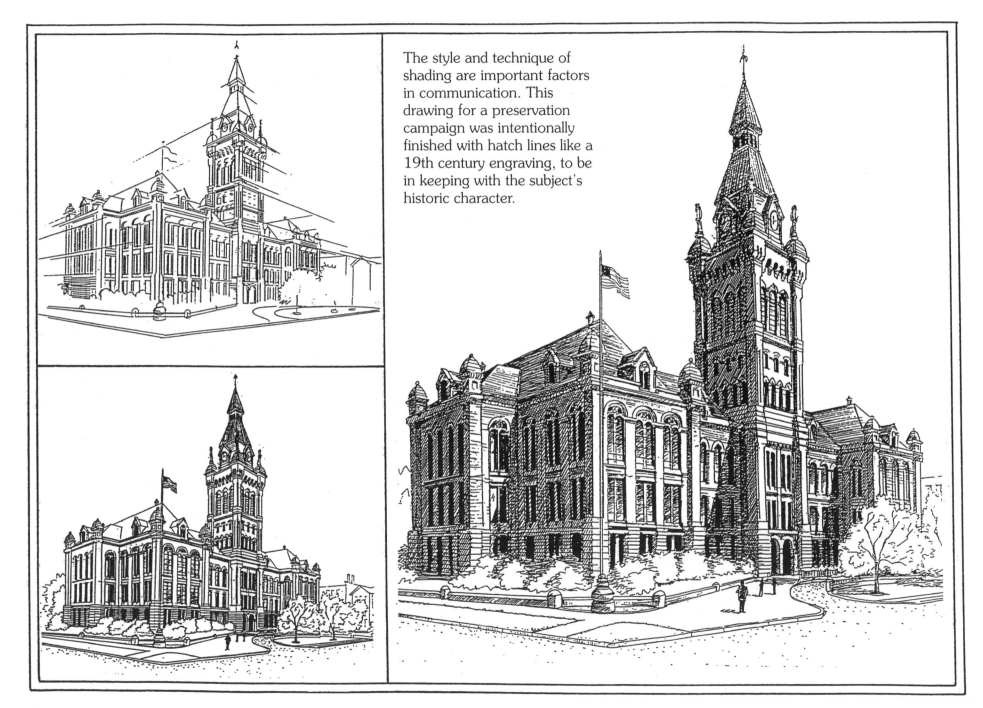

The style and technique of shading are important factors in communication. This drawing for a preservation campaign was intentionally finished with hatch lines like a 19th century engraving, to be in keeping with the subject's historic character.

Perspective Drawing and the Computer

12

The computer has had an enormous impact on drawing and design, just as it has had, on most other areas of modern life. It is not possible in this space to deal with this field in any real depth; besides new and improved hardware and software are constantly appearing accompanied by their own vast literature of instruction manuals and tutorials. However, it is important, in the context of this introduction to perspective drawing, to present a general overview of how computer perspective drawing is done and how it relates to the traditional methods of drawing presented here.

Use of the computer for generating perspectives can be roughly divided into two categories:

A. Computer used as a traditional drawing tool.

B. Computer used to create and display 3-D models.

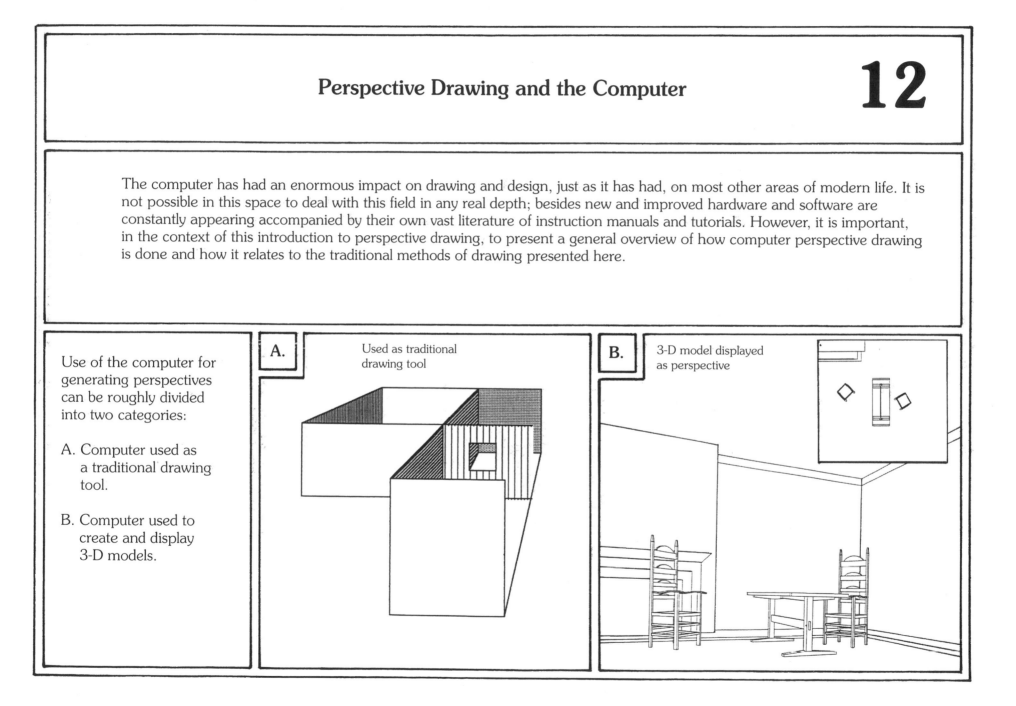

A. Used as traditional drawing tool

B. 3-D model displayed as perspective

All traditional methods of manipulating a 2-D surface are possible in a computer version. Even some of the most inexpensive software packages offer a wide range of tools, from pens to airbrushes, from drafting tools to texture maps. Additionally, the computer screen provides a versatile drawing surface that can be edited, saved, copied, resized, colored, and manipulated in a host of other ways.

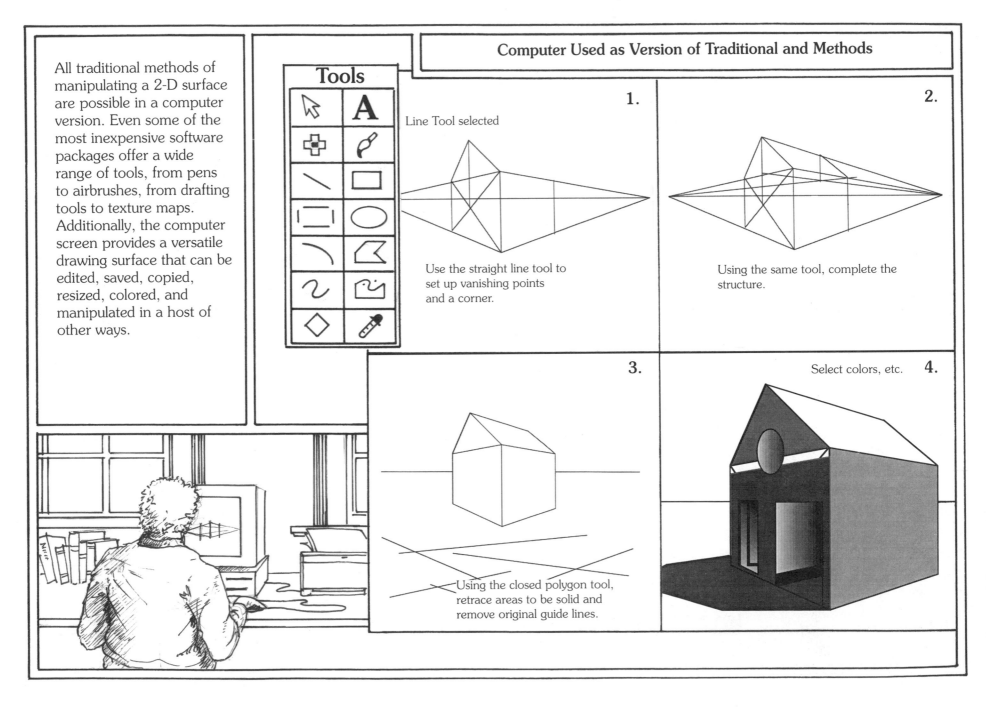

Tools

Computer Used as Version of Traditional and Methods

1.

Line Tool selected

Use the straight line tool to set up vanishing points and a corner.

2.

Using the same tool, complete the structure.

3.

Using the closed polygon tool, retrace areas to be solid and remove original guide lines.

4.

Select colors, etc.

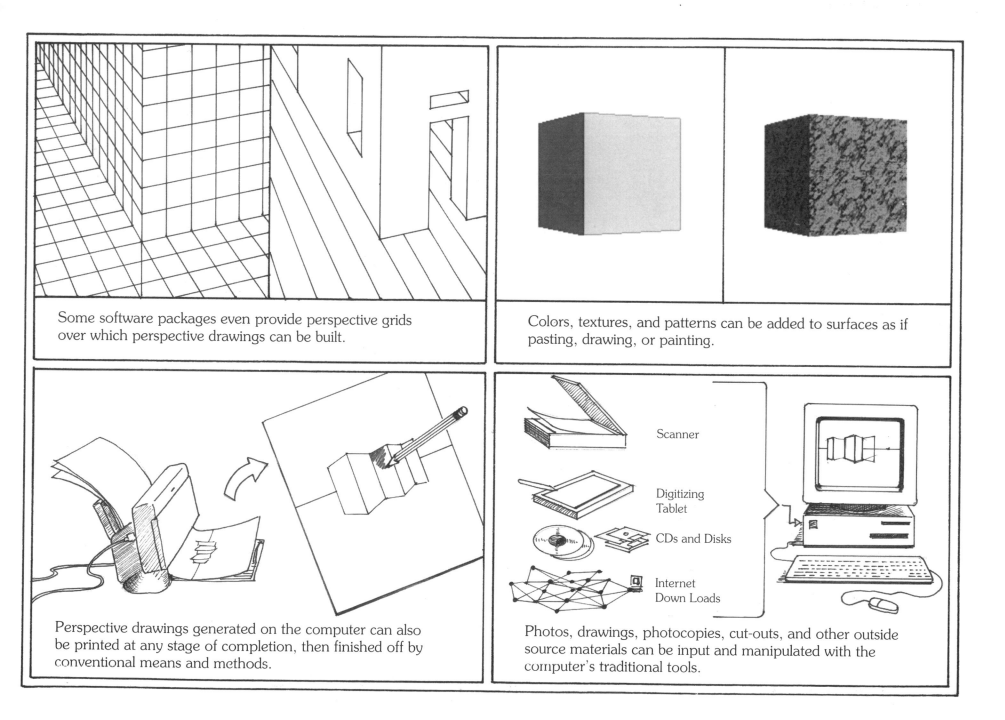

Some software packages even provide perspective grids over which perspective drawings can be built.

Colors, textures, and patterns can be added to surfaces as if pasting, drawing, or painting.

Perspective drawings generated on the computer can also be printed at any stage of completion, then finished off by conventional means and methods.

Scanner

Digitizing Tablet

CDs and Disks

Internet Down Loads

Photos, drawings, photocopies, cut-outs, and other outside source materials can be input and manipulated with the computer's traditional tools.

175

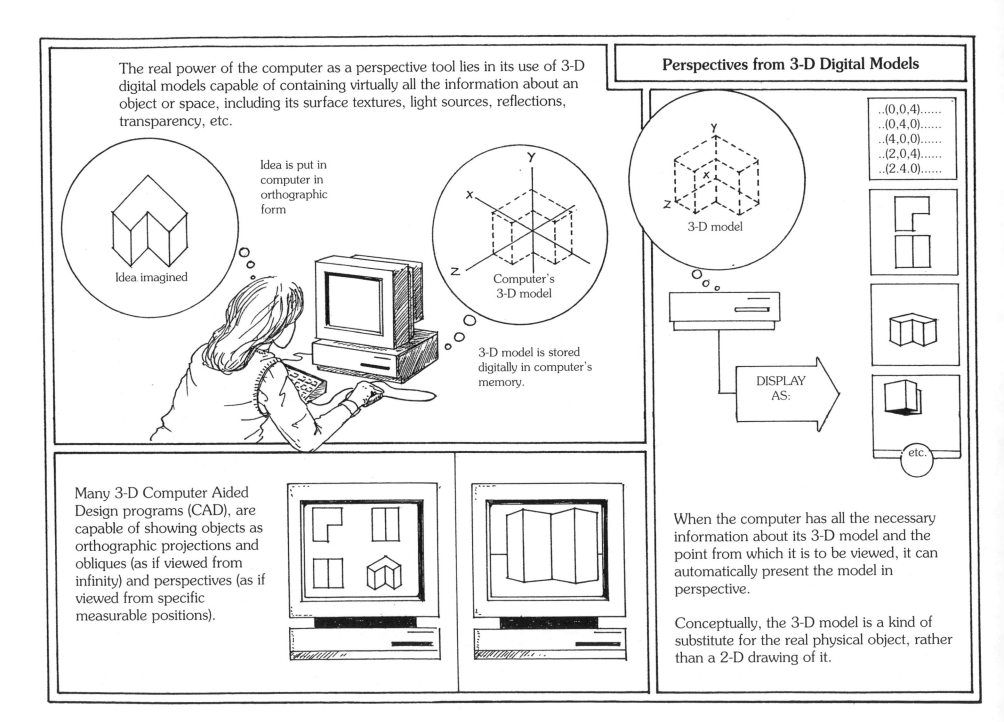

The real power of the computer as a perspective tool lies in its use of 3-D digital models capable of containing virtually all the information about an object or space, including its surface textures, light sources, reflections, transparency, etc.

Idea is put in computer in orthographic form

Idea imagined

Computer's 3-D model

3-D model is stored digitally in computer's memory.

Perspectives from 3-D Digital Models

..(0,0,4)......
..(0,4,0)......
..(4,0,0)......
..(2,0,4)......
..(2.4.0)......

3-D model

DISPLAY AS:

etc.

Many 3-D Computer Aided Design programs (CAD), are capable of showing objects as orthographic projections and obliques (as if viewed from infinity) and perspectives (as if viewed from specific measurable positions).

When the computer has all the necessary information about its 3-D model and the point from which it is to be viewed, it can automatically present the model in perspective.

Conceptually, the 3-D model is a kind of substitute for the real physical object, rather than a 2-D drawing of it.

Designing and editing are usually done in orthographic views, then displayed as perspectives. Any modifications to the 3-D model will automatically be displayed in perspective when the computer is instructed to shift to a perspective view. Thus patterns, textures, shadows, and other details will conform to the perspective of the object.

When this stock brick pattern is added to the two elevations of the 3-D model shown, the patterns conform to the surface changes when displayed in perspective.

It is helpful to think of the 3-D digital model as though it were a physical model constructed and arranged on a stage set, then photographed.

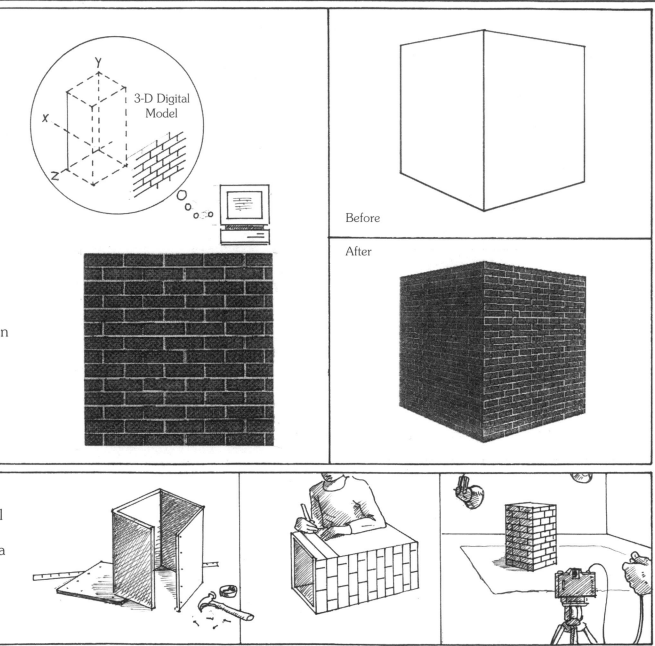

3-D Digital Model

Before

After

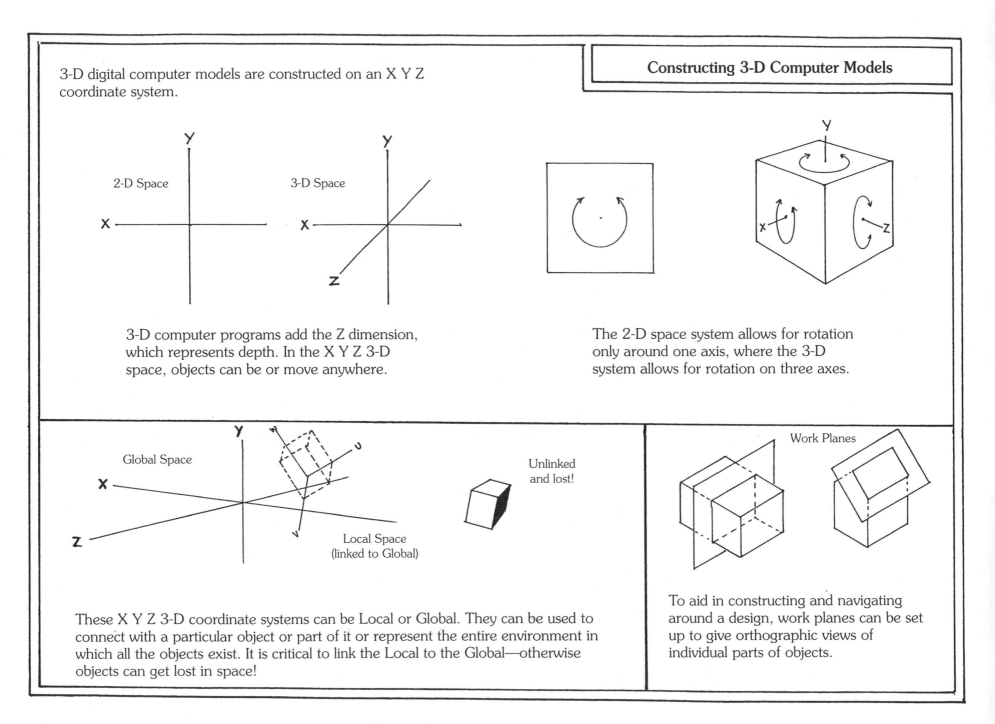

3-D digital computer models are constructed on an X Y Z coordinate system.

2-D Space

3-D Space

3-D computer programs add the Z dimension, which represents depth. In the X Y Z 3-D space, objects can be or move anywhere.

The 2-D space system allows for rotation only around one axis, where the 3-D system allows for rotation on three axes.

Global Space

Unlinked and lost!

Local Space
(linked to Global)

These X Y Z 3-D coordinate systems can be Local or Global. They can be used to connect with a particular object or part of it or represent the entire environment in which all the objects exist. It is critical to link the Local to the Global—otherwise objects can get lost in space!

Work Planes

To aid in constructing and navigating around a design, work planes can be set up to give orthographic views of individual parts of objects.

Wireframe modeling is the simplest method of constructing 3-D models. By defining the edges and vertices (where edges meet) in terms of X Y Z coordinates, one can establish points and boundary lines for objects.

Wireframe models contain information about the edges of objects. And while they contain information about the faces of objects (their size, orientation, and location), they contain no information about the object's surfaces.

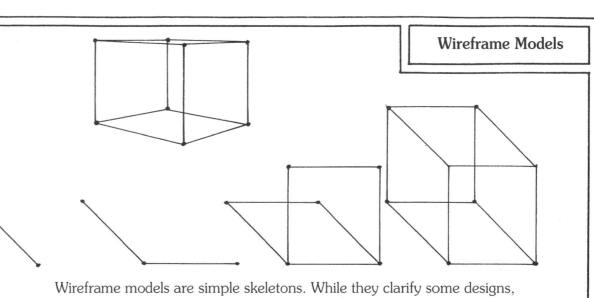

Wireframe models are simple skeletons. While they clarify some designs, their transparency can also be ambiguous and confusing.

Surface modeling defines edges like wireframe modeling but also defines the surfaces delineated by those edges. Through the use of parametric techniques, the computer can calculate and display precisely defined complex surface characteristics.

With the ability to create opaque surfaces, the ambiguities of the wire frame are eliminated and thus a full range of new possibilities are introduced—colors, textures, patterns etc.

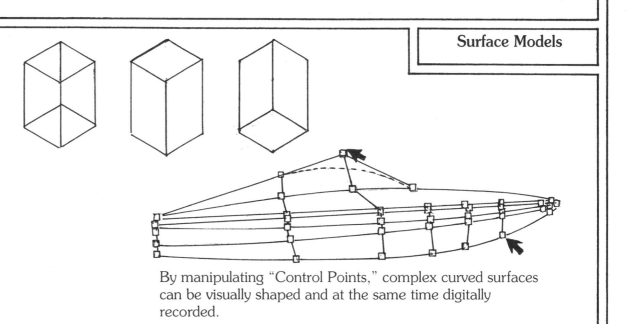

By manipulating "Control Points," complex curved surfaces can be visually shaped and at the same time digitally recorded.

In solid modeling, the computer calculates volumetric data for the object. The model contains information about the insides and not just the edges and surfaces. The data would include the volume of a room, for example, and not just the walls that enclose it.

Geometric "primitives" (prisms, spheres, cylinders, etc.) are often used as building blocks in solid modeling.

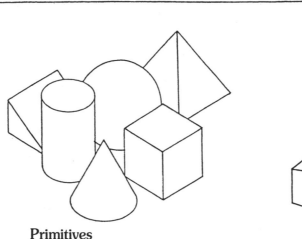

Primitives

Geometric primitives can be sized and joined to generate complex combinations.

"Boolean Operations"

Solid modeling with primitives is a strictly additive process and thus limited. One cannot make holes in things, for example, nor does the computer understand the intersection of solids or when they overlap in the same space. Software that supports what are called "Boolean Operations" solves these problems by providing information about how shapes interact with one another.

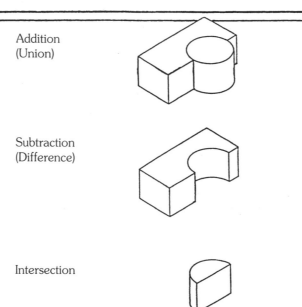

Addition
(Union)

Subtraction
(Difference)

Intersection

Boolean operations can fuse two objects seamlessly into one for later mapping and surface treatment.

One form can be carved out of another. For example, holes can be precisely stamped out of existing forms or a screw can tap its threads into a hole.

The overlap or intersection of two shapes can be used to create yet another new shape.

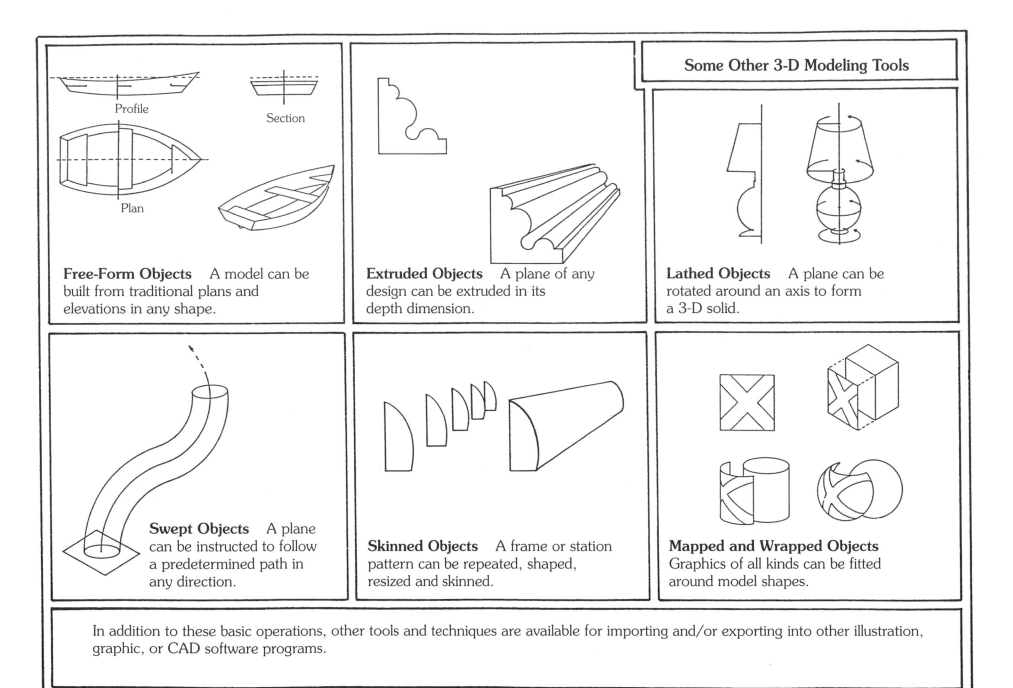

Free-Form Objects   A model can be built from traditional plans and elevations in any shape.

Extruded Objects   A plane of any design can be extruded in its depth dimension.

Some Other 3-D Modeling Tools

Lathed Objects   A plane can be rotated around an axis to form a 3-D solid.

Swept Objects   A plane can be instructed to follow a predetermined path in any direction.

Skinned Objects   A frame or station pattern can be repeated, shaped, resized and skinned.

Mapped and Wrapped Objects Graphics of all kinds can be fitted around model shapes.

In addition to these basic operations, other tools and techniques are available for importing and/or exporting into other illustration, graphic, or CAD software programs.

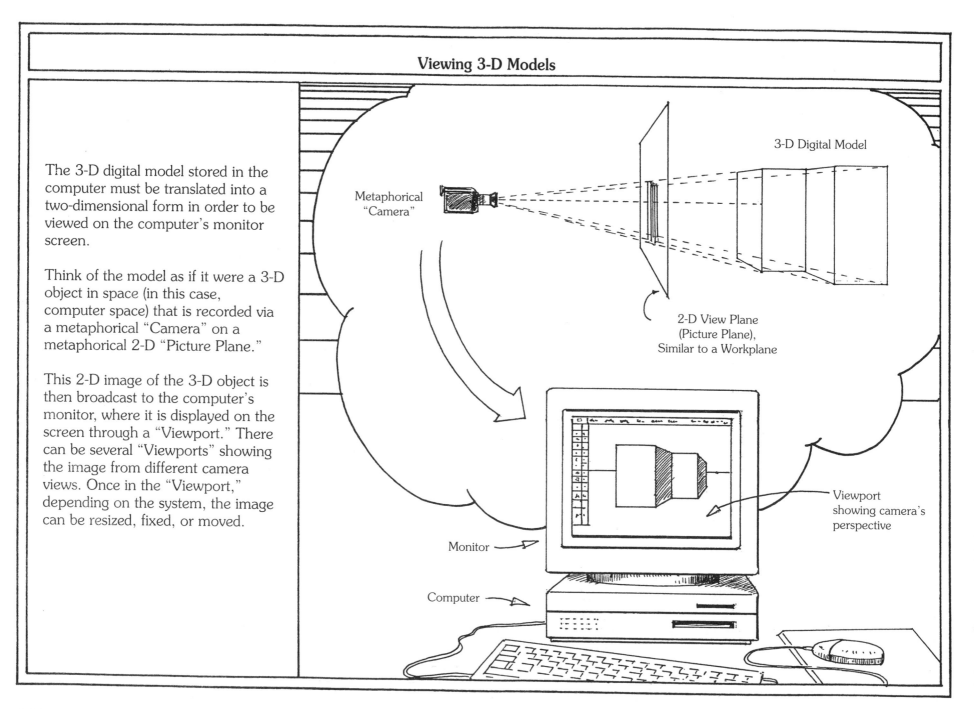

The 3-D digital model stored in the computer must be translated into a two-dimensional form in order to be viewed on the computer's monitor screen.

Think of the model as if it were a 3-D object in space (in this case, computer space) that is recorded via a metaphorical "Camera" on a metaphorical 2-D "Picture Plane."

This 2-D image of the 3-D object is then broadcast to the computer's monitor, where it is displayed on the screen through a "Viewport." There can be several "Viewports" showing the image from different camera views. Once in the "Viewport," depending on the system, the image can be resized, fixed, or moved.

3-D Digital Model

Metaphorical "Camera"

2-D View Plane (Picture Plane), Similar to a Workplane

Viewport showing camera's perspective

Monitor

Computer

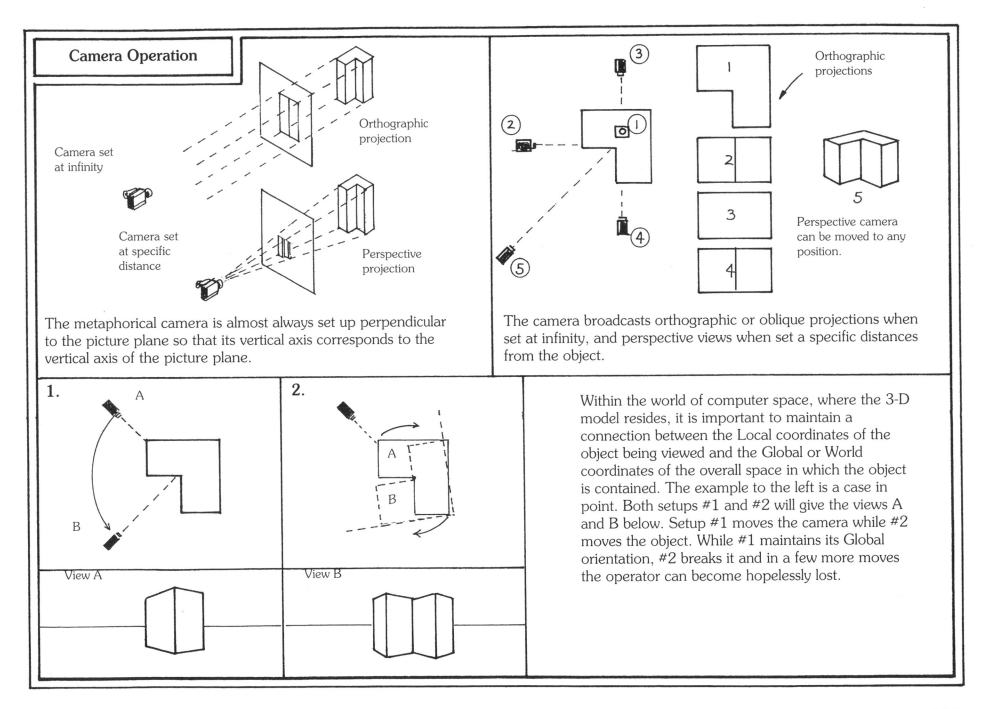

Camera Operation

Orthographic projection

Camera set at infinity

Camera set at specific distance

Perspective projection

The metaphorical camera is almost always set up perpendicular to the picture plane so that its vertical axis corresponds to the vertical axis of the picture plane.

Orthographic projections

Perspective camera can be moved to any position.

The camera broadcasts orthographic or oblique projections when set at infinity, and perspective views when set a specific distances from the object.

1.

A

B

View A

2.

A

B

View B

Within the world of computer space, where the 3-D model resides, it is important to maintain a connection between the Local coordinates of the object being viewed and the Global or World coordinates of the overall space in which the object is contained. The example to the left is a case in point. Both setups #1 and #2 will give the views A and B below. Setup #1 moves the camera while #2 moves the object. While #1 maintains its Global orientation, #2 breaks it and in a few more moves the operator can become hopelessly lost.

183

Once the projection of a model has been established, simple zooms and pans can be executed without changing the model or the position of the camera.

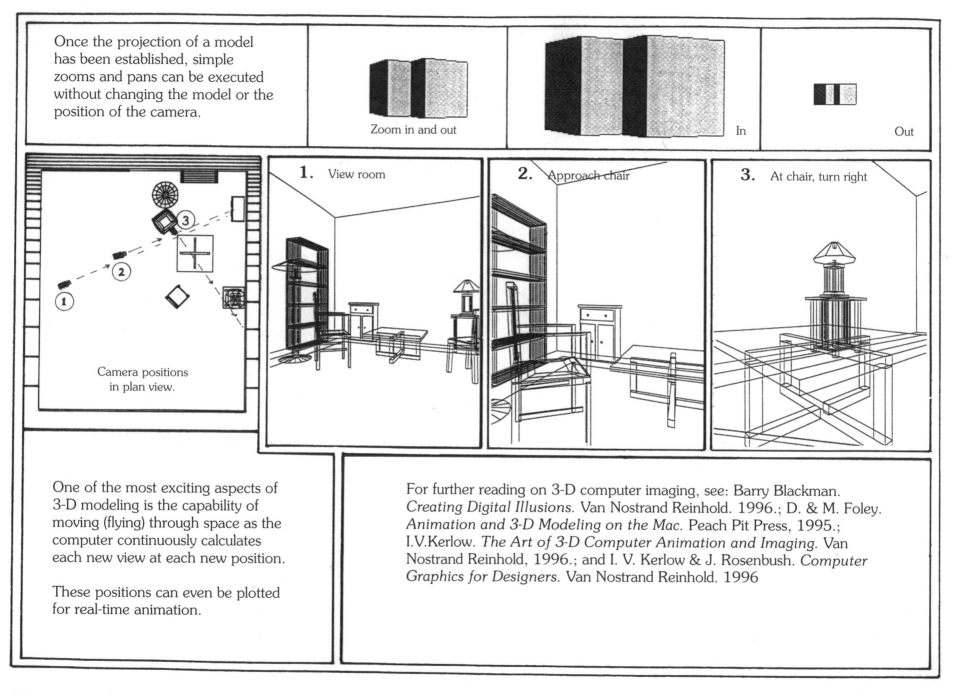

Zoom in and out

In

Out

Camera positions in plan view.

1. View room

2. Approach chair

3. At chair, turn right

One of the most exciting aspects of 3-D modeling is the capability of moving (flying) through space as the computer continuously calculates each new view at each new position.

These positions can even be plotted for real-time animation.

For further reading on 3-D computer imaging, see: Barry Blackman. *Creating Digital Illusions.* Van Nostrand Reinhold. 1996.; D. & M. Foley. *Animation and 3-D Modeling on the Mac.* Peach Pit Press, 1995.; I.V.Kerlow. *The Art of 3-D Computer Animation and Imaging.* Van Nostrand Reinhold, 1996.; and I. V. Kerlow & J. Rosenbush. *Computer Graphics for Designers.* Van Nostrand Reinhold. 1996

Examples of Perspective Views

13

**Step-by-Step Construction
and Analysis**

1. Boxes

2. Table

3. Chair

4. Chair

5. Chair

6. House (Exterior)

7. Bank (Exterior)

8. House (Interior)

9. House (Interior)

10. Church (Interior)

11. Cityscape

12. Cityscape

13. Spiral Staircase

14. Bicycle

15. Motorcycle

16. Classic Automobile

17. Contemporary Automobile

18. Boat Hull

19. Airplane

20. Spacecraft

21. Landscape

22. Human Figures

23. Conference Center (Exterior)

24. Exterior Sculpture

25. Spoon, Cup, and Glass

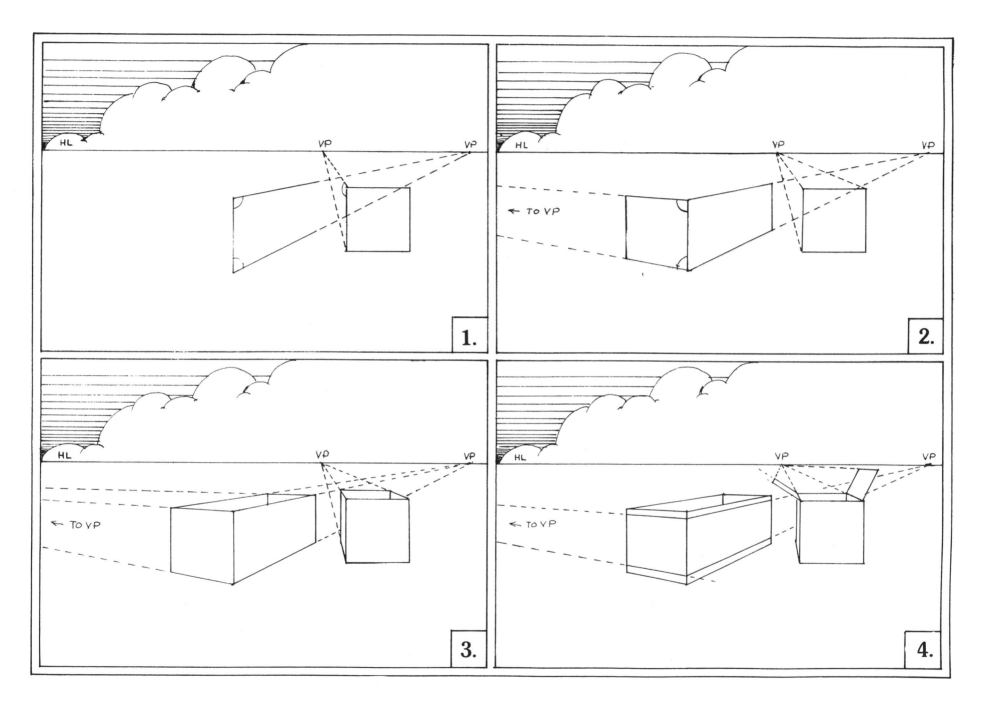

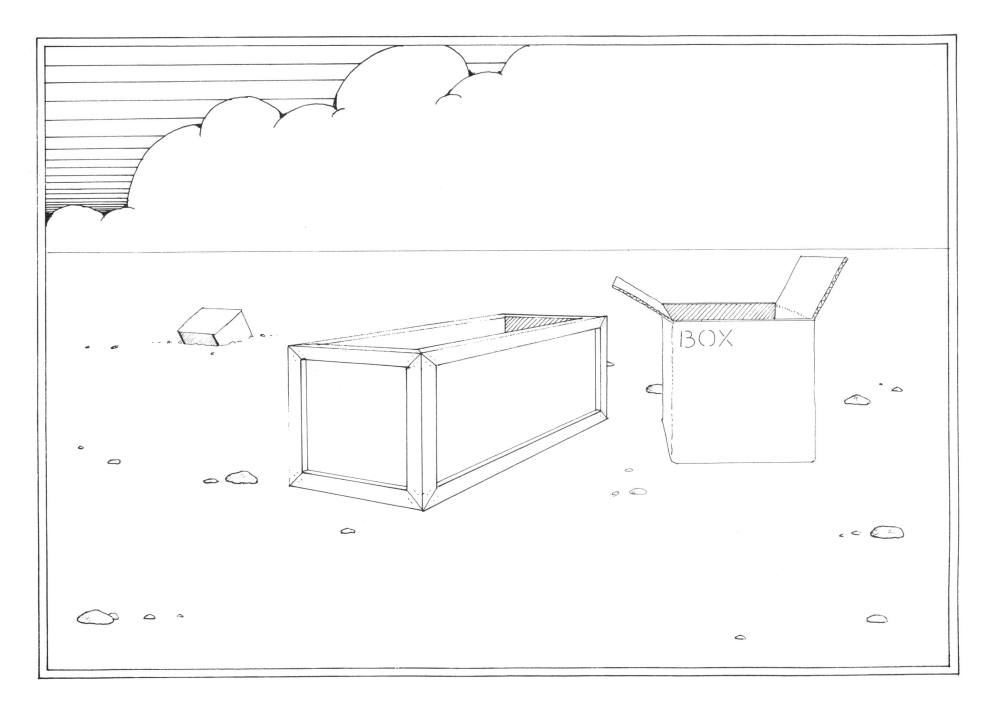

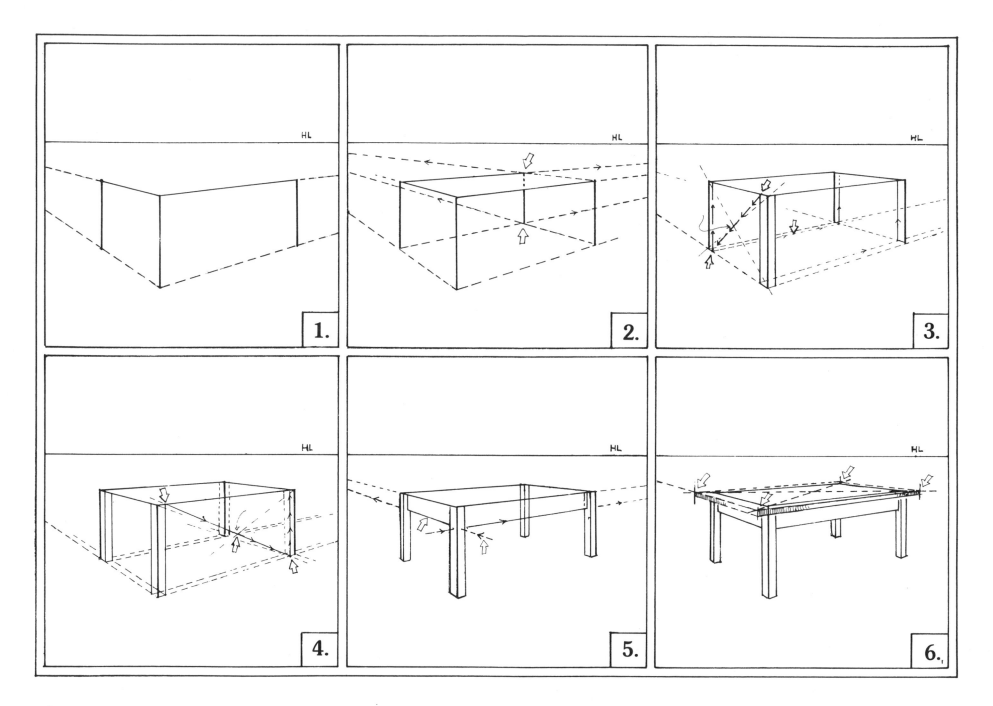

HL

HL

189

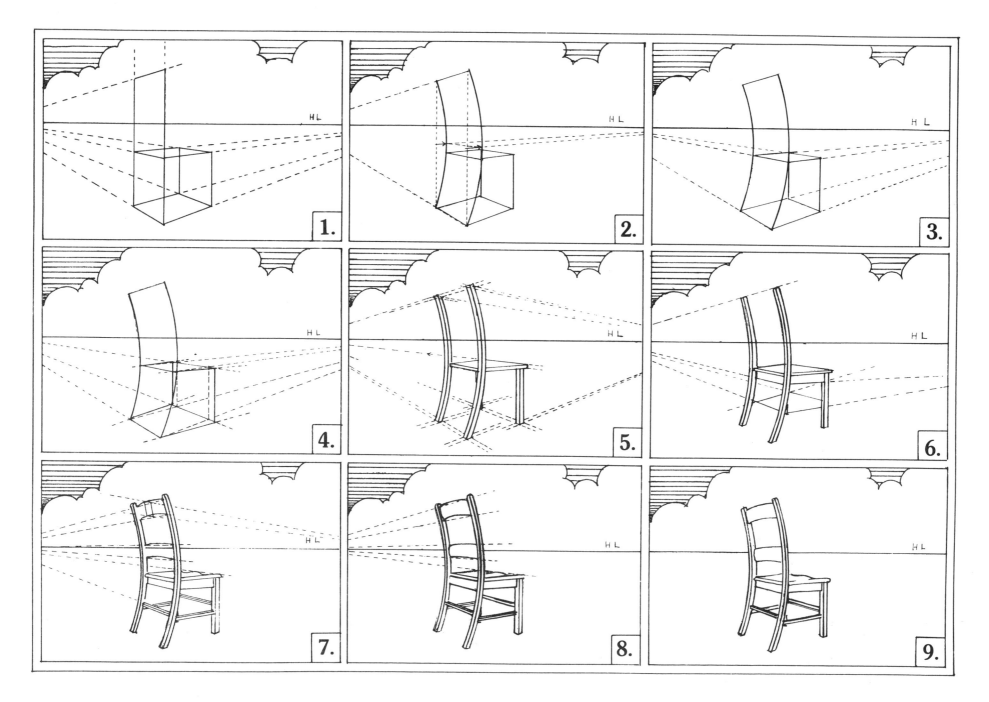

HL   HL   HL
HL   HL   HL
HL   HL   HL

1.   2.   3.
4.   5.   6.
7.   8.   9.

190

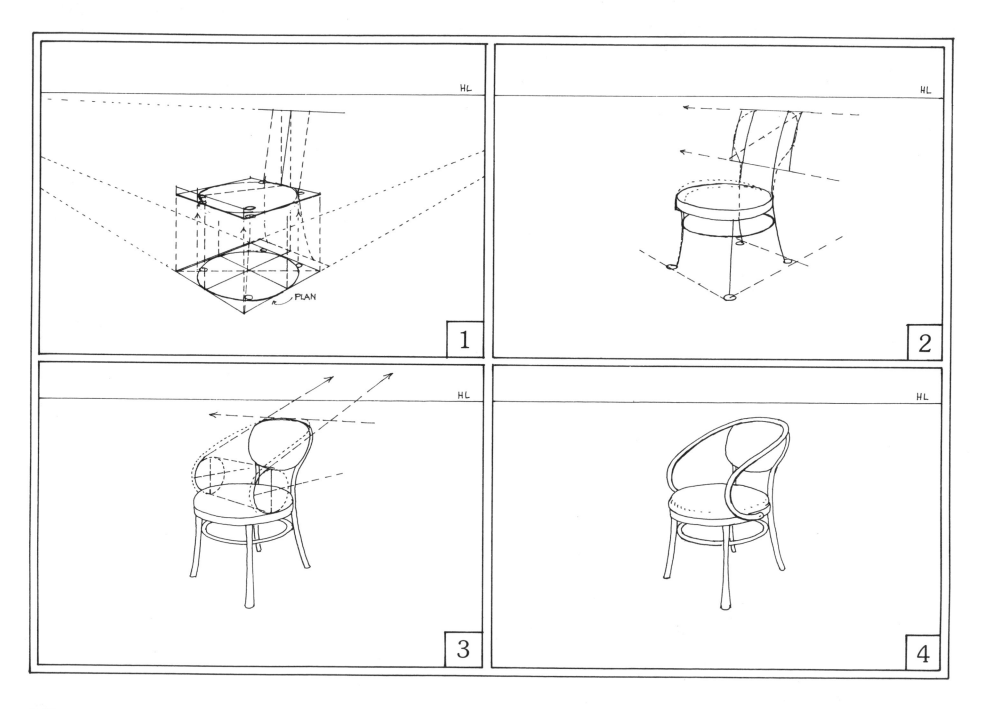

192

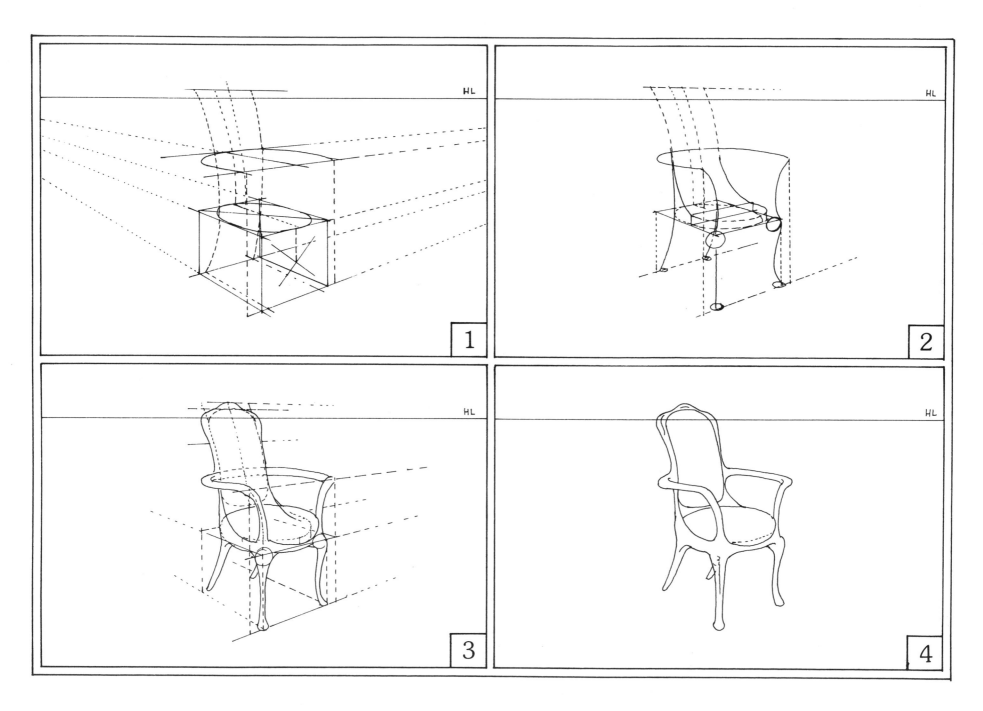

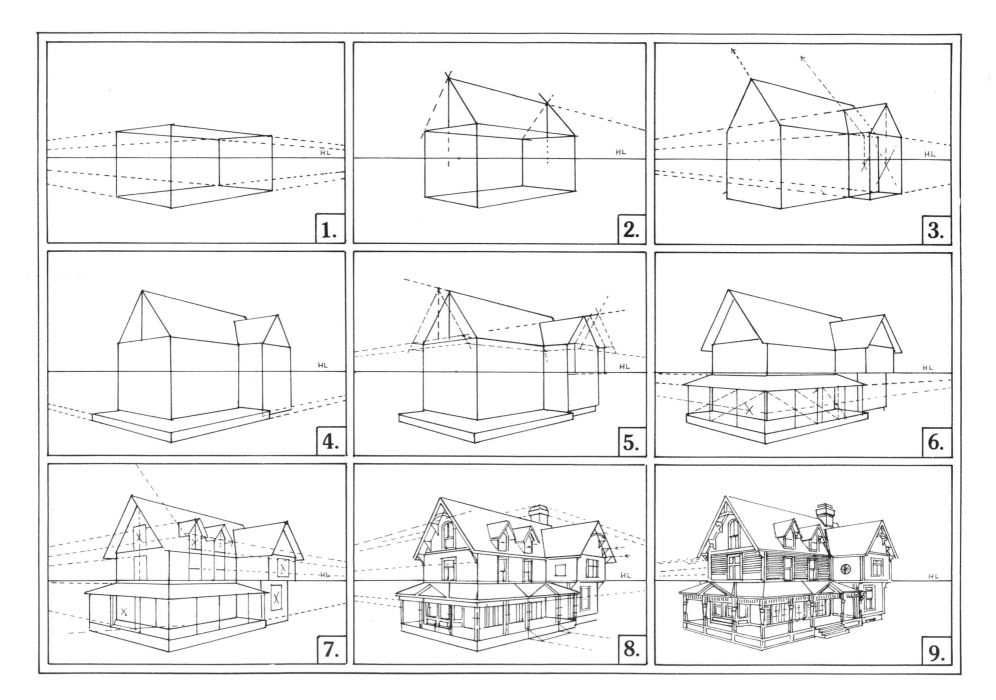

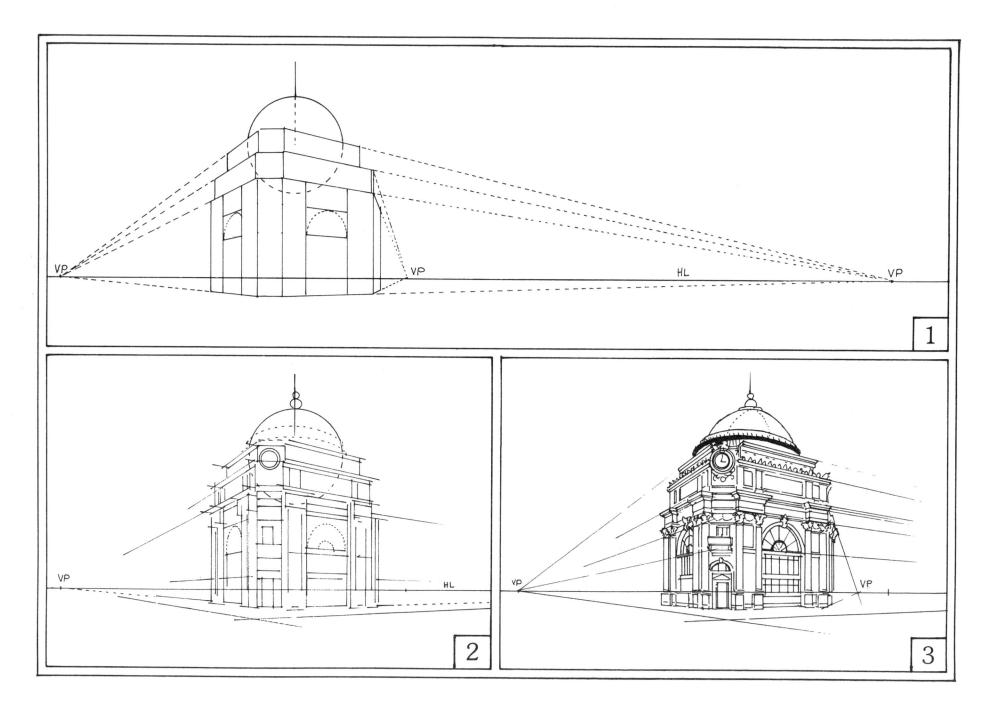

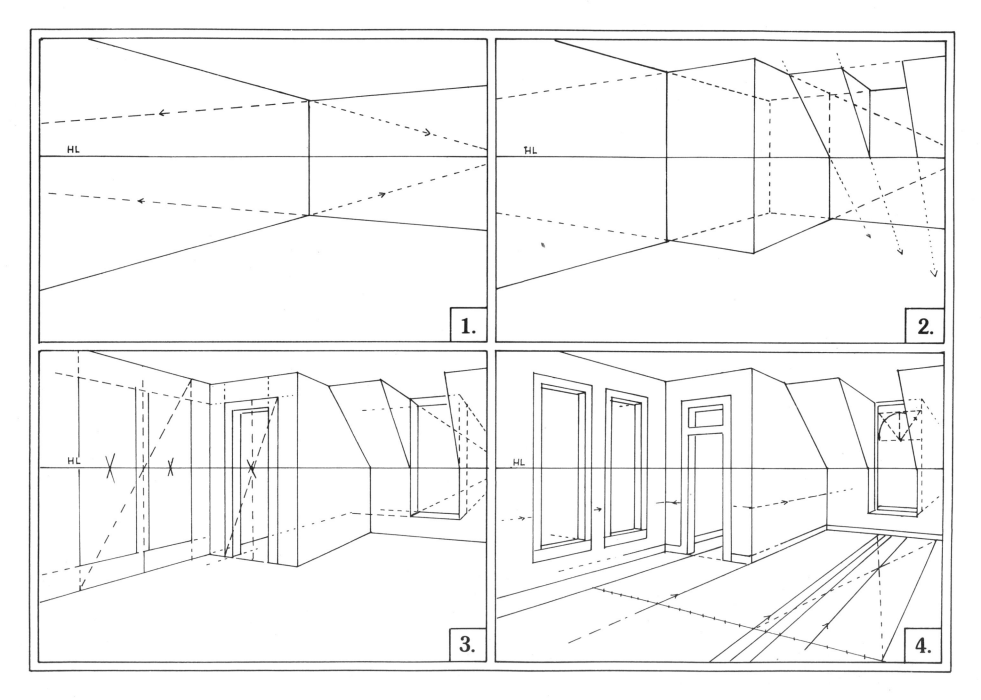

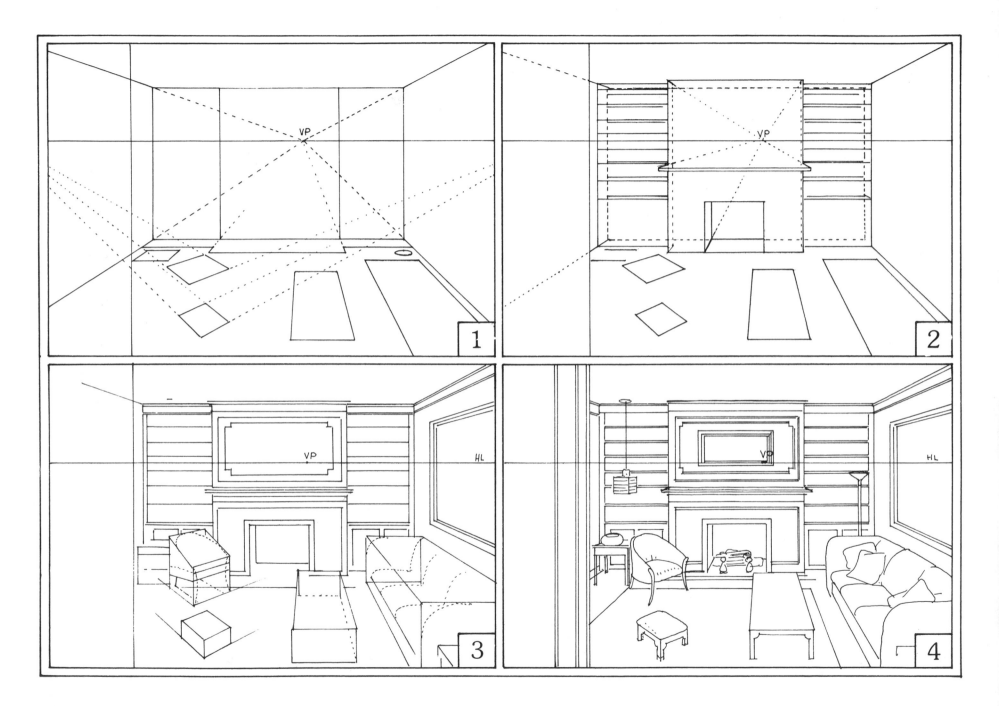

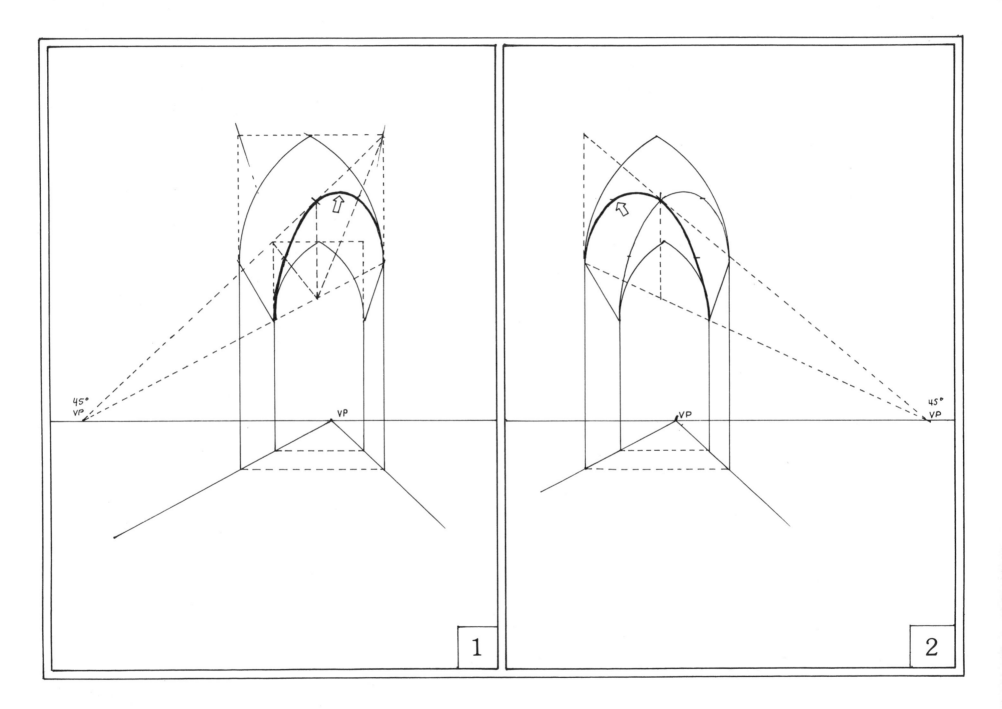

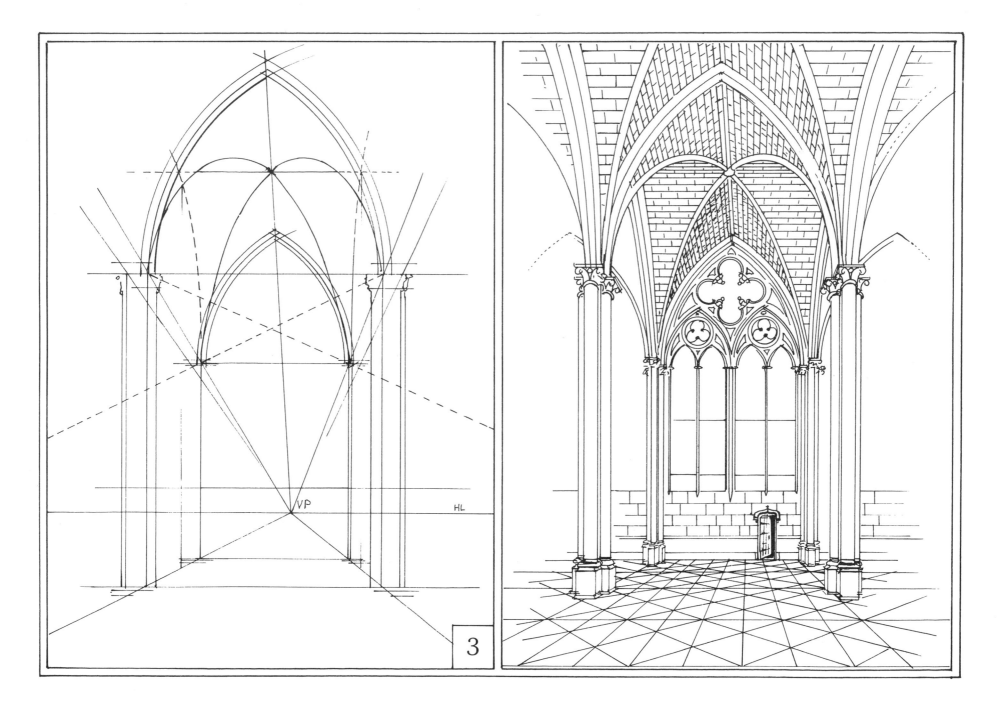

3

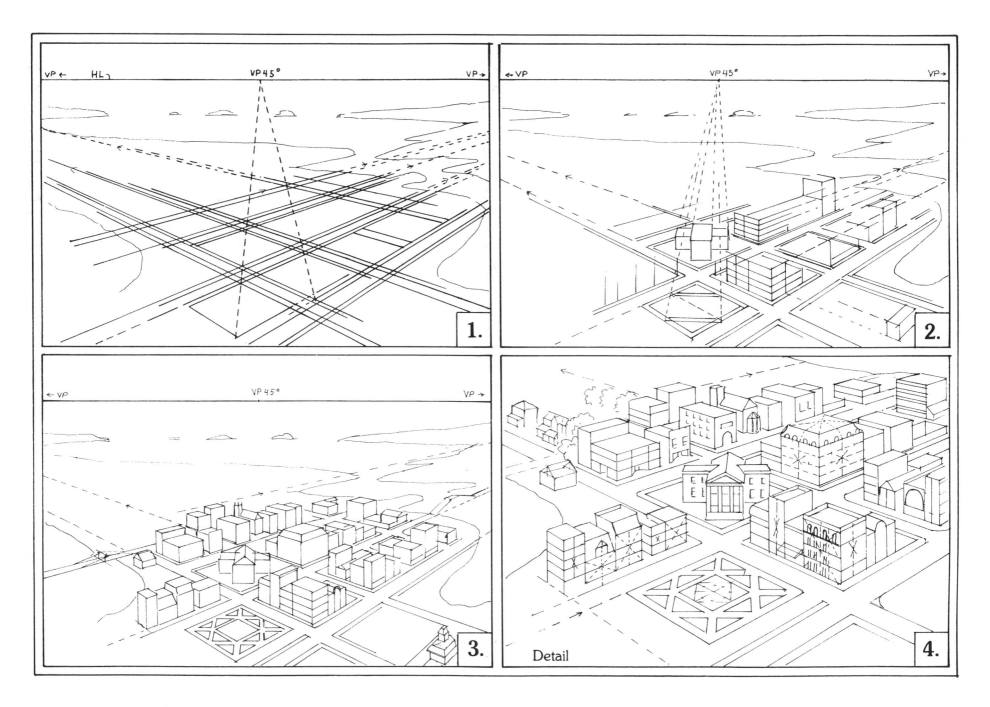

Detail

206

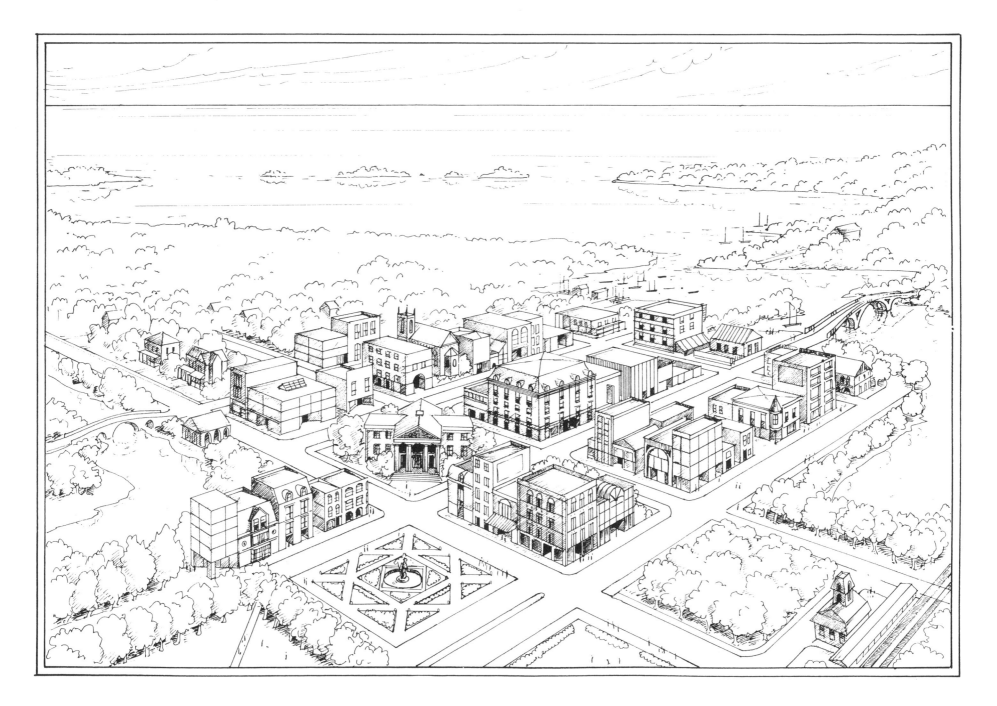

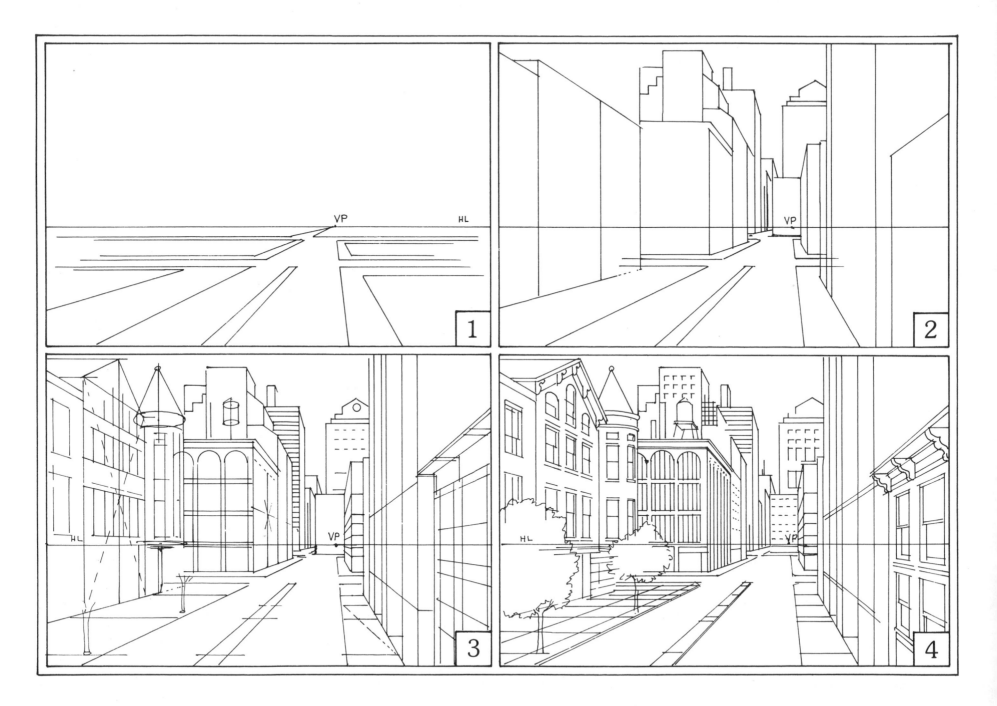

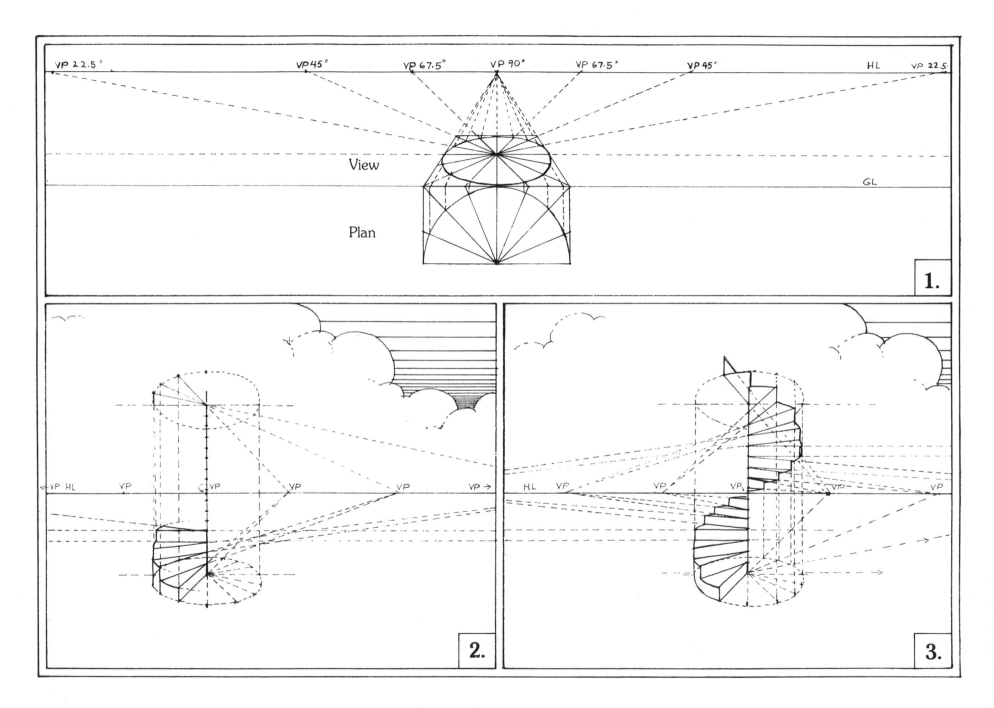

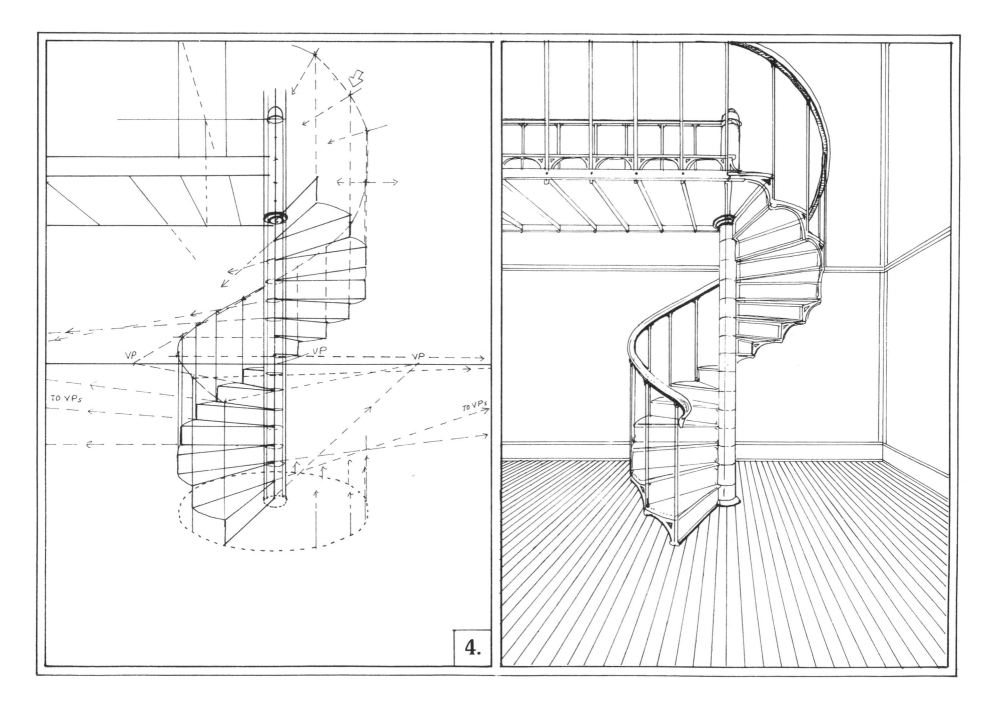

VP VP VP

TO VPs TO VPs

4.

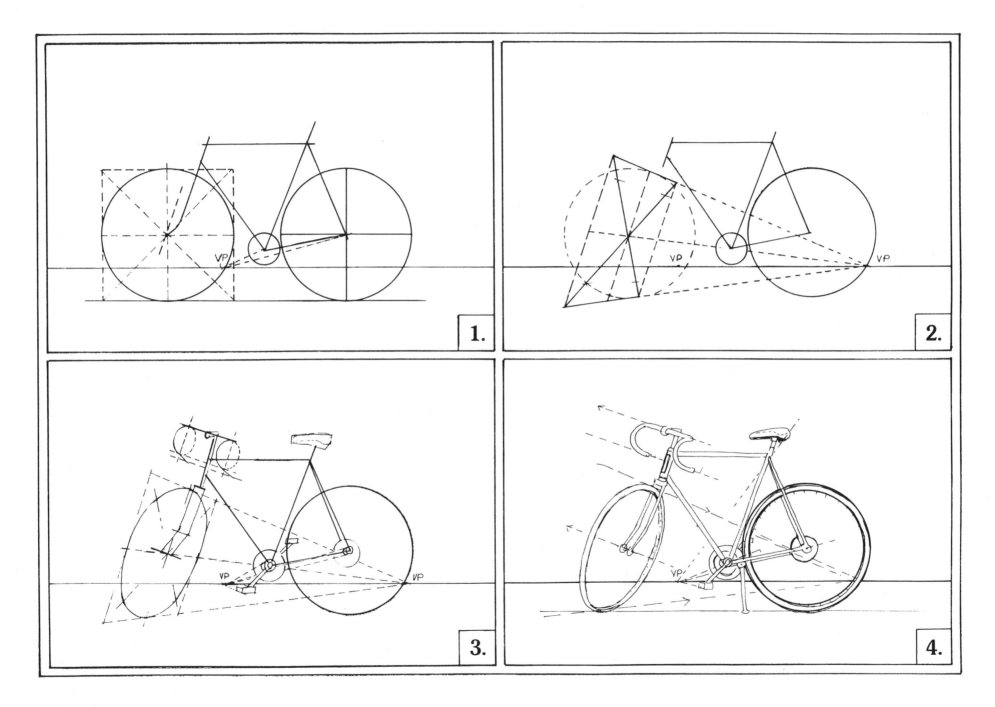

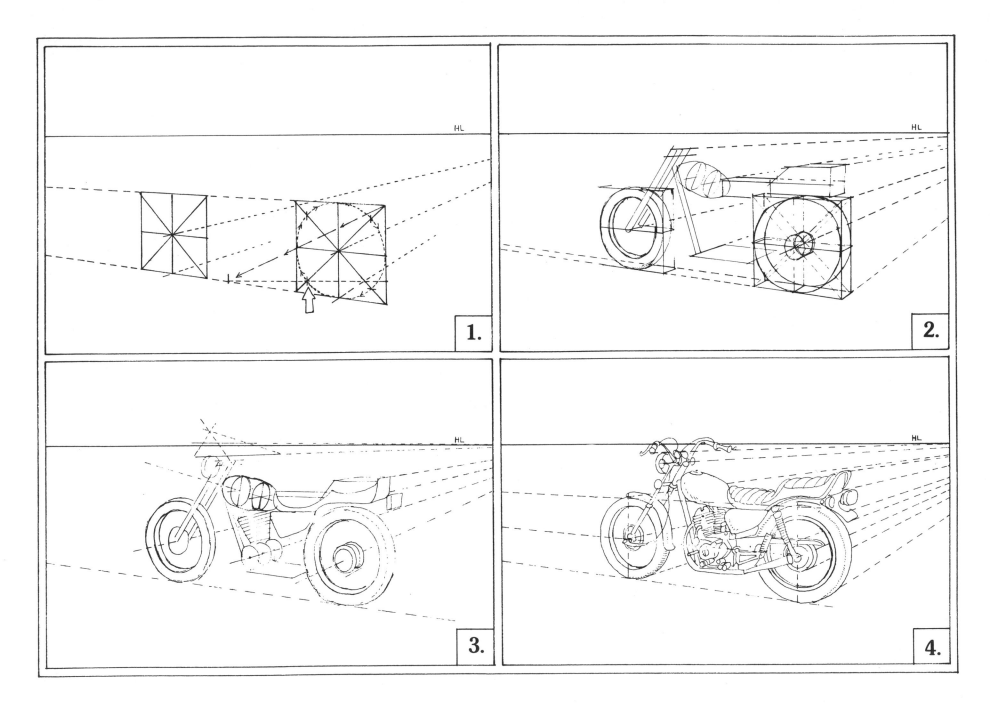

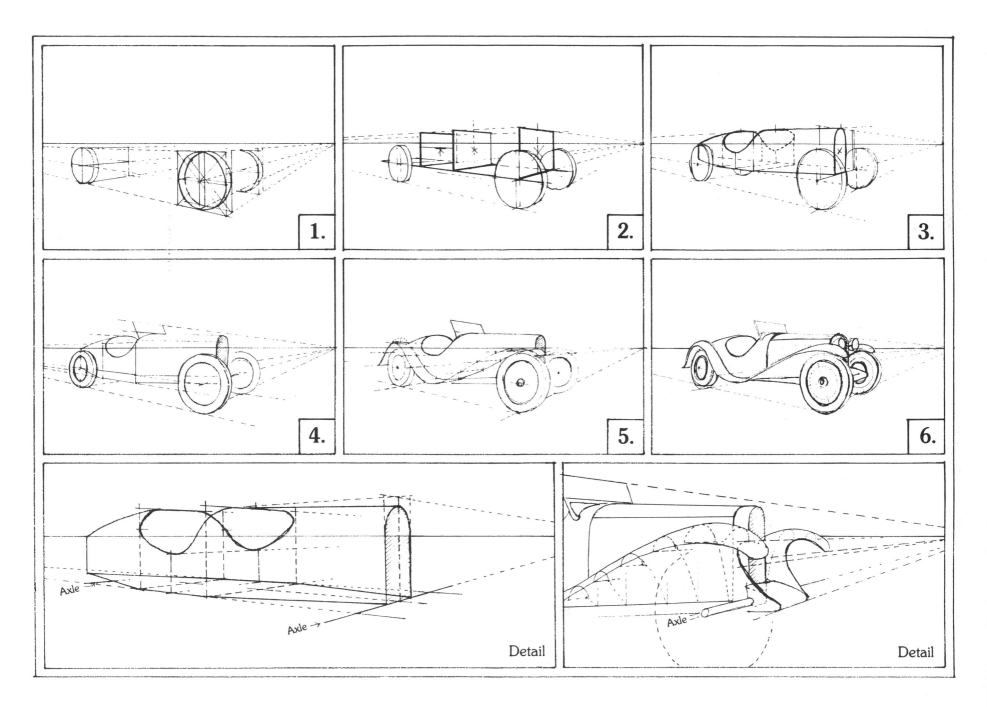

1.

2.

3.

4.

5.

6.

Axle

Axle →

Detail

Axle

Detail

217

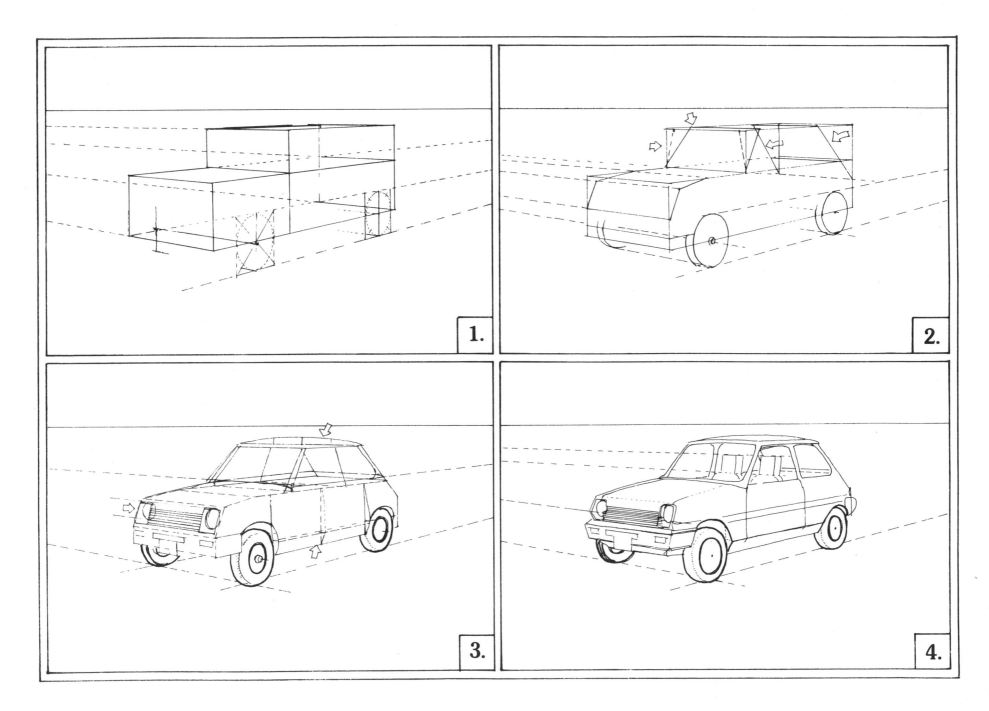

1.

2.

3.

4.

218

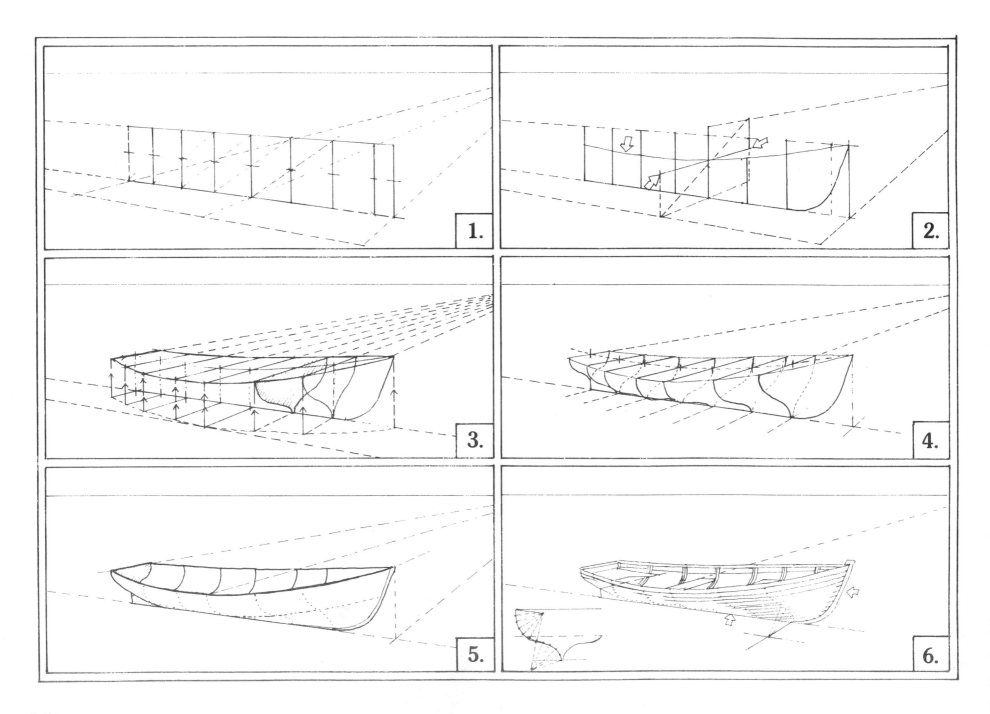

1.

2.

3.

4.

5.

6.

220

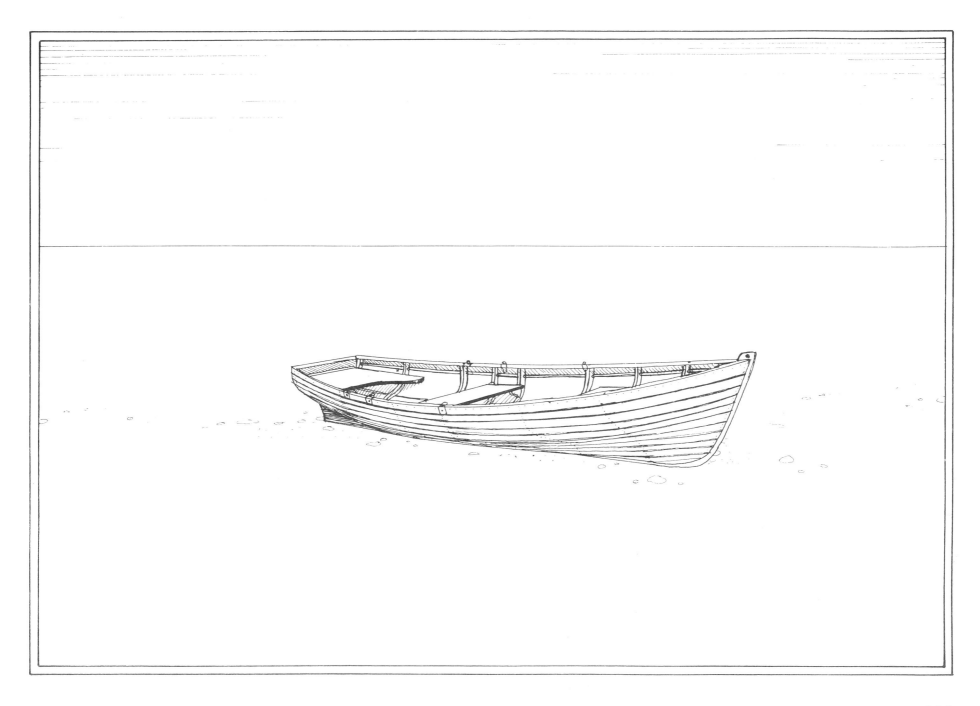

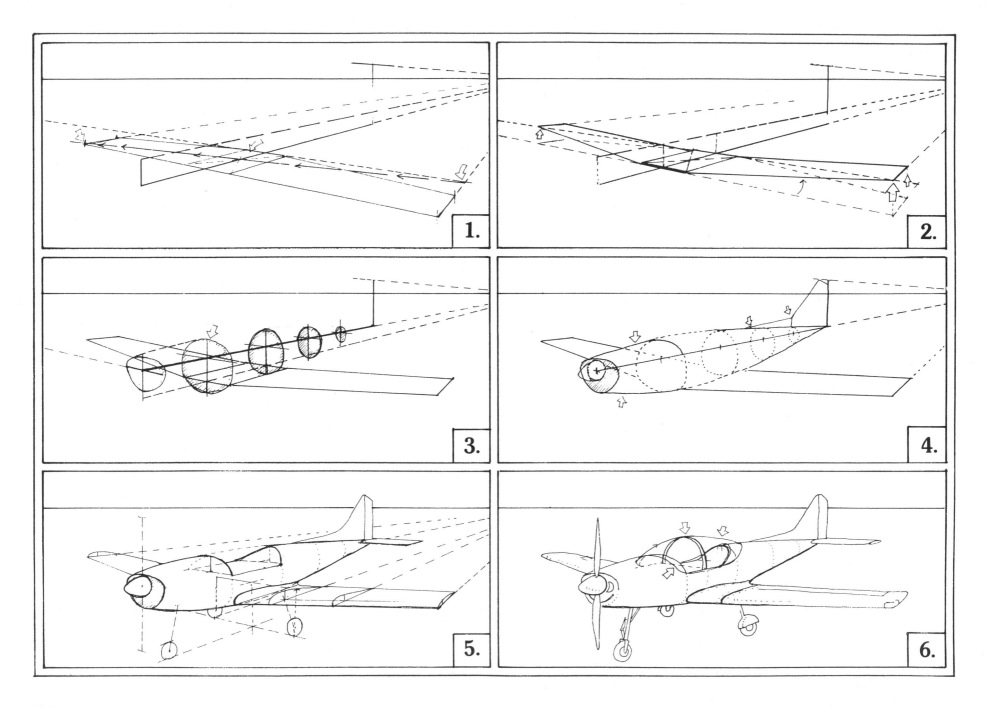

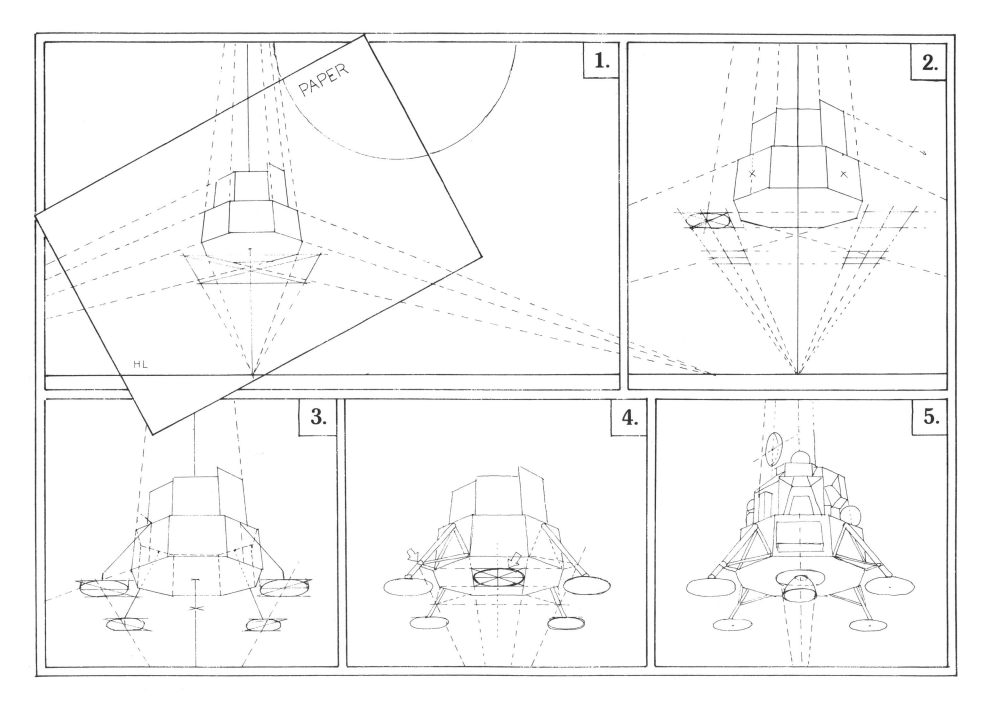

PAPER

HL

3.

4.

5.

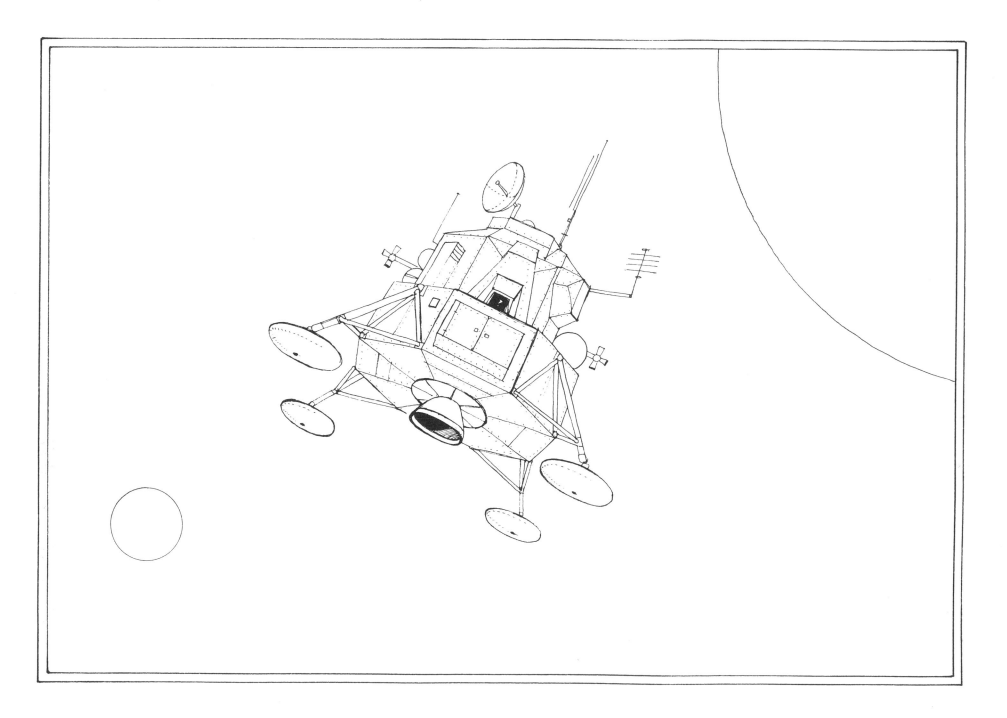

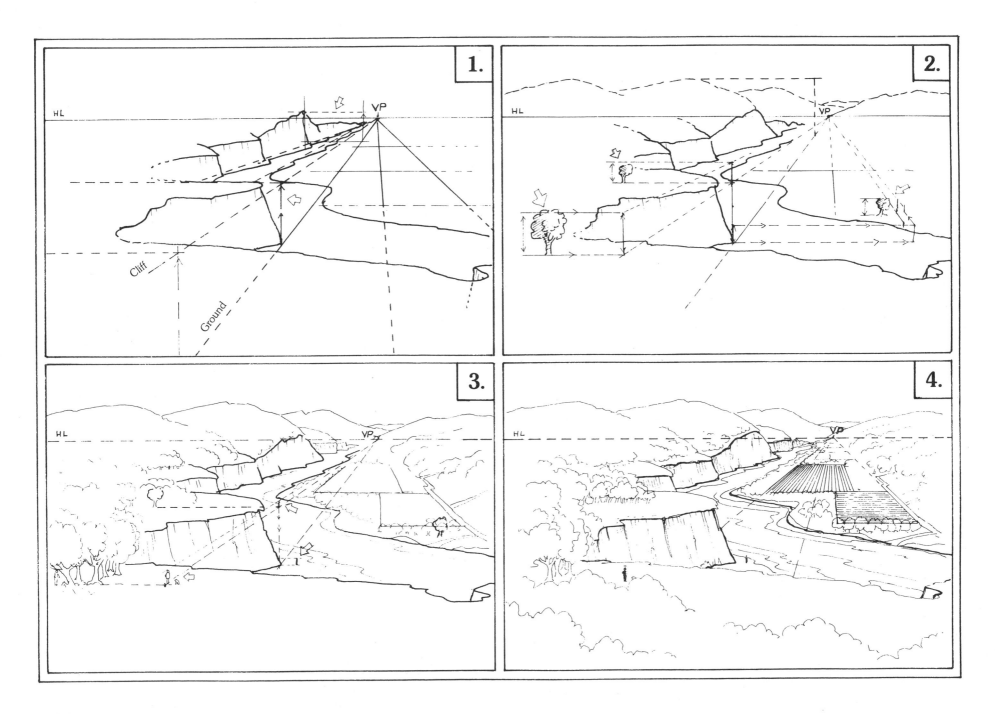

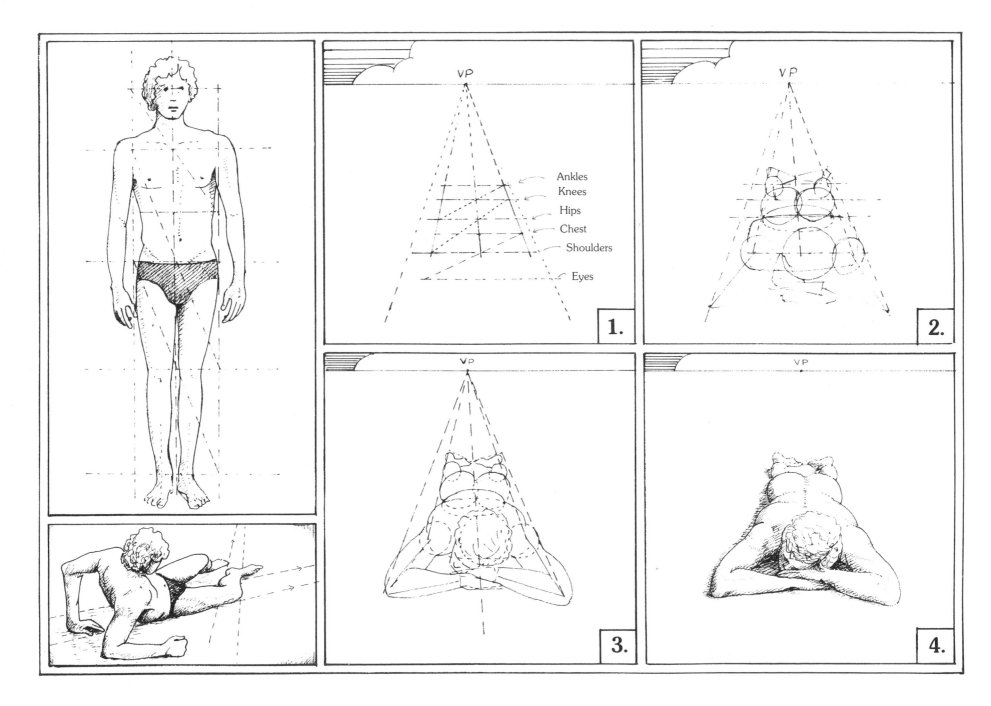

1.

Ankles
Knees
Hips
Chest
Shoulders
Eyes

VP

2.

VP

3.

VP

4.

VP

228

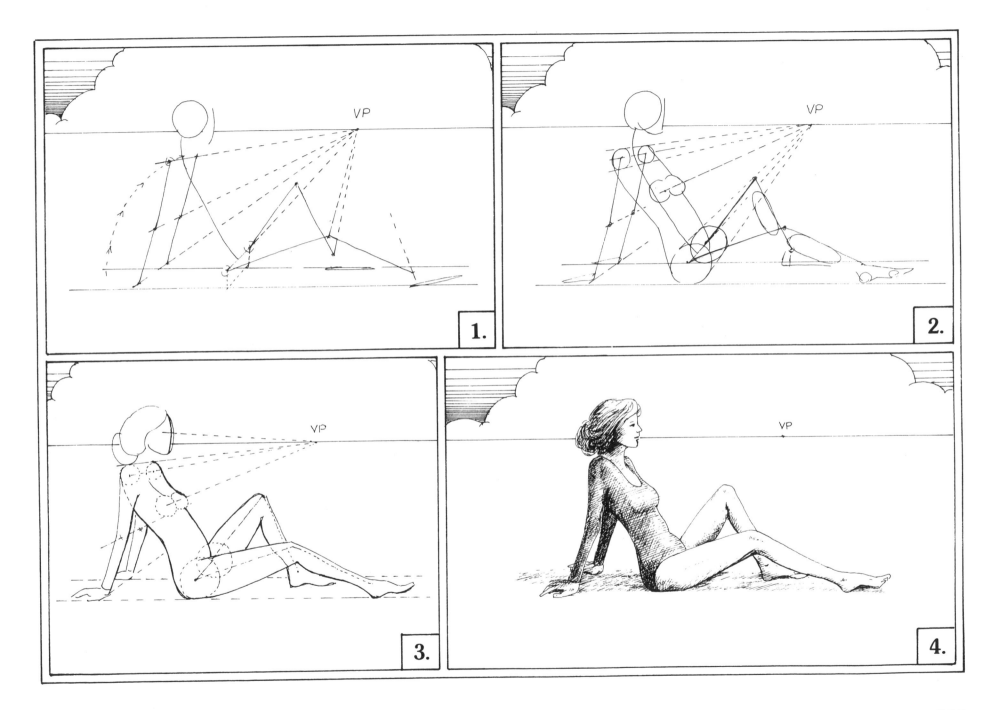

1.

2.

3.

4.

229

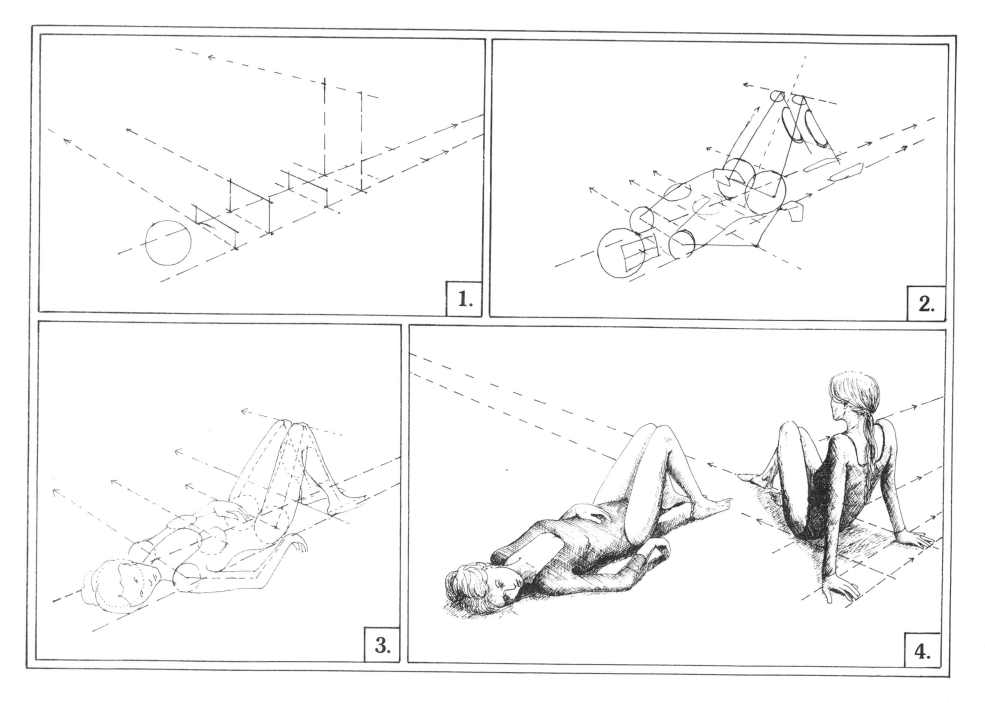

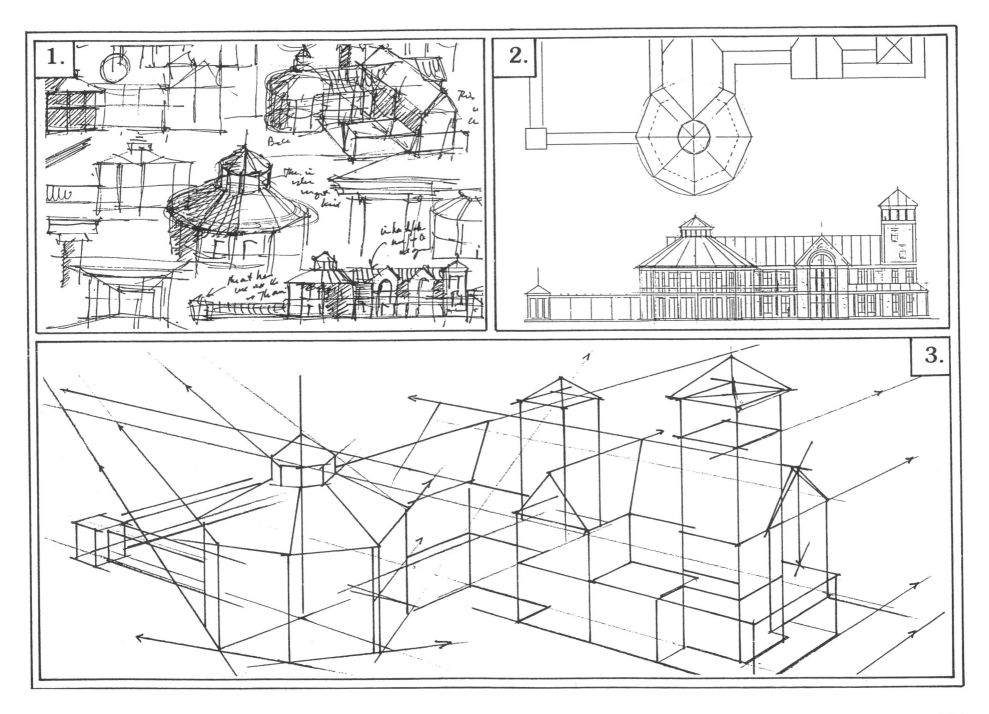

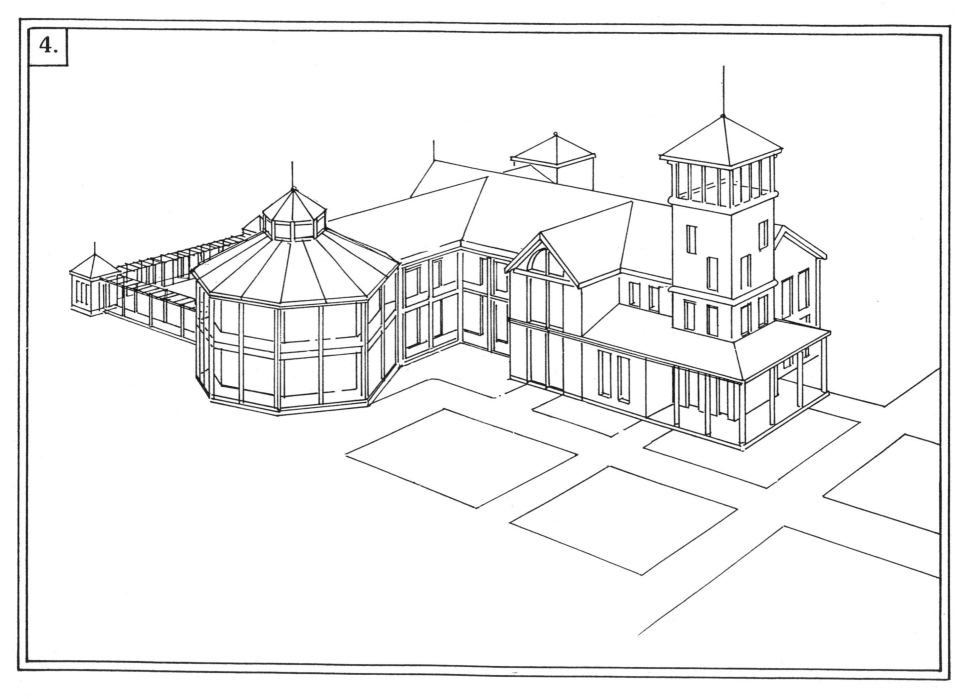

4.

232

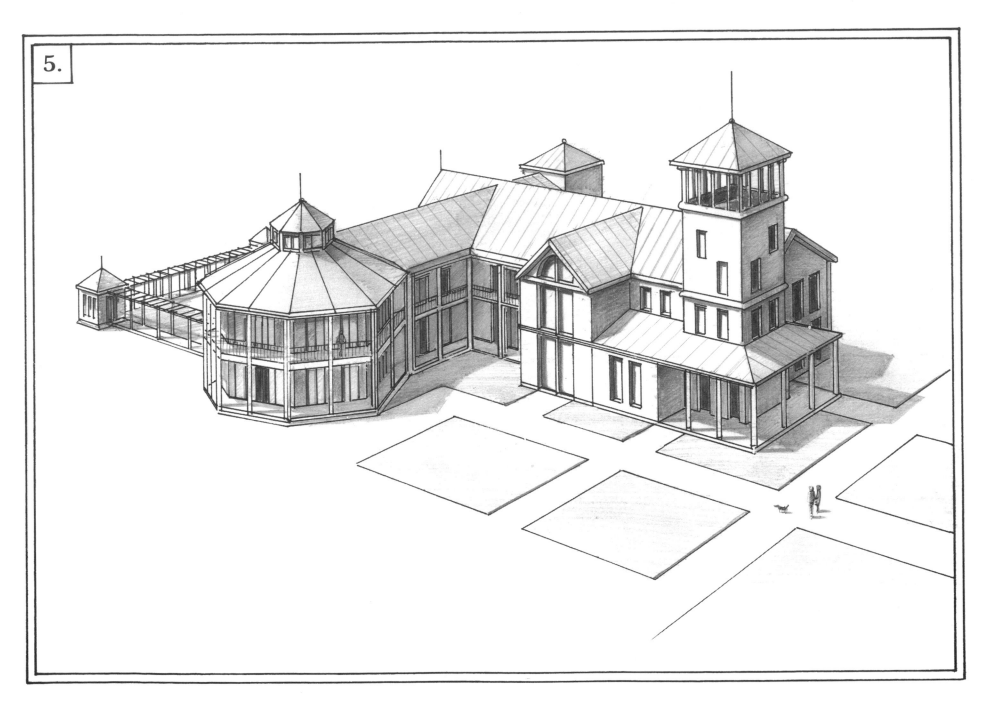

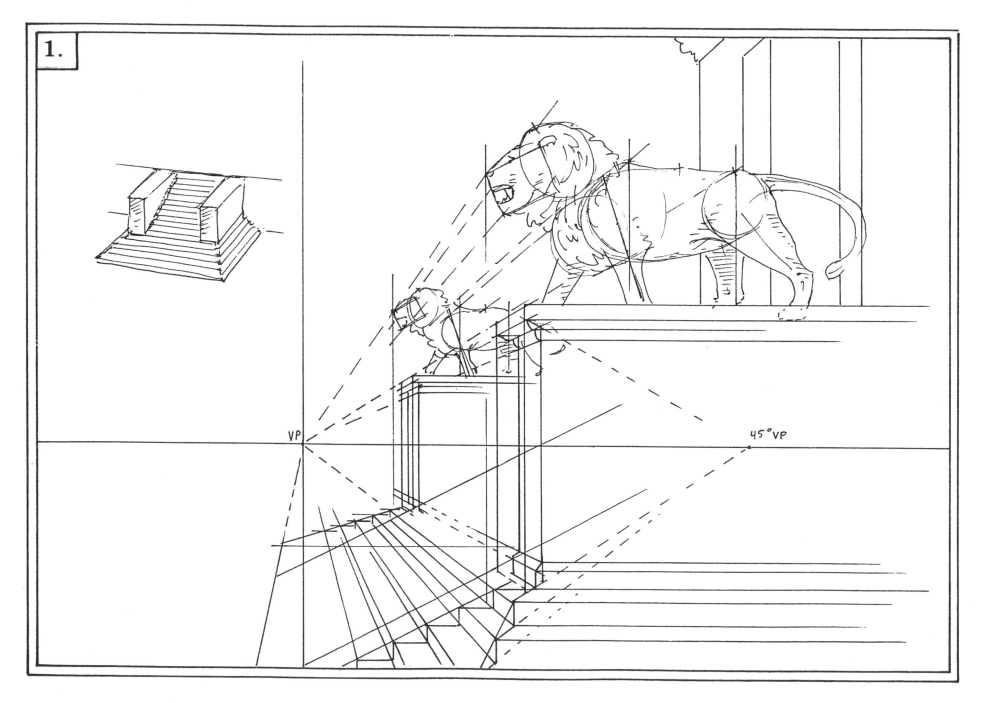

1.

VP

45°VP

234

2.

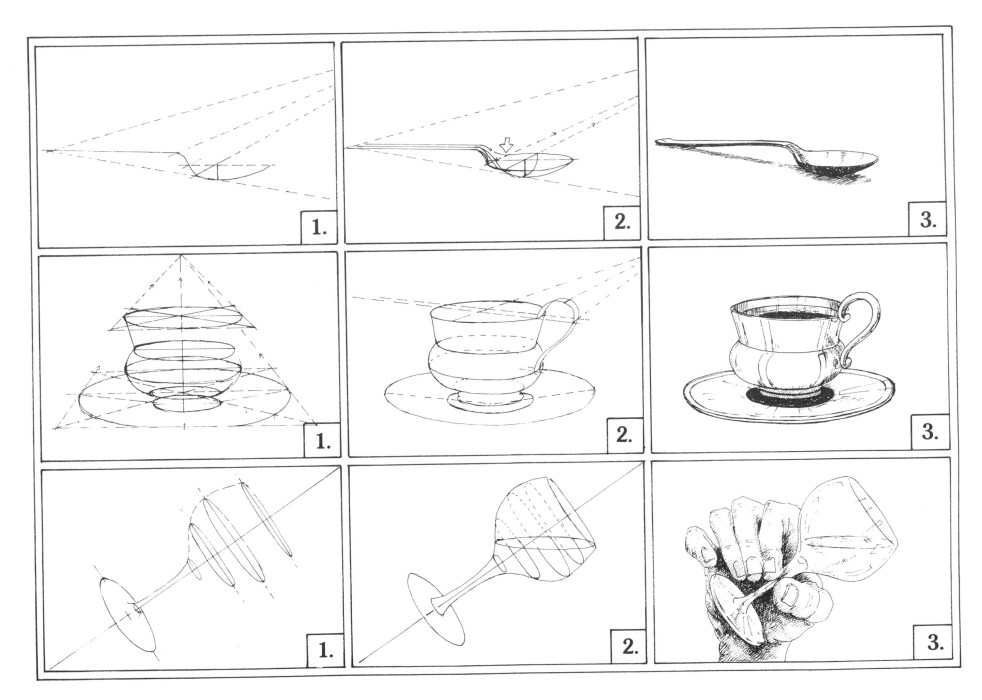

1.

2.

3.

1.

2.

3.

1.

2.

3.

Appendix

Notes on Studying and Teaching Perspective Drawing

Basic Perspective Drawing originally grew out of long experience teaching college courses in perspective drawing to art, design, and architecture students. While the book has been used as a text for both beginning and advanced courses, most of the material can reasonably be covered in one semester, i.e. a three-credit, 15-week studio course meeting 6 hours per week. The following course, like the text, is designed to move from the general to the specific and from the simple to the complex. It relies on rapid visualization exercises, a sketchbook project, and class work, which culminates in a series of final drawing projects due about every two weeks.

Suggested Course Outline

Week 1 Introduction and Overview. Class work: optics/observation (see Tools, Materials, and Aid on page 243). Chapter 1

Week 2 Drawing from Observed Reality. Class work: interior and exterior views. Chapter 2
Project I due: Outside view from life

Week 3 Plans, Elevations, and Paraline Projections. Class work: measure real objects for plans and elevations. Chapter 3

Week 4 Construction of Perspective Views. Class work: one-point perspectives from plans. Chapter 4
Project II due: Measured plans and obliques

Week 5 Construction of Perspective Views. Class work: two-point perspectives from plans. Chapter 4

Week 6 Construction of Perspective Space. Class work: building grids/using measuring points. Chapter 4
Project III due: Perspective interior and exterior from plans

Week 7 Geometric Tools, Slopes. Class work: tools, slopes, roofs, and details. Chapter 5-6
Project IV due: Architectural exteriors/roof details

Week 8 Circles and Curved Forms. Class work: cylinders, domes and arches. Chapter 7

Week 9   Complex Curved Forms. Class work: boat hulls/cars/etc. Chapter 7
          Project V due: Curves, arches/hull

Week 10 Shadows and Shading. Class work: geometry of shadows/basic rendering. Chapters 8 and 11

Week 11 Reflections. Class work: geometry of mirror surfaces. Chapters 8 and 11
          Project VI due: Architectural shadows

Week 12 Scale Figures in Perspective. Class work: basic proportions structure. Chapter 10

Week 13 Introduction to Computer Aided Design. Class work: demonstration of basic 3-D modeling. Chapter 12
          Project VII due: Interior space with figures and furniture.

Week 14 Rendering Problems in Black, White, and Color. Class work: exercises with color pencils/markers. Chapter 11

Week 15 Review and Final Critiques
          Project VIII due: Fully rendered perspective view

Class Sessions

Class sessions are generally divided into two parts: 1) presentation, demonstration, and practice of new material, and 2) rapid visualization exercises.

1) Presentation, Demonstration, and Practice of New Material

Many studio classes tend to be in two-hour sessions. The greater part of each period is taken up with the introduction of new material and in-class practice.

The character of class sessions should be guided by a commitment to building students' self-confidence on the one hand and nurturing a sense of discovery on the other. Finding the right pace in moving from the simple to the more complex is critical. At the same time, it is important psychologically to approach the subject as an experimentation and a probing rather than a mere reception of a finite body of information.

It is very effective, especially in the beginning, to demonstrate the concepts or ideas through aids that encourage individual participation. Slides can be projected on the blackboard while students find the horizon lines and vanishing point by tracing off the picture. 3 x 5 cards with view windows cut in can be used to demonstrate cone of vision. A video camera and monitor or simple perspective machine (window glass with station point attached) can save hours of verbal explanation (see Tools, Materials, and Aids on page 243).

Practice in class is critical. In that regard it is important to identify this class work as "disposable process drawings," for often learning slows down when students become too fearful of making errors. Finally, because perspective drawing is a coherent system, each time a new body of material is presented, the foundations on which it depends should be briefly reviewed and reinforced.

2) Rapid Visualization Exercises

As part of each class period, usually at the beginning and end of a session, students are given intense timed drawing assignments (ten minutes or less), designed to increase awareness and develop new ways of seeing and thinking. By creating a momentary artificial pressure to solve a problem, students often see the issues much more clearly. If treated more like a game than a test, these short sessions are useful for setting up problems and getting students to start thinking about them well before they are addressed in class. These rapid visualization sessions not only can raise consciousness of what is to come but also can be very effective reviews to reinforce previous material.

One of the most valuable ways these sessions can be used is in spatial perception practice. For example, students can routinely be asked to look at an object, then draw it from where someone else is sitting, rotate it, and draw how it would look from the inside. Sometimes these rapid visualization exercises are most effective and most stimulating when, like TV commercial breaks, they are inserted into the middle of the class session as complete nonsequiturs.

Assignments

1) Final Drawing Projects

The final drawing projects are designed as the culmination of the material covered in the previous two weeks of class. Unlike the process drawing in class or the rapid visualization exercises, these drawing are carefully finished to clean professional standards with the purpose of demonstrating the students grasp of the concepts and skill of execution. These drawings figure prominently in the evaluation system, but they too are works in progress, as students have the opportunity to rework or redo as necessary. Final drawings are normally submitted on 18" x 24" layout bond.

2) Sketchbook Project

The sketchbook is a device for encouraging the habit of drawing. It is evaluated on energy input, not on correctness or quality per se, and it is also a place where variety and experimentation are encouraged. Through the sketchbook, students locked into routine ways of drawing things are encouraged to move in new directions. These are not graded but checked several times per semester, and the commitment they reflect is connected to the final grade (see Contract on page 242). They should be done on $8^1/_2$ x 11 paper or on more convenient sizes to encourage use.

Learning Process and Evaluation

In language study, fluency is achieved by those willing to take risks and make mistakes. Fluency in drawing is achieved the same way. In fact, when coupled with a determination to try again, a wide tolerance of error is essential. With this in mind, a method of evaluation has been developed that not only makes error a positive learning strategy but also shifts the ultimate responsibility for learning to the student, where it properly belongs and where it is most effective.

PASS/REDO System of Evaluation

In brief, all assignments to be graded are designated as either a PASS or a REDO. A PASS reflects what the instructor feels adequately reflects reasonable knowledge or skill expectations. A REDO is accompanied with an indication of what the problems are and what needs to be done to bring the work up to a PASS. Through this system, each project is a learning experience. If something needs to be fixed, it is pointed out, guidance is given, and it is then the student's decision to act.

As students all start at different levels, this system addresses the fact that some need more work than others. The needs, problems, and responsibilities are individualized.

The final grade for the course (a necessary evil in most systems) is achieved by simply adding up the number of PASSES previously indicated as equivalent to a specific grade. For example, 8 PASSES = A, 6 PASSES = B, etc.

To further encourage student responsibility, students are offered a contract after a few weeks of class, through which they may indicate what they hope to take from the course. The students can realistically assess what they are willing to commit to and what that means in terms of a final grade. Obviously, to get one's "money's worth" one should contract for an A, but in the real world this is not always possible. The option is also left open for a change of mind, as circumstances may change during the semester, as confidence rises, or as outside forces interfere. If students are to take responsibility for their own learning, it is important that they always know what needs to be done in order to achieve a given result.

Through this system, a REDO is not a failure but a learning opportunity, and the taking the opportunity is ultimately the student's choice. Even if the student chooses not to take the maximum value from the course, the grading system does not interfere with the actual process of learning. In fact, experience has proven the working relationship between students and teachers is more honest, more positive, more open, and more effective.

A Typical Contract for a One-Semester College Course in Perspective Drawing

CONTRACT

All final drawings done in consecutive order as assigned. Projects must be handed in on due date to qualify. All projects may be redone and resubmitted as many times as necessary until the last week of the semester. Drawings that receive a PASS will count for the final grade tally.

The chart below represents minimal numbers required for a given grade, i.e., 8

	A	B	C	D
FINISHED PROJECT DRAWINGS	8	6	4	2
SKETCH BOOK PAGES	60	40	20	10
CLASS PARTICIPATION & EXERCISES	X	X	X	X

Grade_____ Signed_____

This contract can be modified at any time and resubmitted.

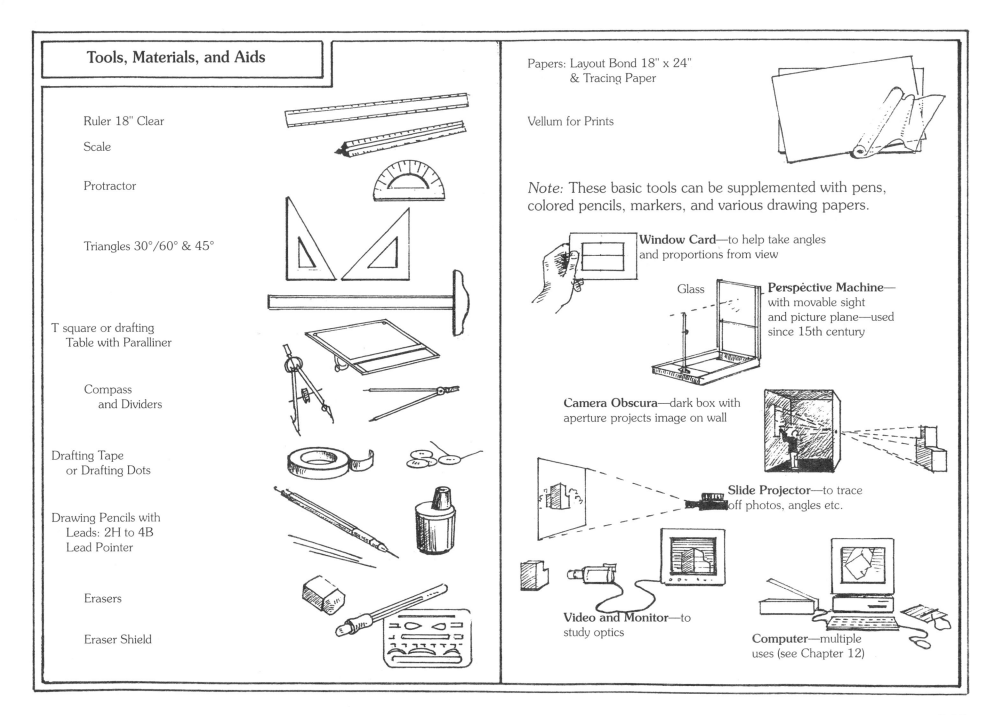

Tools, Materials, and Aids

Ruler 18" Clear

Scale

Protractor

Triangles 30°/60° & 45°

T square or drafting
   Table with Paralliner

Compass
   and Dividers

Drafting Tape
   or Drafting Dots

Drawing Pencils with
   Leads: 2H to 4B
   Lead Pointer

Erasers

Eraser Shield

Papers: Layout Bond 18" x 24"
    & Tracing Paper

Vellum for Prints

Note: These basic tools can be supplemented with pens, colored pencils, markers, and various drawing papers.

Window Card—to help take angles and proportions from view

Perspective Machine—with movable sight and picture plane—used since 15th century

Glass

Camera Obscura—dark box with aperture projects image on wall

Slide Projector—to trace off photos, angles etc.

Video and Monitor—to study optics

Computer—multiple uses (see Chapter 12)

Index